BROADWAY THEATRE

"I do not think there is anyone more qualified to write about the Broadway theatre than Andy Harris."
Bernard Jacobs, *President of the Shubert Organization*

". . . a fascinating history of Broadway . . . a highly informed, well researched, canter down the Avenue; indispensable."
Mike Ockrent

"Broadway" has been the stuff of theatrical legends for generations. In this fascinating and affectionate account of a unique theatrical institution, Andrew Harris takes a searching look at both the reality *and* the myth behind the heart and soul of American drama.

Broadway Theatre takes a look at the aims and achievements of such major writers as Tennessee Williams, Eugene O'Neill, David Mamet, Edward Albee, and Arthur Miller.

What, Andrew Harris asks, are the processes a play goes through from preliminary draft to opening night? What are the roles played by those behind-the-scenes figures such as producers, agents, managers and reviewers? How does writing for Broadway relate to acting on Broadway?

Broadway Theatre is a *tour de force* of writing about the theatre. It combines the love of the theatre-goer for the magic of Broadway with the knowledge and wit which can only come from an insider's understanding. A must for anyone interested in how theatre *works*.

Andrew Harris has chaired Theatre Departments at Columbia University, SMU and TCU. His production credits include works by most of the playwrights in this volume, most recently the world première of *Albee's Women*.

THEATRE PRODUCTION STUDIES
General Editor: John Russell Brown

BROADWAY THEATRE

Andrew B. Harris

London and New York

First published 1994
by Routledge
11 New Fetter Lane, London EC4P 4EE

Simultaneously published in the USA and Canada
by Routledge
29 West 35th Street, New York, NY 10001

Typeset in Times by Intype, London
Printed and bound in Great Britain by Biddles

British Library Cataloguing in Publication Data
A catalogue record for this book is available from the British Library

Library of Congress Cataloging in Publication Data
Harris, Andrew B. (Andrew Bennett)
Broadway theatre / Andrew B. Harris
p. cm. – (Theatre production studies)
Includes bibliographical references and index.
1. Theater–New York (N.Y.)–History–20th century. 2. American drama–20th
century–History and criticism. I. Title. II. Series.
PN2277. N5H35 1994
792'.09747'1–dc 20 93–19344

ISBN 0–415–06039–7 (hbk)
ISBN 0–415–10520–X (pbk)

Broadway Theatre is dedicated to my wife, Ann, whose love and support have helped make this book happen.

CONTENTS

ILLUSTRATIONS

PREFACE

They want to hear something that concerns themselves, and the
delineation of the present age is what they demand.

Alexis de Tocqueville

Our interest in the life of our times must lead us to the discovery
of those methods that would must truly convey this life through the
theatre.

Harold Clurman

Everyone in the theatre talks about Broadway, but few people know
what it really is. One hundred years ago, when publisher Samuel French's
son, T. Henry French, built the American Theatre on Eighth Avenue
and 41st Street, the Broadway district was residential. The theatres were
spread along twenty-five blocks of city streets to the north of Union
Square. Times Square was Longacre Square. During the next quarter-
century, theatres were built at an amazing rate until there were more
than eighty of them huddled in the district. Broadway became more than
a street. It became a state of mind. It came to mean the biggest stars
appearing in glittering productions which meet the highest artistic standards, or the lowest form of pandering and rank commercialism imagin-
able. Broadway is the American musical (a subject worthy of an extended
treatment in another volume) as well as the style of realistic popular
theatre which is the subject of this volume. Over the years, the two
theatres, one lyrical, the other realistic, have coexisted in a symbiotic
relationship on the "Crossroads of the World," Times Square. Today,
the musical seems to dwarf the straight play, but it was not always so.
In America, the word "Broadway" has been used to modify both. For
de Tocqueville, an eighteenth-century French aristocrat steeped in neo-
classicism, there was something both horrifying and exhilarating about
this kind of theatre. He was appalled that works of quality might be
overshadowed by those which simply pleased the masses. He lamented,
"You may be sure that if you succeed in bringing your audience into the

presence of something that affects them, they will not care by what road you brought them there."[1]

Yet de Tocqueville was sensitive to the virtues of a democratic stage which might function as a kind of forum for ideas. In the 1930s, with the nation in the midst of the Depression, the Franklin D. Roosevelt administration sought to stimulate theatrical employment through the Works Progress Administration's Federal Theatre Project. The Federal Theatre evolved a theatrical forum called the Living Newspaper. But plays such as Arthur Arent's *One-third of A Nation* (1938), depicting wretched social conditions, stirred up a hornet's nest of adverse criticism among conservative constituents. Rather than censor the theatre, the United States Congress simply stopped funding it.[2] Today's controversy over the funding policies of the National Endowment of the Arts merely mirrors this earlier debate.

For all of its shortcomings, the Broadway theatre has remained surprisingly free from censorship and government intervention. In spite of controversy, the paradoxical state of striving for timeliness through what purports to be timeless art has been an integral part of Broadway history. To introduce this volume, I begin with a highly selective view of the theatrical landscape from colonial times through to the quintessential producer of the 1920s, Jed Harris. Rather than mire the reader in detail, I chose to use a broad brush, picking up only a few of the most vivid colors. The second chapter provides some additional background about Broadway and the various roads that led to it. I include brief considerations of such artists and reformers as Eugene O'Neill and Harold Clurman, individuals who opposed the Broadway of their times but who contributed to the making of today's Broadway.

The remainder of the volume is made up of individual production studies, one per decade. The plays were selected based on a variety of criteria: popularity, literary merit, and durability. With a theatre that is perceived as functioning in the broad way, popularity must rank first. Although some attention was given to awards such as the Pulitzer Prize in Drama, this writer did not find the Pulitzer to be a "mirror of the age." Obviously, the popular success of plays such as *Who's Afraid of Virginia Woolf?*, denied the Pulitzer, argue against using it as a primary criteria.[3] I was more concerned with another measuring stick, revivals. Here, I was not only concerned with box-office success, but how the play has contributed to the ethos of Broadway.

Although I choose plays by playwrights who had significant reputations (Clifford Odets, Kaufman and Hart, Arthur Miller, Tennessee Williams, Edward Albee, David Mamet, and Neil Simon), I focused on productions that permitted me to explore the workings of the Broadway collaborative process. In describing this process, I have tried to give a balanced picture of what happened, keeping in mind that on Broadway this is determined by "who has the muscle." My understanding of this term goes beyond the obvious. To this critic, "muscle" is the force or rationale behind the *entire* production.[4] What this study shows is that this will vary from production to production. There is no one right way to mount a Broadway production.

Broadway Theatre is written to appeal to the general reader, student, teacher, and theatre professional. It deals with how productions are conceived, developed, and transformed from text to performance under the unique pressures of a commercial system that considers artistic work "product." The constant friction between these forces in the arena of live production makes for a fascinating story. It is a story rich in theatrical lore and filled with personalities that are as large as the theatre itself. My aim as author has been to give my reader a glimpse of what goes on in "the smoke filled rooms," "behind the scenes," and "in front of the footlights." The plays and productions selected for this volume are not simply representative, they are exemplary. I hope the reader will enjoy reading about them as much as I have enjoyed writing about them.

Andrew B. Harris

ACKNOWLEDGMENTS

I am indebted to many people for their assistance in preparing this volume. I owe a particular word of appreciation to Michele Baker, a former student, who worked as my editorial assistant during a crucial stage of this endeavor and to my sister Joan Torres, an author in her own right. I also owe a debt of gratitude to former students Emily Davis and Stephen Pickover, both of whom helped to assemble research materials for me in New York. For his encouragement and support, I wish to thank John Russell Brown, the General Editor of the Theatre Production Studies series. For his faith over the years, I owe thanks to Glenn Young, Founder and President of Applause Books. At critical stages during the writing of this book, I also received encouragement and help from Ann L. Rhodes, Helen M. Guditis, Annette Niemtzow, Randolph Goodman, Glenn Ellman, Shirley Herz, Kent Paul, David Keller, Ada Rotkiewicz, Craig Belknap, and Susan Yecies. Since a book of this kind develops out of years of observation and experience, I need to thank my former colleagues at Columbia University and theatrical mentors: the late Bernard Beckerman, Bernard Gersten, Peter Entin, Bernard Jacobs, Martin Meisel, and Gerald Schoenfeld. I also wish to thank the American Society for Theatre Research for encouraging me to moderate the Twenty-fifth Anniversary Playwrights Panel. Several of the playwrights in this study were fellow participants. I also owe a debt to my professional organizations such as New Dramatists in New York and the Playwrights' Project of Dallas for giving me the time and encouragement to think about theatre. Research, editorial assistance, and photographic reproduction costs were made possible in part by a grant from the Joseph Goldring Foundation and Allen Goldring, President. The grant was administered by the Broadway Theater Institute, Helen Guditis, Executive Director.

For specific assistance in photographic research, I wish to thank Melissa Miller-Quinlan, Assistant Curator Theatre Arts Collection, Harry Ransom Humanities Research Center, the University of Texas at Austin; Marty Jacob, Acting Curator, Theatre Collection, the Museum of the

City of New York; Richard M. Buck, Assistant to the Executive Director, Billy Rose Theatre Collection, the New York Public Library for the Performing Arts; Lauren Bufferd, Archivist, Chicago Theatre Collection, Chicago Public Library; and Culver Picture, Inc. For access to recordings, I wish to thank the Dramatists Guild, Inc. and David Anthony, President, Premiere Post Production, New York. For special permissions with copyrighted material: the Estate of Jo Mielziner, Bud H. Gibbs, Executor; Al Hirschfeld and the Margo Feiden Galleries, Ltd. Special thanks also to Edward Albee for his permission to view archival material and access to the unpublished manuscript of his producer, the late Richard Barr. For his help with material on the Theatre Development Fund, Stephen Benedict. For his valuable time in discussing the career of David Mamet, I wish to thank his designer and my college classmate, the late Michael Merritt.

In addition to my formal study of the theatre, I have been fortunate over the years to have gained experience as a playwright, director, and producer. To all those who have contributed to my knowledge, thank you.

1 The centerfold of the *Broadway* souvenir program shows the various sensational scenes of this melodrama. The images are the climactic moments of scenes, tableaux when the action of a particular scene is realized. Cartoons by E. J. Fry, courtesy of the Museum of the City of New York Theatre Collection.

1

CURTAINS UP!

With me the play is not only the thing – it's absolutely everything.

Jed Harris

Our journey begins in the 1920s, because not only was this Broadway's golden era, but it was also the literary beginning of Broadway's modern realistic stage tradition. However, it is necessary to discuss prior periods since much of what is Broadway from theatre buildings to labor relations, has its origins even earlier. Before the 1920s Broadway theatre was best known for light entertainment: farces, melodramas, and musicals. As diverting as these plays were, they were for the most part devoid of any serious literary merit. Although Broadway had spawned several promising playwrights, the most notable was Clyde Fitch. Others worthy of consideration were Edward Sheldon, Percy MacKaye, Augustus Thomas, Langdon Mitchell, James A. Herne, and William Vaughn Moody. However, none of these writers was ever able to break away from the formulaic constrictions inherited from the nineteenth century.

The period of development we will deal with is where Broadway producers, directors, designers, and writers attempted to combine ideas derived from European models such as the Moscow Art Theatre with American practice. The result was a manifestation of a stage realism tempered by expressionistic and other theatrical devices. Eventually, this evolved into a style which has become identified with Broadway. It was a time when the post-First World War generation of writers – which we extend to include playwrights such as Eugene O'Neill, Maxwell Anderson, Elmer Rice, Philip Barry, Sidney Howard, Marc Connelly, Paul Green, S. N. Behrman, Rachel Crothers, Sidney Kingsley, Lillian Hellman, Samson Raphaelson, and Robert Sherwood – were idealistic enough to believe that a popular theatre could not only soar higher and probe deeper but could bring together art and commerce.

The 1920s were unique on Broadway. There was an energy and a restless enthusiastic spirit that questioned conventional wisdom. The First World War had given America a new feeling of confidence in herself.

1

The "Yanks" who came home from "over there" came home knowing they'd met the test of Europe's older civilizations. They saw this new age as the American Century. Industry, art, science, education, manners, and literature would now reflect that change in western civilization. At the center of this American democratic ideal was the life and times of the average American. He was a working man, proud that his ancestors had fled the decadent world of Europe. The courage, boldness, and muscularity of carving an urban industrial empire out of the wilderness needed to find expression in a tough, honest, and unpretentious drama. These ideas came to dominate Broadway's realistic theatre for the remainder of the century.

Never before or since has there been a decade that could equal the 1920s. Broadway was ablaze with theatre marquees. Walking north along the Main Stem across from the Metropolitan Opera, there was the Empire Theatre where the "carriage trade" would queue to see America's reigning first families, the Barrymores and the Lunts. Along Forty-second Street, the theatres were packed in like sardines. On the Great White Way itself were the bigger musical houses – theatres named after the famous musical stars of the day such as George M. Cohan and Al Jolson. In all there were more than seventy-six "legit" houses in operation, and the building boom was not over.[1] Even though Broadway virtually closed down over the summer, except for the girl-and-comedy revues such as Flo Ziegfeld's *Follies*,[2] in 1927 there were 268 openings. That meant that on some nights there were as many as five different shows vying for the attention of the daily critics.[3] The best seats in the house were still under $5, and the balcony seats went for as little as 50¢.[4] Playwrights could earn a royalty of $700 a week in an era when 10 percent of that sum was a handsome wage. If a show was a success and ran for more than one hundred performances (the century mark), there was a possible movie sale. After the playwright's split with the producer, he still stood to make "a tidy little fortune."[5] In those days, production costs were running between $10,000 and $20,000.[6] Although circumstances changed by the end of the decade, producers and investors had a one in three chance for a success.[7]

The entire district had the look and feel of a carnival "midway." There were nickelodeons, vaudevilles, burlesques, peep shows, and movies of various kinds. Hotels in the district boasted nightclubs and restaurants with live entertainment. The theatres had cabarets upstairs in roof gardens and casinos. Crowded in patchwork patterns were gaming parlors, Ripley's Believe It or Not "Curioddities" and a Wax Museum. News bulletins flickered around the Times Building while other electric signs jittered, danced, blew smoke, and cascaded before the eyes of awe-struck millions. Broadway was the nation's primary entertainment marketplace. Tin Pan Alley, home to songsmiths and lyricists, was within Broadway's precincts. Marketing songs through shows was an obvious method to gain exposure, but it was only valuable if Broadway appealed to the masses – performances by the hundreds to audiences of thousands.

Broadway remains distinct among American theatres because of the element of competition. Due to its location on expensive Manhattan Island real estate, the competition for space readily converted into a competition for attractions, actors, publicity, and ultimately for audiences. From the eighteenth century until the present, theatres have had to struggle against other kinds of land use. Therefore Broadway was and is, first and foremost, a commercial theatre. It exists not to create art, but to create profits.

As early as 1732, with fewer than ten thousand inhabitants in the colony, when the present Broadway district was a farm with a manure dump, there were already two theatres in New York. One represented the British Crown, and the other represented Dutch settlers and those in favor of home rule. The rivalry began when Rip Van Dam, who owned a building that might serve as a theatre on Nassau Street, refused to pay William Cosby, the new Royal Governor, the emoluments he had received in his term as interim governor. Although Cosby won his case in court, many colonists stopped patronizing the theatre on Broadway near the governor's palace to show support of Van Dam.[8] This early commingling of political, ethnic, and commercial interests became a distinguishing feature of Broadway theatre.

In spite of this early rivalry, the first truly professional theatre in America was not established until twenty years later in Williamsburg, Virginia. William Hallam, a manager who ran afoul of the London licensing act, organized a troupe of ten actors headed by his brother Lewis Hallam (the Elder). The form of organization of this theatre was typical of a small eighteenth-century stock company and stands in marked contrast to what we now call Broadway theatre. In Lewis Hallam's company, Hallam acted the leading roles, his wife was his leading lady, and their three children were available for the smaller parts. This form of organization had certain artistic limitations. For instance, Master Lewis Hallam, the son, was required to play Romeo opposite his mother's Juliet. The elder Hallam was a traditional actor-manager, which meant he handled all the financial and the artistic affairs of the company. Producer, director, leading actor, and general manager, his was the only position of authority. The rest of the troupe included actors and actresses who, if not members of the Hallam family, were shareholders in the company. An actor received his remuneration according to his share. Each adult was wed to the fortunes of the actor-manager as well as to the troupe as a whole for it was impossible to sell one's share without the approval of the manager and the company. This method of organization created loyalty as well as assuming a fixed repertory. During this period, repertory meant established plays (Shakespeare, Steele, Rowe, Lillo, Cibber, and Farquhar) and current comedies. Each actor would have a group of stock parts which constituted that actor's "line" (a technical term as in a "line of business"). The "lines" in a typical eighteenth-century acting company were the Juvenile Lead and Ingenue, First and Second Light Comedians and Soubrettes, First and Second Low Comedians, Heavies of both sexes ("for villainy, tragedy, blood, and thunder"), Aristocratic Father and Bourgeois Father (or First and Second Old Man and Old Woman), Walking Gentlemen, Walking Ladies, and Utilities.[9] The Hallam Company established the basic pattern of theatrical organization in America, a pattern that sustained itself until the last three decades of the nineteenth century.

In spite of being greeted by neighbors as "the synagogue of Satan"[10] the Hallam troupe (now the American Company), took up regular residency. With the construction in 1798 of the Park Theatre (designed by French architect Joseph Mangin), New York possessed one of the finest facilities in the colonies.[11] In the fifty years that followed, the population of New York grew to half a million. Waves of German and Irish immigrants came ashore and settled into the tenements of what today is known as Chinatown. To meet this rapid expansion, thirty theatres were constructed, the number of performance days increased to six a week, and theatrical bills changed nightly. By 1810, the increased competition sparked a quest for novelty and Stephen King (dubbed "King Stephen" by humorist Washington Irving) broke with tradition and imported the first English star, George Frederick Cooke. To help recoup the costs of the transatlantic passage and Cooke's princely salary, King set up a tour of several cities.[12] The Cooke tour proved so successful that it established a pattern soon followed by other English stars, including James Wallack, Edmund Kean, Junius Brutus Booth, Charles Mathews, William Charles Macready, George Holland, and Charles and Fanny Kemble.

Although English stars did little to help the growth of American theatre, they did attract large audiences, overshadowing the efforts of the local actors. When the theatre did not have a star, attendance fell off so drastically that the booking of stars became a more deeply entrenched practice. In this earlier era, American audiences were not so easily won over by visiting talent. A sense of cultural inferiority combined with anti-English sentiment sometimes created life-threatening situations. Although it was a major coup to bring Edmund Kean to America, the great actor was not prepared for the small houses he encountered. In fact, he was so appalled that he refused to play *Richard* one night in Boston. The crowd became so incensed by his arrogance that they erupted, forcing him to leave the city out of fear of violence.[13] Years later when he returned for another American tour, the slight was remembered. In New York, he was greeted with so many hisses and cat-calls that he was driven

4

from the stage. Regaining his composure, he decided to brave the oranges and rotten apples and was hit on the shoulder by a bag of sand. In Boston, the crowd reacted even more violently. A riot ensued, furniture was smashed, and Kean was not allowed to play.

But if Kean had difficulties with American audiences, they were minor compared to those William Charles Macready encountered during his final farewell appearance in May of 1849. Macready had quarreled with the native-born tragedian, Edwin Forrest. Forrest's style of acting was in direct opposition to the idealization and noble demeanor practiced by the English Macready. Forrest's nationalistic stance had attracted a rowdy following of young fans many of whom were Irish. They were known as the "Bowery B'hoys." The B'hoys heckled and howled Macready with such vigor at the Astor Place Opera House on May 8 that they forced the visitor from the stage. The aristocratic members of the New York audience were incensed and unwisely prevailed upon Macready to make a second attempt on May 10. To assure a friendly reception for this performance, they bought all the tickets in the house. This left an angry and threatening mob of fifteen thousand in the streets outside the theatre, which vented its frustration by rock-throwing. A regiment of infantry was called forth. Upon their arrival, they were greeted by a barrage of bricks. The command to fire into the crowd was given. Several rioters were hit. The mob went berserk attacking the soldiers. A second volley was fired. Panic followed and thousands stampeded from the square. When the smoke cleared, there were twenty-two dead and thirty wounded. Macready fled New York in disguise never to return again. The Astor Place Riot occurred on land that is now next to the New York Shakespeare Festival's Public Theatre. It was the worst riot in the history of American theatre.

The rough-and-tumble treatment given to Kean and Macready gave resident managers pause, but it was the exception and not the rule. Still, these reactions were significant, for they showed that American audiences were not going to be patronized by even the greatest of English stars. They also indicated how strongly the first American-born star Edwin Forrest played upon nationalistic feelings to elevate his stature. The idea of "taking the theatre" as the Bowery B'hoys had was but one variation of a continuing pattern.

Forrest's desire to win and hold an American audience found expression through another nationalistic idea, the awarding of an annual cash prize for an American play, which would then serve as a vehicle for his own unique talents.[14] In the years that followed, Forrest awarded $20,000 in prizes for American plays which helped to spark an interest in native dramaturgy. Unfortunately, very few of the plays were successful and most have disappeared. But the actor's idea, soliciting plays as vehicles, has become one method for American plays to reach the

5

public.[15] Today Hollywood, which has taken over and adapted many Broadway business practices, continues this tradition.

Through the nineteenth century, natural geographic limitations and the public transportation network helped to foster the formation of distinct districts: dry goods on Pearl Street, jewelry on Maiden Lane, newspapers on Park Row, and banks and exchanges on Wall Street. Theatres gravitated to Broadway, the City's most important shopping street. When the Academy of Music was erected at Fourteenth Street (Union Square),[16] the theatres began their north-westerly march up Broadway. They found their new locations in those areas that were to become the City's most elite neighborhoods. In 1883, a London visitor commented:

> The plan adopted in New York has been to bring them [theatres] as nearly as possible together, so that the overflow of one house finds another theatre ready at hand. Hence the New York houses are nearly all situated in the Broadway, and have therefore a continual stream of life passing backward and forward before their doors.[17]

The commercial advantage of districting not only helped to attract audiences, but also facilitated the daily transaction of business. Actors, musicians, and managers knew where to go to find work. A strip of Broadway designated the Rialto became a shopping place for out-of-town managers in search of available talent. By the mid-nineteenth century, the business of the theatre was becoming more and more specialized.

In the days before adequate copyright law, George C. Howard, who managed a stock company in Troy, New York, arranged to have George L. Aiken adapt Harriet Beecher Stowe's novel *Uncle Tom's Cabin* (1853). What Howard saw in the novel was the opportunity for his daughter Cordelia Howard to become a star in the role of Little Eva. From Troy, the play made its way to New York where it played the National, achieving a run of over two hundred performances. A father's hopes were vindicated when Miss Howard went on to stardom. So stirring was the final scene that management realized they did not need an afterpiece, a standardized feature of the traditional stock company:

> Gorgeous clouds, tinted with sun light. EVA, robed in white, is discovered on the back of a milk-white dove, with expanded wings, as if just soaring upward. Her hands are extended in benediction over ST. CLARE and UNCLE TOM, who are kneeling and gazing up to her. Expressive music. Slow curtain.[18]

Soon spectacular final scenes became the norm and within twenty years the afterpiece which had served as the acting company's signature disappeared from the American stage forever.

In 1857, Dion Boucicault, actor, manager, and playwright, furthered the tendency towards the unique and spectacular. He adapted *Les Pauvres*

6

de Paris to become *The Poor of New York*.[19] He not only recreated settings of recognizable New York streets but he managed to have a house destroyed by fire on the stage. Boucicault's play toured widely, becoming "the poor" of just about any place. Title, costumes, and local color were altered to suit the engagement. It was "the play" for American playwrights to imitate because it apparently dealt with contemporary issues and used local characters. Technological advances such as limelight provided what were in essence the first spotlights. The need to keep pace with these demands placed increasing financial burdens on the local stock companies. But the new scenic contrivances could not be utilized without a certain amount of risk. There were several theatre fires.

After one such occasion in 1866, William Wheatley, manager of Niblo's Garden, decided to incorporate a large troupe of stranded imported ballet dancers into Charles M. Barras' *The Black Crook*. The result was a spectacular musical entertainment. The public, delighted by the play's fairyland setting and the scantily clad ballet girls, kept the show running for a record sixteen months. To keep the audience coming back for more, Wheatley continued to add feature performers and specialty numbers when available. Critics found this reprehensible, but Wheatley is now credited with the birth of the Broadway musical.

Once the American Civil War was over the growth of the railroads occasioned by the war effort made large-scale theatrical touring not only appealing but affordable. Railroad speculation and corrupt business schemes were also responsible for the Panic of 1873. Peter A. Davis (*Theatre History Studies* 8 (1988): 3–6) has described how within the first three years of this downturn over 60 percent of the nation's fifty stock companies failed. Within ten years, only seven stock companies remained.[20] The loss of so many stock companies did much to strengthen management and booking. In the stock company, the actor-manager selected plays because they helped him to display his talents. In the new arrangement, a manager or producer selected plays with the box office in mind. Augustin Daly was one of the transitional figures in this development. His combination of talents as a playwright, director, and manager earned him a special place as America's first great director-manager.

Daly began as a newspaper reporter and rapidly advanced to drama critic. In the days when no one gave a second thought to the notion of a conflict of interest, he wrote plays and did publicity for the stars while serving as drama critic for five different newspapers, all in New York, including the *Times*.[21] In his theatrical ventures he tried to eliminate the tendency towards the histrionic in favor of natural acting.[22] Ten years before the reforms of Sir Henry Irving in London, Daly was already insisting on precision of detail, completeness of surroundings, and the general unity of company and performance.[23] He placed great emphasis on scenery, costumes, lighting, and music, and he reshaped the plays he produced for his company so that the play's story unfolded through sustained action.[24] He achieved what the century had hitherto lacked; productions where the acting was memorable because it was integrated with the other elements of the play.

Daly nevertheless further undermined the stock company when he and his chief rival, A. M. Palmer, began extending the runs of hit plays. Palmer put his contracted actors to work in productions in other cities such as San Francisco and Chicago.[25] Next came the idea of the *combination* company, assembling a group of actors specifically to do a single play. An actor was hired because of his ability to perform a specific role. From the single-play company, it was only a short step to the creation of the *duplicate* or *touring company*. Touring companies essentially permitted management to mass produce "the product" and to send it out on "the road" all over America. This signaled the greatest change in American theatre during the nineteenth century, the reliance on "the road."

Theatre owners in cities across America found it less expensive to import a New York production than to attempt a local production with lesser-known talent. In the 1890s, the slogan "Direct from New York" became the death knell for the local stock companies. The combination companies of stars and touring actors grew rapidly from 282 at the beginning of the decade to 420 by 1904.

Alfred L. Bernheim in *The Business of the Theatre*, written on behalf of Actors' Equity Association (1932), estimates that it took approximately thirty years for what he called the "industrial revolution" to occur:

> The breakdown of the stock system and its replacement by the combination system were of momentous importance in the economic development of the legitimate theatre in this country. They changed the character of the theatre business as completely as the advent of power machinery and the evolution of the factory system had changed the character of manufacture.[26]

Although it has become fashionable of late to object to Bernheim's metaphor, comparing the reorganization of the theatre to the manufacturing sector, there can be little question that the impact of these changes was comparable. There was obviously a fortune to be made in touring if one could organize a system. The business Panic of 1893, occasioned a New York meeting of seven of the most powerful theatre owners and producers. Following a fateful dinner at the Holland House, the "Theatrical Syndicate" was born.

The Syndicate consisted of Abraham Lincoln Erlanger, Marc Klaw, Charles Frohman, Al Hayman, William Harris, Fred Nixon-Nirdlinger, and Fred Zimmerman. So effective were these men at reorganizing the theatre business that within a year they had completely revolutionized it.

Before their arrival, the booking of out-of-town theatres had been in the hands of individual theatre owners or freelance agents. None of these agents controlled enough of the turf to be able to book a consecutive tour. However, the Syndicate with its superior resources could lay out a tour plan that included the best theatres in the big cities as well as small town theatres *en route*. These houses were known as one-night stands or split-week houses depending on the size of the town, and they provided a way to defray the costs of the tour. Not only was the new system more efficient than the haphazard system of freelance agents or the star manager's improvised arrangement, but the Syndicate could command a "standardized" contract. Attractions and theatres signed on, and it was not long before the Syndicate controlled 95 percent of theatrical bookings in the United States and Canada, about 2,000 theatres in all.

The fly in the ointment was the Napoleonic greed of Erlanger, who with Klaw handled the day-to-day operations of the Syndicate. Unlike Charles Frohman[27] who retained a strong artistic interest in the theatre, Erlanger's chief interest, like so many after him, was strictly money. To his credit, he did bankroll the early careers of George M. Cohan, Florenz Ziegfeld, and Charles Dillingham. But he is best known for insisting that both star and producer sign "exclusive" contracts to appear only in Syndicate-controlled houses. He sewed up control of the road by also demanding "exclusive" booking agreements with all the local theatre owners. The Syndicate gained absolute control over both sides of the business, a monopoly. In his defense, one could say Erlanger and partners were only following a national trend, for this was the "robber baron" period in American business, spawning the likes of Rockefeller, Gould, Harriman, Mellon, and Carnegie.

It wasn't long before theatre owners discovered that they no longer had a say in the running of their businesses. Although Erlanger initially requested only 5 percent of the gross, once the theatre owner joined up this figure rose to as much as 50 percent. If the theatre owner balked, the Syndicate would either cut him off or threaten to build its own theatre. The independent producer of attractions found that there was really no such thing as a "standardized" contract. Syndicate-backed attractions were given privileged treatment: the most profitable tour routes, the best dates, and the best terms. If an independent hoped to succeed, he had to give the Syndicate a piece of the action – a large piece. Several stars did not wish to have the terms of their contracts dictated to them, the most notable being Richard Mansfield, Joseph Jefferson, Nat C. Goodwin, James O'Neill, Francis Wilson, James A. Herne, and Mrs Fiske.[28] For two decades these insurgents revolted against the new order, clinging tenaciously to their right to manage their own affairs.

Minnie Madern Fiske is best remembered for her Ibsen heroines.

Naturally, this "Nora" was not about to be told how to run her life by a syndicate of "Torvalds." Her manager and husband, Harrison Gray Fiske, was a man of independent means. He bought the Manhattan Theatre in New York and as publisher and editor of the *Dramatic Mirror*, he fought a pitched battle against the Syndicate. Every attempt was made to prevent the *Mirror* from reviewing Syndicate shows. Managers took to threatening actors who were caught even reading a copy of the renegade newspaper. Fortunately, Mrs Fiske was not alone. Mansfield took to making curtain speeches denouncing the Syndicate to audiences. In time David Belasco, Henry W. Savage, and James K. Hackett joined in what became a nation-wide outcry against the Theatre Trust.

Then the Shubert brothers, three young men from humble conditions, founded a rival theatrical chain based out of Syracuse, New York. At first the Shuberts avoided direct conflict with the Syndicate by booking local stock companies and not relying on touring attractions. However, after accumulating five theatres, they made the decision to produce and tour their own shows. To give their product credibility, they needed to have a New York City theatre. They leased the Herald Square Theatre, accepting an arrangement with the Syndicate as part of the deal. After surviving several unsuccessful Syndicate bookings, they hit pay dirt when August Thomas' *Arizona* (1900), one of the first western plays, turned into a surprise hit.[29] Fortune again smiled on the brothers when Mansfield, who was still at war with the Syndicate, played their Herald Square Theatre. These and other early successes made it possible for the Shuberts to increase their holdings to ten theatres. They were becoming a major force which Abe Erlanger swore to destroy.

But on December 30, 1903, just as the war between the Shuberts and the Syndicate was heating up, Erlanger's Iroquois Theatre in Chicago went up in flames. Within a matter of minutes, there were six hundred dead, mostly women and children. Bodies were piled twenty deep in front of unyielding steel doors and in tiny cramped exit corridors. The Iroquois fire became a national scandal when it became apparent that the "fireproof theatre" was actually a firetrap. In the wake of the disaster, theatres across the country were closed for inspection. New building codes were written to provide clear escape routes for patrons.

Erlanger had chosen this season to withdraw and cancel all production and touring agreements with the Shuberts. He thought this would eliminate the Shubert brothers as a business threat. Relations between the Syndicate and the brothers were anything but cordial, and the Shuberts rightly viewed Erlanger's move as a betrayal. Joining forces with David Belasco, they began planning an "Independent Movement." With increased financial backing, Jake (J. J.), the youngest brother, moved to Chicago to begin a theatre building program in the mid-west. Sam, the middle brother, was *en route* to Pittsburgh to battle a Syndicate lock-out when he was killed as a result of a train wreck. Lee, the eldest, who had adored Sam, was devastated. Having lost all interest in fighting the Syndicate, he decided to meet with Erlanger to negotiate a buyout. The only condition Lee placed on the table was that Erlanger honor Sam's memory and go ahead with the out-of-town bookings that had been set up with Belasco. Erlanger refused, stating, "I don't honor contracts with dead men." Lee stalked out of Erlanger's office and the war was on.

The "open door policy" became the Shuberts' battle-cry. All suitable theatres were to be open without prejudice or favor to all attractions. Mrs Fiske and the "Divine" Sarah Bernhardt promptly joined the Shubert camp. While the Syndicate was rebuilding old theatres to meet the new fire codes, the Shuberts were able to raise capital and compete successfully.

Since the Shuberts, like the Syndicate, were also involved in producing, the much-touted "open door" began to close on producing rivals using their theatres. Not surprisingly, Shubert-produced shows received preferential bookings. Soon the Shuberts were being accused of the same strong-arm tactics they had attributed to the Syndicate. However, the Shuberts had succeeded in breaking Erlanger's stranglehold. The Syndicate's attempt to take over vaudeville, which they later surrendered to the B. F. Keith and E. F. Albee monopoly,[30] together with the increased popularity of film, did much to diminish their hold over the theatre.

At the height of their power in the mid-1920s, the Shubert circuit consisted of eighty-six first-class theatres in New York, Chicago, Philadelphia, and Boston, and twenty-seven in other major cities. They could seat one hundred and thirty thousand ticket buyers a night with a weekly box office of $1,000,000. Besides their real estate holdings, the Shuberts booked seven hundred and fifty theatres or about 60 percent of all legitimate theatres in the United States and Canada. This accounted for two-thirds of their income, while their own productions accounted for the remainder. The Shuberts were big business, the first theatrical chain to sell their stock on Wall Street.[31]

This is the prelude to the 1920s, Broadway's golden era. The "Broadway producer" had become an independent businessman and an artist of the theatre. The actor-managers had vanished and the director-managers, such as Daly, Frohman, and Belasco, were already falling by the wayside. Theatre owners such as the Shuberts had a regular staff of playwrights and directors to put together and package musical shows. However, straight plays (without music) originated from independents. The independent producer optioned the dramatic property and gathered the creative team, frequently playing the all-important role of the guiding force behind the production. When the producer was satisfied with the product, he would arrange to bring it to market and hold backers' auditions. Raising capital was done by forming a limited partnership with

11

"angels" or "backers." The producer served as the general partner and assumed the liability for the production. Only when the production had been fully capitalized ("vested") would the producer allow the director to cast and go into rehearsal. To perfect the product, the producer would then seek an out-of-town try-out. If the try-out failed, the production would be abandoned. If it succeeded, it opened on Broadway.

Until the invention of the talking motion picture in 1927, Broadway dominated the national cultural arena. It was during the 1920s that "publicity" came of age in America and Broadway created the myth of the overnight success. The epicenter of Broadway banter was the Algonquin Hotel's Round Table, where the wits gathered to either talk up or down the Broadway shows. The charmed circle had many regulars, such as Heywood Broun, Dorothy Parker, Harold Ross, Alexander Woollcott, George S. Kaufman, Marc Connelly, Robert Sherwood, Donald Ogden Stewart, Franklin Adams, Robert Benchly, Edna Ferber, Neysa McMein, and Margolo Gillmore. They either wrote for the newspapers or the trendy magazines: *The New Yorker*, *Vanity Fair*, and *Smart Set*.

The "Jazz Age" was in full swing. New fashions were designed to shock. Hemlines went up just high enough to reveal hip flasks. "Speakeasies" were "in" and "flaming youth" yearned to be part of "Café Society." As the decade wore on, traditional small-town values seemed more and more irrelevant and naive. By the end of the decade, the words "New York" and "Broadway" had come to embody all that was smart, urban, and sophisticated. Denizens of the underworld, the Gatsbys and the bootleggers, went unchecked, gaining political power while servicing the "speaks" and clubs with prohibited alcohol. A play that could capture the gaudy excitement and violence of the underworld, and yet be true to life, would be a sure-fire hit.

Jed Harris grew up in Newark, New Jersey and was educated at Yale. Ivy League universities were not particularly hospitable to Jews and Jed Harris remained at Yale just long enough to develop an intellectual patina. He entered the theatre as a publicist, and after a brief stint on the road in Chicago was ready for bigger and better things. He began producing at the age of 25. He was determined to be greatly respected. Although he was still wet behind the ears, he had learned the patter of Broadway insiders. If the Yiddish word *chutzpah* (unmitigated gall) had been in vogue then, it would have been used to describe Jed Harris' bold and abrasive manner. Although not motivated only by financial gain, he seemed to find it personally distasteful to pay partners, collaborators, and employees. Evidently what bothered him was acknowledging their contribution to his production. The "billing" on the showcard read "Jed Harris presents . . ." and this seemed to mean that only Jed Harris had the moral right to take command over the writing, directing, designing, etc.

It was Jed Harris alone that seized upon a dross idea and spun it into theatrical gold. Whether an idea arose out of an inspired reading of a play or out of his own need to control all aspects of the production, he was incapable of undertaking a production without seeking to totally transform it in the process. He would option properties which challenged existing conventions of the theatre.[32] His ingenious concept of weaving two different kinds of plays together, a revenge melodrama with a back-stage romance, became the smash hit *Broadway*.

Jed Harris started with a script entitled *Bright Lights*, written by Philip and Virginia Dunning. According to George Abbott, who would be brought on to direct and "co-author" the project, "It was a confused script, full of wonderful characters and wonderful scenes. . . . The main plot was exciting and topical."[33] *Bright Lights* made the rounds to every producer on Broadway before it reached S. N. Behrman, Harris' reader. Behrman found the play "offensive . . . the vision of life offered by this play would make you see the (atomic) bomb as a cleanser."[34] But at 26 Harris saw another kind of explosion, a Broadway hit. Though he did not have the $500 for an option, he was determined to produce the play he called *Broadway*.

Short on cash but long on ambition, Jed Harris needed every penny for this venture. Upon learning that there were still funds left from his maiden production (*Weak Sister*, 1925), he forbade his general manager, Herman Shumlin, to pay any of its bills, including the cartage fee for hauling away the set. Jed Harris rationalized, "The show's past history, it lost every penny."[35] He then took on as an equal partner, Crosby Gaige, a real-estate man who dabbled in producing plays. Gaige only seemed to become truly interested in producing when there was a play that might have a role for a mistress, in this case Eloise Stream. Miss Stream was cast in the role of Pearl, even though director George Abbott protested she was "not very good."[36] Jed Harris insisted and then inflated the cost of Gaige's half interest to $16,000. (In fact the entire production only cost $13,000.)[37] Jed Harris never put up one cent to qualify for his half share in the profits. Fortunately, Gaige's other interests, which included his wife Hilda, kept him at a distance from the production.

Although the play *Broadway* was cast along the lines of an old-fashioned melodrama, it had a journalistic intensity that spelt truth. Jed Harris had Abbott direct each scene of the play until its most intense moment could be expressed as a tableau. The illustration from the souvenir program reproduced in this volume proves this point. The actors were creating serial pictures, each of which told its own story in bold physical and emotionally exciting terms. This technique was an extension of the concept of "realization" of nineteenth-century representational art.[38] The play's backstage setting, although not novel, had been recast with characters that looked and sounded true-to-life. In fact, Dunning, a stage manager of musicals, had based the character of the lead, Roy Lane, on a friend, actor Roy Lloyd. Lloyd later played the role in London. Jed Harris added to the play's topicality by demanding director/co-author George Abbott remove all of the "cheap jokes" and instead treat the subject matter with absolute conviction and sincerity.

Broadway marked the first appearance on the American stage of organized crime. In the first act, a gangster, "Scar" Edwards (John Wray), is shot in the back by rival gangster Steve Crandall (Robert Gleckler). In the last act, Pearl (Eloise Stream), Scar's sweetheart, empties her pistol into the murderer. Between the murders, there would be room for a backstage romance between cabaret dancers, tough-talking Roy Lane (Lee Tracy) and sunny "Billie" Moore (Sylvia Field).

Jed Harris realized that a play-within-the-play structure would strengthen both story-lines. This required a naive but harder Billie. Only she could provide the necessary linkage between the free-spending Crandall and the would-be vaudevillian Roy. To make it work, Roy had to be so irritating that the audience would understand why Billie accepts Crandall's invitation to a gangster soirée. In fact, that encounter could be used to prove Billie's virtue. She returns the gangster's diamonds when fellow chorines tell her what she must do for the "gift." Inflamed by jealousy, Roy confronts Crandall but is saved by the opportune entrance of "cop" Dan McCorn (Thomas Jackson). In the final act, McCorn again makes a timely appearance, discovering Pearl, smoking gun, and Crandall's body. McKorn, "It's a suicide." Jazz plays up. Roy and Billie dance off. Curtain.

When the curtain rose at the Broadhurst, the audience experienced the Paradise Night Club, a speakeasy that might have been around the corner from the theatre. It was an orange-lit, tinseled room populated by showpeople, hoofers, gangsters, bootleggers, and cops, pulsating with jazz rhythms. The characters spoke the picturesque language of Damon Runyon. For the uninitiated, the souvenir program contained a gloss, "The argot of subterranea," but the message was clear to all: "live for today and forget about tomorrow."

Amidst the thunderous approval of the opening night throng, frenzied daily critics bumped and pushed their way to the theatre doors. What could they say that would communicate their experience to the readership? *Broadway* wasn't just plot and performance. From his vantage point in the balcony young Harold Clurman said to his roommate: "Don't miss the point of this, Clifford [Odets]. This is more than a 'meaningful' play. This is of these times, it is these times."[39] Allen Churchill, chronicler of 1920s theatre, dubbed it "the play of the decade."[40] For drama critic

Alexander Woollcott it was "the one which most perfectly caught the accent of the city's voice."[41]

Broadway ran a total of 603 performances at the Broadhurst. It spawned six American road companies, and it took London and a dozen other foreign capitals by storm. It made both Jed Harris and Gaige millionaires. It made possible a whole series of Hollywood gangster movies in the 1930s. It laid the foundation for the careers of such film stars as Jimmy Cagney,[42] Humphrey Bogart, Edward G. Robinson, and George Raft.

Broadway wasn't so much art as it was a species of highly pictorial jazz journalism. Jed Harris knew that his audience would not necessarily see beyond the surface of his form of pyrotechnical theatrics. He had set out to conquer the new urban audience of his day, and he had succeeded. In many respects, Jed Harris represents the best and the worst of Broadway producers, and the late 1920s was his era. At the age of 27, he had three smash hits playing the White Way: *Broadway*, *Coquette*, and *The Royal Family*.[43] Each play was different, one a gaudy melodrama, one a tear-jerker, and one a high comedy. The following season, he would crown these achievements with the blockbuster, *The Front Page*.[44] And by September 3, 1928, Jed Harris would become what he always wanted to be most: an icon and a legend – the first Broadway producer to warrant a *Time* magazine cover story.

Jed Harris became the quintessential Broadway producer with an income of $100,000 a month and an ego twice as large. From his day to the present, all Broadway producers have sought to have something akin to his control over the artistic process. But few are as gifted or as outrageous!

2

CHANGES IN THE ROAD

I would be a very sick and unhappy man if I were not a writer. Nothing else can satisfy this hunger to be useful, to be used for the common good.

Clifford Odets

Beginning as early as 1910, Broadway producers began to feel the competition of silent films. Although the losses were far less than those experienced after the "talkies," box-office receipts were down, indicating important changes taking place in the theatre business.[1] Road-houses that used to book live theatre were changing over to movies. Even though gate receipts on a per performance basis were less than one quarter of a "legit" attraction, tireless celluloid could be shown four times more often than any living performers. Moreover, the action-packed adventure films and the slapstick comedies appealed to all ages. The silent film was truly family entertainment. The use of visual images without spoken dialogue appealed to many for whom English was a second language. Also, the touring theatrical productions were frequently retreads of past successes. The actors who were sent out to do time in the provinces were not celebrities. So, it was difficult to whip up enthusiasm for the eighth company of *Blossom Time* or *Abie's Irish Rose*. The Syndicate and Shubert tours had all of the characteristics of assembly-line mass production with little in the way of "quality control."

According to Kenneth MacGowan in *Footlights Across America*, the Little Theatre Movement owed its genesis to two factors: "The development of dramatic taste all over the country and [to] the decay of the professional theatre outside New York."[2] Spearheaded for the most part by amateurs, an ardently anti-commercial theatre movement grew up in the shadows of the great road-houses. Following the leadership of the European Independent Theatre Movement, the Little Theatres selected plays by Ibsen, Shaw, and Chekhov. Only on rare occasions, when a touring star of Mrs Fiske's independent stamp came to town, had hinterland audiences been treated to professional productions of these modern

16

classics. It was the desire to see these plays that led to the formation of America's first regional theatre movement. With regard to contemporary American plays the Little Theatres, more often than not, looked to New York and the Syndicate and Shubert tours. In spite of hometown chauvinism and a spirit of anti-commercial rebellion, local audiences did not trust themselves to know what was good and what was not good. Broadway set the standard.

Therefore, the Provincetown Players was unique among theatrical companies in the era before the First World War in that this group was devoted to the discovery of American writers. The Players was one of two Little Theatres destined to have a major impact on the future of Broadway. The other was the Theatre Guild, which began in 1914 as the Washington Square Players. Eugene O'Neill, who worked first with the Provincetown Players and then with the Theatre Guild, would even play a minor role in supporting a third theatre company, the Group Theatre, in 1928.[3] Although the Group Theatre could not be called a Little Theatre, it had a similar impact on the future of Broadway. These three theatres helped to shape the future of Broadway in several ways. Each served as a training ground for theatrical talent. In several instances, each produced specific plays that either transferred or were produced directly for Broadway. But perhaps the most important influence was also the least direct. Each theatre altered the way Broadway saw itself. The theatres altered the underlying rationale behind commercial production. Whether it was through their emphasis on experimentation, artistic process, or social interaction, the theatres worked to redefine the way the professional viewed his profession. Whatever their specific theories were, none of these theatres saw their work as simply "product."

By 1915 Provincetown, a picturesque little fishing village on the tip of Cape Cod, had already become the site of a summer colony of artists and social reformers. Many of these individuals were among the avant-garde of their generation. The Players were a diverse lot, but three of them – Floyd Dell, George "Jig" Cook, and Susan Glaspell – hailed from Davenport, Iowa. Their interest in theatre owed much to the pioneering efforts of Maurice Browne, the founder of the Chicago Little Theatre (1912). Browne was a disciple of Gordon Craig and was an outspoken advocate of theatrical reform. His theatre was an amateur operation with a strong anti-commercial bias. However, in time he bowed to necessity and paid actors a modest $16.50 a week,[4] just enough to encourage a commitment.

Dell, Cook, and Glaspell envisioned the Provincetown Players as an experimental theatre. Cook, the spokesman of the group, was also its leading visionary. He believed that through the revival of Greek ideals the Players could reform the modern American stage. He stressed "a kindredness of minds, a spiritual unity underlying their differences, a

17

unity resembling the primitive unity of the tribe, a unity which may *spontaneously* create the unity necessary to the art of the theatre."[5] Ironically, although the Players was organized to foster native talent,[6] they began without any plays. Fortunately, Terry Carlin, an early associate, knew that Eugene O'Neill, also summering in Provincetown, had a trunk full of scripts. Cook invited O'Neill to his home. The young playwright read *Bound East for Cardiff* aloud to the group and, as Susan Glaspell has stated, they knew what they were there for.[7]

Buoyed by the success of their summer efforts, the Provincetowners decided to continue their work in New York City. They made their winter quarters in Greenwich Village, where they performed in living rooms until they acquired a space at 133 Macdougal Street which they named the Playwrights' Theatre. The enthusiasm of the effort bore fruit and a variety of scripts were produced. However, it soon became apparent that only a few of the members – O'Neill, Glaspell, and Edna St Vincent Millay – warranted public presentation. In spite of discussions about spontaneous unity, Dell found that in practice the collegiality of the group was undermined by a "meanness, cruelty and selfishness."[8] More important, there were other calls on the idealism of these young people. America was on the eve of her involvement in the First World War, and many members of the Players were eager to volunteer "to make the world safe for democracy." Next, there were problems with New York's Building Department, which forced the theatre's closure in the midst of a season. And finally, with America's entry into the war there was crippling inflation. By 1920, there were only four of the original twenty-nine active members left.

Simultaneously, Eugene O'Neill was gaining recognition far beyond the confines of the Provincetown Players. His work was being published. Frank Shay published the *Provincetown Plays* (1916),[9] Boni and Liveright published a volume of sea plays (1919), and H. L. Mencken published *The Long Voyage Home*, *'Ile*, and *The Moon of the Caribbees* in *Smart Set*. The fact that Mencken and George Jean Nathan, *Smart Set*'s influential drama critic, published these plays was an indication that the young playwright had arrived. After another magazine, *Seven Arts*, printed his story *Tomorrow* and his play *In the Zone*, Broadway producer George Tyler, a friend of James O'Neill, Sr, the playwright's actor father, approached the young playwright with work. Tyler made his living producing star vehicles similar to *The Count of Monte Cristo*, the play that James O'Neill had starred in for thousands of performances. What he wanted the young O'Neill to do was to adapt melodramas. Although the young playwright was severely tempted since he was desperate for money, he refused the offer. He clung tenaciously to the hope that a young producer, John D. Williams, who like himself, had attended George

Pierce Baker's "47 Workshop" at Harvard University, would exercise his option to produce his full-length *Beyond the Horizon* on Broadway.

Although O'Neill despised the thought of being beholden to a star's ego, it was nevertheless through Richard Bennett, father of future movie stars Joan and Constance, that his first play was produced on Broadway. Bennett, who was appearing in Williams' production of *For the Defense* by Elmer Rice, happened to pick up O'Neill's script in the producer's office. He read it and liked it. Bennett recognized that *Beyond the Horizon* had great roles for actors and was amazingly free from melodramatic plot contrivances. The actor was so enthusiastic about the play that he persuaded the other members of the cast to perform O'Neill's play at a special matinée (March 3, 1920). Although O'Neill had carefully sketched his ideas for the scenery in the margins of his manuscript, Bennett chose to ignore these notes. Instead he threw together stock scenery and drops from a rental house. It is ironic that Eugene O'Neill, the noted realist, made his Broadway debut with sets designed for a fantasy ballet of forest sprites and nymphs.

In spite of its length, the O'Neill afternoon at the Morosco had an immediate positive impact on the audience. *Beyond the Horizon* made the other one hundred plays previously seen by the critics that season look pale and hollow. The critics attending were quick to note that O'Neill had written a real tragedy. Woollcott, already an O'Neill enthusiast, proclaimed, "The play has greatness in it and marks O'Neill as one of our foremost playwrights."[10] Professor Baker made the trip in from Harvard to see the work of his former pupil and recounted his thoughts to O'Neill in this letter:

A public which heartily welcomes *Beyond the Horizon* is not the old public. It seems now as if there really were in New York an audience large enough to make successful any kind of drama worthy of attention. With that newer public created out of the War . . . with the promise shown by the newer writers, this is no time for pessimism. . . . Surely we have the right to hope that the next decade will give us an American drama which, in its mirroring of American life, will be more varied in form, even richer in content.[11]

Williams, seeing an opportunity to double receipts, had thought of running *Beyond the Horizon* as a series of matinées on Mondays, Tuesdays, Wednesdays, and Fridays. Since *For the Defense* continued, Bennett was acting in twelve performances a week instead of eight, but he was not protesting. When Rice's play began to falter at the box office, Williams closed it. He continued *Beyond the Horizon* for a run of 111 performances. The play grossed $117,071, but O'Neill's share was only $6,264 (which was still more money than he had ever earned).[12] The play went on to win the first of O'Neill's four Pulitzer Prizes.[13]

The Provincetown Players could now produce O'Neill's expressionistic *Emperor Jones* (1920), and it became the greatest success the Players ever had. Ironically, it was this success that ended the initial and most exciting phase of their development. Philosophically, the theatre had clearly stated it preferred work that would extend and stretch the physical limits of theatre, in essence work of pure theatrical experimentation. O'Neill had accepted this credo literally and, when writing *The Emperor Jones*, had decided to use physical production elements – sound and light – to move the audience into the mind of the play's central character. It was something that had never been done before. Cook was enthusiastic and committed virtually the entire resources of the theatre to the production. Fortunately, the production was an instantaneous success. Unfortunately, it had to be kept running for weeks beyond its scheduled run, which compromised the plans for the announced subscription season. Finally the play and its cast were transferred for an open-ended run on Broadway.

With *The Emperor Jones*, O'Neill's career was prominently in the ascendent. Even though the Players gathered a huge subscription list as a result of the success of *The Emperor Jones*, Cook no longer felt free to explore and create. He realized that he now had a responsibility to produce a comparable season. Cook and Glaspell had never thought of the Players as a showcase for Broadway. It went against what Cook believed to be the purpose of art. He called for an "interim" and, with Glaspell, set sail for Greece where the two hoped to rediscover the roots of holy theatre.

After a year the Provincetown Players, reorganized by O'Neill, opened with three directors: O'Neill, Kenneth MacGowan (an editor of *Theatre Arts* which published *The Emperor Jones*), and Robert Edmond Jones (a designer who co-authored *The Theatre of Tomorrow* with MacGowan). Although the Players still outwardly advocated experimentation, their field of vision had narrowed. Their new aesthetic was "expressionism," which they conceived of as exploring the psychology of the unconscious along the lines set down in the writings of Freud and Jung. O'Neill's *The Hairy Ape*, offered the season before the new directorship took charge (1921–2), had already fulfilled the theatre's stated mission. So, although the Provincetown went on to produce an O'Neill masterpiece (*Desire Under the Elms*, 1924), it no longer fulfilled a vital role as a developmental theatre.[14]

The technical demands required by O'Neill's increasingly complex scripts demanded a greater and greater degree of professionalism. O'Neill turned to the Theatre Guild (formerly the Washington Square Players) to produce his plays. The Provincetown Players might have withstood the loss of its primary playwright were it not for the economics of the time; increased production costs coupled with a loss of revenue due to the

Great Depression. Like her sister Little Theatres across the country, the Players fell victim to hard times. Out of this once robust movement that had numbered member theatres in the hundreds with admissions totalling over a million per season, only one theatre, the Cleveland Playhouse (1916), survives to the present. Broadway, for all of its woes, both real and imaginary, has achieved a much better survival record even during the worst of times.[15]

Following the highly successful amateur efforts of the Washington Square Players, the Theatre Guild began its operation in December 1918. From its beginnings until 1940, the Theatre Guild maintained a consistent management.[16] At the end of the 1930s, the Guild, America's first subscription theatre, had 85,000 subscribers in sixteen cities in the United States and Canada of which 35,000 resided in Metropolitan New York.[17] The so-called vintage years of the Theatre Guild (1928–39) resulted from actions taken during the first ten years its existence.

At first, the Guild had no interest in Broadway at all. Three out of the six directors were products of Professor Baker's "47 Workshop" at Harvard. They saw themselves as young playwrights outside the Broadway mainstream. As the Washington Square Players, members of this group had produced sixty-two one-act plays, a form consistently rejected by Broadway as non-commercial. The name "guild" stressed the kind of "co-operative organization" associated with medieval trade guilds. In its early days, the Guild emphasized its old-world traditions by going to Europe to select its repertory. Since the group was reform-minded, their mission statement talked about improving the working conditions of actors, directors, designers, and playwrights. They wished to found a repertory theatre which would offer long-term contracts to actors. In their theatre, it would be possible for actors to improve their craft by playing a variety of roles each season. Not surprisingly, the Guild also hoped to open a training school. All these ideas were aimed at raising the standard of American theatre so that it might be considered an art. Unlike the Players, the Guild never committed itself to experimentalism. In fact, they wished to avoid being thought of as "artsy." They believed that if art were well managed, it would pay for itself.[18]

During its first season, the Guild produced St John Ervine's *John Ferguson* (1919). It was an enormous success and the management made the precedent-setting decision of moving *John Ferguson* uptown to the Fulton Theatre on Broadway.[19] Coincidentally, the newly formed Actor's Equity Association declared its first major strike. The Equity Strike was long and violent. George M. Cohan, who opposed Equity, was threatened, and his mansion in Great Neck was riddled with rifle bullets. The strike closed all legitimate theatres in New York *except* the Guild's. Equity had made this an exception because the leadership wanted to show their strong approval of the "co-operative" nature of guild organization. For the duration of the strike, *John Ferguson* was the only play on the New York stage.

St John Ervine's support encouraged a wavering George Bernard Shaw to license the Guild to produce the world première of *Heartbreak House*.[20] Shaw thought the idea of producing *Heartbreak House* was "lunatic," but if this fledgling organization was prepared to seriously undertake the project, he would not stand in the way. Before the First World War, Shaw had been good box office in America.[21] Following the war, Shaw was in disfavor with English audiences because of his outspoken opposition to the War. From the Guild's perspective, Shaw's political pronouncements did not seem as troubling as they might have been to an English management. Shaw made a series of tyrannical demands regarding the sanctity of his written word, and the Guild agreed to pay a whopping high royalty of 15 percent!

The Guild took special care in producing *Heartbreak House*. They hired Broadway actresses Lucile Watson and Effie Shannon, both of whom would add luster to the occasion. They reasoned that they needed an actress of Shannon's theatrical reputation to carry the evening. The Guild's gamble succeeded and *Heartbreak House* was a hit, although not comparable to *John Ferguson*. The production ran for 125 performances.[22] By the end of the second season, subscriptions for the Guild almost tripled, nearing thirteen hundred.[23]

In its first two seasons, the Guild had made three major decisions that would shape its future: one, they had transferred a production for a long run to Broadway for the express purpose of making money; two, they had sought and then produced a play from the best-known playwright in the English language and agreed to pay him high royalty payments for the privilege; and three, they had cast the leads of this play with guest stars, actresses who were not Guild members, to impress New York critics. These decisions, all of which made good business sense, were definitely at odds with the co-operative art theatre mentality that had established the Guild in the first place.[24]

But with the increased subscription income the Guild was now in the enviable position of having all of its production capital in hand at the start of its third season. It did not need charitable gifts or investment partners. It had subscribers. Success had altered the Guild's aims ever so slightly. It had now taken on an obligation to produce art theatre that made money. By its fifth season (1922–3), the Guild was still fulfilling subscriber expectations superbly. To prove that they still warranted the title of an art theatre, the Guild produced a series of difficult plays (Karel Capek's *RUR*, A. A. Milne's *The Lucky One*, Claudel's *The Tidings Brought to Mary*, Ibsen's *Peer Gynt*, and Elmer Rice's *The Adding Machine*) which it balanced by a resubscribe revival of Shaw's *The Devil's Disciple*.

The Guild was so proud of its production of *Peer Gynt* that they invited Constantin Stanislavski, the founder of the fabled Moscow Art Theatre then on tour in New York, to attend a performance. *Peer Gynt* was a play familiar to the great Russian director, teacher, and theoretician. After the performance, the Guild went out of its way to solicit criticism from Stanislavski, whom they very much admired and respected. Although he was polite, he was candid. Stanislavski felt that they had given only a surface interpretation to *Peer Gynt*. He was particularly critical of the style of acting. His criticism troubled the Guild, which had set as one of its aims the creation of a company which would one day equal the famous Moscow Art Theatre. In their defense, the Guild was quick to cite their frustration with the lack of production facilities and classroom space. They had no place to train actors, nor could they produce plays in rotating repertory as they had originally planned. They were saddled with an old theatre, the Garrick, which they now found too cramped to accommodate their new larger audiences. The Guild missed the point of Stanislavski's criticism. Their practical response, to set about raising money for a new theatre, was fateful.[25]

The Guild's new theatre was in the Broadway district. To finance the theatre, the Board of Directors decided to sell cumulative interest bonds. The next season (1923–4) the Guild had two successes. Shaw's *Saint Joan* moved to the hallowed Empire where it played for almost a year before a commercial management took it out on the road. Because of these successes the building bond sale went well, and the Guild now had the $600,000 it needed for a new theatre. Putting everything they had into the new building, they were left with a meagre $1,000 to defray operating costs for the season.

Board member Theresa Helburn had a bright idea: to try a young couple in a play by Ferenc Molnar which had failed when first presented on Broadway (in 1913) with the singularly inauspicious title *Where Ignorance Is Bliss*. The new title of the play was *The Guardsman* and the acting couple, Alfred Lunt and Lynn Fontanne, became theatre legends. *The Guardsman* was a tremendous hit and provided an incredible springboard into the Guild's seventh season (1924–5). As Roy Waldau notes in *Vintage Years of the Theatre Guild, 1928–1939*, "What is perhaps more important than the 271 performances it ran was the fact that *The Guardsman* marked the beginning of the most fruitful and compelling relationship between performers and management ever known in the American theatre."[26] Eventually, Lunt would join the board of directors. And more than once in the next two decades the Lunts would be called upon to save the Guild just as they did that season.

The Guild Theatre at 245 West Fifty-second Street (renamed the ANTA and now called the Virginia Theatre) was completed in the middle of their seventh season. With designers Norman Bel Geddes and Lee

Simonson in control of the architects, the Guild unknowingly entered into one of its greatest failures. The stage was made so large that there was little room left for dressing rooms or even audience space. "We made the ghastly mistake," Langner wrote, "of providing a theatre with all the stage space necessary for a repertory of plays without seating capacity to provide the income necessary to support the repertory."[27] There were only 914 seats, about half the size of most Broadway houses. On April 13, 1925, President Coolidge officially opened the theatre by pushing an electric button in Washington, DC, turning the lights on Helen Hayes and Lionel Atwill in Shaw's *Caesar and Cleopatra*. The production ran for a respectable 128 performances.

One aim in building the Guild Theatre was the creation of a permanent acting company which would develop artistically by running shows in rotating repertory. The Guild chose to ignore what Beerbohm Tree had to say about repertory when he answered a question, "When is a repertory theatre not a repertory theatre?" He replied, "When it is a success."[28] But the Guild was determined to have their dream of repertory even if the cost of union labor made it prohibitively expensive. To facilitate this idea, they decided to rent an additional Broadway theatre. Rather than changing sets, they rotated casts back and forth from the Guild Theatre to the rented theatre. It was a bold solution, but an expensive one.

In the Guild's "Golden Era," 1926–8, they produced fourteen artistically successful productions,[29] even so, they had to abandon the idea that the play came first. Although alternating repertory was fun for actors, it wasn't for audiences. They wanted to see the *reviewed* actors in the roles and not a second (rotated) cast.[30]

Initially, the Guild had planned to control costs by opening each play at its own theatre, where it planned to run the show for at least fifty performances. This was just enough to take care of the subscribers and a certain amount of walk-up business before either moving the play to another theatre or terminating the run. However, the Guild had underestimated the cost of playing repertory and overestimated the New York audience's tolerance for plays which received poor reviews. The scheme was too inflexible to permit the Guild to profit from extended runs. With success after success, long runs, touring companies, and its own theatre, the Guild could not claim to be a group of artists organized around an art theatre philosophy. By the close of this golden decade, the Guild had certain fixed costs that were non-theatrical in nature. It had financial obligations to bondholders, building costs, and taxes. In addition, it now attracted subscribers who were not interested in art theatre but in low cost tickets to highbrow hits.

In the early days of the Guild, it was possible to list a group of plays that were considered representative of the art theatre movement, but once the Guild successfully produced those plays and transferred several of them to Broadway, were they still art? Or was the term "art" reserved only for Guild productions that failed? What was the difference between "art theatre" and "good theatre"? The highbrow aims of the Guild concerning its artistic standards and literary pretensions made it an easy target for critical hazing by the daily press.

The commercial theatre was never "anti" art. It was simply "pro" profit. The Guild's own definition, that art is that which is too risky for commercial management to produce, no longer characterized their play selections. The Guild had to have its share of hits just the way other managements had to have theirs. Only they believed their motives for producing plays were not governed by the play's commercial viability. But with fixed costs running so high, hadn't the Guild, in practice, chosen safer plays, including Shaw revivals, simply to please audiences? The Guild was not committed to a training philosophy, and its ensemble did not even have a unified style. At the end of the decade, the Group Theatre, led by Guild employees Harold Clurman and Cheryl Crawford, would raise these very questions.

But even before the Group, the Guild had unfinished business with a disappointed constituency of American playwrights. They complained that far too many scripts were being "imported" by the Guild. It was a criticism to which the Guild was vulnerable. The Guild had listed one of its founding purposes: to encourage and produce American playwrights. During its first ten years, the Guild produced sixty-six plays of which fifty were by foreign authors.[31] S. N. Behrman, later a successful Broadway playwright, discussed his first interview with Guild director Helburn in his autobiography *People in a Diary*. The interview concerned his first Guild production, *The Second Man* (1927). "She didn't put on plays just because she liked them," he wrote, "It had to be a passion. And even if she were impassioned, she was helpless unless her colleagues were equally impassioned."[32] Behrman, who had had successful Guild productions, shared the impatience of other American writers. He disliked working with a board of directors all of whom had to agree about all artistic decisions. It was an unwieldy, impersonal system that worked best for a foreign writer who had already put the finishing touches on a play and who would be divorced from the Guild's production process.

In addition, the Guild's production plans limited the possibility for extended runs to only bona fide blockbusters. This limited a playwright's opportunity to make money from a moderately successful production. These frustrations would motivate Behrman and several of his colleagues into forming their own production company, the Playwrights Company.

Obviously, not all American playwrights suffered at the hands of the Guild. Eugene O'Neill was openly courted. The Guild was proud of the fact that as the Washington Square Players, they could claim credit for one of the master's early achievements, the one-act play *In the Zone*. By the Guild's tenth season, O'Neill delivered two important scripts to them: *Marco Millions* and *Strange Interlude*. These were difficult works to produce and neither was thought to be commercial. The Guild decided the risk was worth the gamble and opened the two plays within fourteen days of each other. This "mini O'Neill festival," it was hoped, might soften the anticipated critical attack.

Strange Interlude had Lynn Fontanne as the lead. Starting at 5.15 in the afternoon with a dinner intermission after Act Five, the entire nine-act drama concluded shortly before the witching hour. *Marco Millions* had Alfred Lunt in the title role and was very lavish. Although the notices for *Marco* were somewhat mixed, *Strange Interlude*, which because of its length had been thought of only as a curiosity, was deemed the "finest, the profoundest drama of [O'Neill's] entire career."[33] Brooks Atkinson of the *New York Times* (January 31, 1928) was more guarded and felt the drama's technical innovation – the "aside" – was not always used well, yet he reached the conclusion that O'Neill had, with the talents of actress Lynn Fontanne, given the audience a "complete" character. By 1928, Broadway audiences wanted an in-depth portrait of an American heroine. Many saw their own lives reflected in the sobering picture of Nina Leeds, who had lost her love and her feelings of innocence in the First World War. Admittedly, O'Neill had cribbed from Freud and psychological novels and created a loquacious play, but he had produced the fullest study of a woman in the American theatre.

Strange Interlude defied all expert opinion and ran for a year and a half without an empty seat in the house (426 performances). It was a turning point. The Guild's gamble that Broadway would appreciate a play of this quality had been answered. *Strange Interlude* was the beginning of a highly successful relationship between O'Neill and the Guild. It was to yield significant achievements, such as *Dynamo* (1929), *Mourning Becomes Electra* (1931), and *Ah, Wilderness* (1933).

Exploiting the success and extending the run of O'Neill's play moved the Guild still further away from its early goals as an art theatre. There was simply no way to alternate productions around this mammoth work. They were forced to abandon their alternating repertory system entirely.[34] Although the Guild remained a subscription theatre, its history now came more and more to reflect the history of Broadway. During the next decade, the Guild and Broadway underwent an intense change as new audience needs arose.[35]

Even more than either the Provincetown Players or the Theatre Guild, the Group Theatre continues to have a direct influence on today's Broadway. It changed the American approach to acting. It stressed the idea that theatre had to be of its time, and it also contributed the plays of Clifford Odets to the repertory. But the most lasting of these contributions by far has been in acting, for it was the Group that popularized Stanislavski's "Method" in America. With the Group, "ensemble" became the watchword of the day. Open casting of roles, which had been one of the strengths of Broadway production, was an anathema to this actor-centered theatre. To put this plan into action, the Group required not only a *range* but *depth* in acting talent. They embarked on their own actor training program. During its ten-year history, the Group included actors such as Stella Adler, Morris Carnovsky, Luther Adler, John Garfield, Elia Kazan, Lee Cobb, Bobby Lewis, Sandy Meisner, Franchot Tone, and Clifford Odets. Because several were to become directors and teachers, the Group's influence continued long after its producing days were finished. Lee Strasberg, Stella Adler, Bobby Lewis, and Sandy Meisner would be listed among America's foremost teachers of acting. Harold Clurman and Elia Kazan became known as directors and writers. Several Group members went on to found theatrical institutions of their own, including: the Actors Laboratory, the Actors Studio, even the Lincoln Center Repertory Theatre. These institutions helped to promote Group ideas and foster the talents of Marlon Brando, Montgomery Clift, James Dean, Julie Harris, Anne Jackson, Sidney Lumet, Karl Malden, E. G. Marshall, Patricia Neal, Paul Newman, Geraldine Page, Joe Papp, Martin Ritt, Jerome Robbins, Kim Stanley, Maureen Stapleton, and Eli Wallach. In fact, if one were to continue this list to include subsequent generations of students, such as Robert De Niro, Robert Duvall, and Al Pacino, the list might truly become endless.

Like the earlier theatres, the Group did not wish to become a part of the Broadway commercial system. Although they wished to be successful in the Broadway market, Group members did not look upon their theatre as a business. If this seems contradictory, it was. In fact, Harold Clurman felt that this basic contradiction between art and commerce was the cause for the eventual collapse of the Group. As his closing notice in the *New York Times* (May 18, 1941) stated, "Our means and our ends were in fundamental contradiction . . . while we tried to maintain a true theatre policy artistically we proceeded economically on a show-business basis."[36]

The demise of the Group was not strictly speaking a matter of subsidies. The Group Theatre, like the Provincetown Players, was tied to a particular time and place, New York in the 1930s. The forces that helped to bring it into existence were the same forces that would contribute to bringing it to an end. Like the Federal Theatre (a federal government program under the Works Progress Administration, also a reaction to the Great Depression) the Group Theatre made its greatest contribution through its optimistic program for social change during very adverse times. Moreover, the central idea at the heart of the Group was "groupness." This tied the theatre to a larger movement within American society, based on a need to organize and belong. "Groupness" went far beyond the limited appeal of unionism. It had to do with people as a unit forcing changes to the system. They did not see the theatre as bricks and mortar the way the Theatre Guild had, nor did they see the theatre as a body of plays as the Provincetown had. The defining element of their theatre was acting, acting with an "inner life," bound to an aesthetic that demanded a moment-to-moment stage reality.

Two plays by Clifford Odets, *Waiting for Lefty* and *Awake and Sing!* were probably the Group's most significant productions, plays that even today continue to have an influence on Broadway theatre. The Group truly came together over the three summers the members spent taking Lee Strasberg's classes outside New York City, on country properties. Since Strasberg held such a strong control over the Group, much of what the Group stood for had to do with his (not Stanislavski's) theory of acting. And while other factors would come into play, it would eventually be Lee Strasberg's "method" combined with Odets' plays that would so profoundly influence Broadway theatre and through it American cinema.

Strasberg demanded from his actors that they create from their *own* "physical and emotional memories," a reality for everything they did on stage. The exercises Strasberg taught were designed to help the actor explore emotions, emotions the actor would eventually use as the means to create the "inner life" of the playwright's character. To motivate actions, the actor had to find personal experiences ("a substitution") that would cause his character to behave the way the script suggested. The idea was to meld the fictional construct with the actor's own psyche so as to make the performance psychologically believable and convincing. Only in the last weeks of rehearsal would Strasberg allow his actors to use the actual words written by the playwright. Until that time, the burden of creation fell squarely on the actor's shoulders.

Harold Clurman, the other major ideological force of the Group, spent the summers seeking to inspire his fellow members to address political and social issues of the time. The Group not only had to have a unified craft but it also had to have plays that would appropriately express its point of view. Clurman did not see the actor as technician or as a facile manipulator of psychological experience. For Clurman the actor was a spokesman who expressed in word and deed "a general concern with our lives and the life of our time."[37] Clurman and Strasberg, although they shared a desire to change the theatre, did not necessarily agree on just how that change should come about.

Though it seems obvious in retrospect that only a play written by a member of the Group could hope to fulfill their needs, it did not seriously occur to either Strasberg or Clurman that they ought to be encouraging their membership to write plays. Instead, the directors scoured every known source for plays including the Shuberts, the most commercial of commercial managements. It took them four years to recognize that

Clifford Odets, a mediocre actor in the company, was in fact a gifted playwright. Until that time the Group had relied on plays written by independent authors such as Paul Green and John Howard Lawson who, although they were sympathetic to the Group's social and political point of view, were not familiar with the exercises used by Strasberg to develop the Group's unique acting style. Odets, on the other hand, who had spent years mastering the Strasberg/Stanislavski method, knew what a writer had to do to maximize the Group's unique approach to acting. Moreover, he shared the Group's ideal of collective action the way only an "insider" can.

Clifford Odets, Elia Kazan, and several other Group actors had become members of the Communist Party, and like many idealistic young people during the Depression, they were caught up in Party efforts to strengthen the labor movement through an appeal to collective action. Within the Group, they formed a writer's collective. As such, they were contacted by the Theatre Union, an activist theatre, to perform a piece at a benefit for *New Theatre*, a magazine devoted to worker's theatre. Motivated by the opportunity to have one of his works acted, Odets wrote *Waiting for Lefty* in three nights.

While Group rehearsals for *Gold Eagle Guy* were going on upstairs, Odets and Sanford Meisner were supervising their own rehearsals of *Waiting for Lefty* in the theatre basement. The project was intended to be a collaborative work, but the attitude towards agitation and propaganda plays, dubbed "agitprop," was so exceedingly negative among the Group's leadership that Odets found himself in charge of this renegade operation. The mimeographed program for the event reflected Odets' ambivalence about assuming responsibility. There was no mention of the author's name, nor of the actors who appeared in the play. All the sheet said was that *Waiting for Lefty* was to be presented by members of the cast of *Gold Eagle Guy*. In fact, the evening was put together in such haste that the lighting cues had to be worked out the night of performance during the intermission (the interval). At the last minute, Odets was able to persuade the promoters that a dance company originally slated to go on last should go on before his play. No one expected anything except another indifferent piece of agitprop thrown together for a good cause.[38]

The plot of *Waiting for Lefty* was simple. Union committee men wait at a strike for Lefty, a leader, who never appears. As they wait, Harry Fatt, the corrupt union leader, talks to his henchmen on the platform about why he does not want to have a strike vote. He is jeered by actors playing hecklers planted in the theatre auditorium. He leans out and addresses these unseen voices, "Stand up and show yourself, you damn red! Be a man, let's see what you look like! [*Waits in vain*]."[39] Fatt goes on speaking. By placing actors in the audience, Odets was able to give the stage event a new level of actuality. Odets adapted Strasberg's affective memory exercises so as to have each character seated on stage tell why he had come to the meeting. As Kazan states, "Over the years, in our acting classes, we'd all done scores of scenes like the ones Clifford had written."[40]

There were several things that distinguished the Odets' piece from other agitation and propaganda plays. The most obvious was the quality of Odets' writing. Union members who had attended rallies were startled to hear dialogue spoken that sounded as if it came from the hearts and minds of real working people, not actors. "The emotions were those in our hearts," writes Kazan, "The lines didn't sound learned; they leaped out of the mouth at the moment."[41] The play took forty minutes to perform, and throughout the performance spontaneous outbursts of applause began to sweep the actors forward. Fifty years later, Kazan recalled the experience as vividly as if it happened yesterday:

> It was the kind of reaction that sometimes occurs at the performance of a favorite opera singer, where every aria is well known and eagerly waited for. . . . Bits of dialogue were cheered. The scene where the wife threatens to leave her husband unless he goes on strike brought forth a salvo of cheers . . . it was like a roar from sixteen-inchers broadside, audience to players, a way of shouting: "More! More! More! Go on! Go on! Go on!"[42]

With each scene the intensity increased until the character of Agate Keller, the labor agitator, appeared on stage exhorting the audience to take action, saying, "Working class, unite and fight! Tear down the slaughterhouse of our lives. Let freedom really ring." With that, he turned on the anti-labor thugs who had been trying to silence him: "What are we waiting for. . . . Don't wait for Lefty! He might never come. . . ." At that moment Group actor Bobby Lewis rushed onto the stage with the news Lefty had been murdered. The actors and the audience exploded with rage. Agate shouted:

HELLO AMERICA! HELLO. WE'RE STORMBIRDS OF THE WORKING-CLASS. WORKERS OF THE WORLD. . . . OUR BONES AND BLOOD! And when we die they'll know what we did to make a new world! Christ, cut us up to little pieces. We'll die for what is right! Put fruit trees where our ashes are! [*to audience*] Well, what's the answer?

ALL

STRIKE!

AGATE

LOUDER!

ALL

STRIKE!

AGATE and OTHERS on stage
AGAIN!
ALL
STRIKE, STRIKE, STRIKE!!!
[*Curtain*][43]

But there was no curtain. The audience went crazy. The cast was kept on stage for forty-five minutes as the pandemonium continued. When they couldn't applaud any more, they stomped their feet until the balcony shook. Clurman likened it to a birth, "It was the birth cry of the thirties. Our youth had found its voice."[44]

One week later, the Group announced its decision to produce Odets' *Awake and Sing!* on Broadway. Strasberg, who had dismissed the play before the performance of *Waiting for Lefty* by saying, "You don't seem to understand, Cliff. We don't *like* your play," had been silenced. Clurman would direct the new play, and Kazan would stage manage. Unlike other Group efforts which had rehearsed for as long as sixteen weeks, *Awake and Sing!* opened with only four weeks of rehearsal. Ironically, a handbill announcing the Broadway opening of *Awake and Sing!* states that it is a "new play by the author of *Waiting for Lefty*." Broadway would not get to see *Lefty* until March 26, a good month after the opening of *Awake and Sing!*, and even though there had only been one critic in the audience to cover the January 6 Benefit, the word had gone out. If the Group had planned *Lefty* as an event to publicize *Awake and Sing!*, they could not have come up with a more successful promotion.

Odets had been working on *Awake and Sing!* on and off ever since his first summer at Group camp.[45] The play had originally been titled *I Got the Blues*, which reflected the mood of the piece. Clurman had disliked the gloomy script and had worked closely with Odets to restructure the second act. The Group heard the second act in the summer of 1932 and members had voiced their approval. Even so, Odets had been stymied in his work on the third act (a problem that continued to plague him with subsequent plays). Now, with the positive reception of *Lefty*, Odets moved forward, determined to make the role of Ralph, his own persona, a strong "affirmative voice." "The change had occurred in me," Odets wrote, "a growing sense of power and direction. If I was going up, everything had to go up with me."[46]

The $5,000 financing for *Awake and Sing!* came from a Group actor, Franchot Tone, who was then working in Hollywood. Cheryl Crawford somehow found the $1,500 necessary to remove the *Gold Eagle Guy* set from the stage of the Belasco Theatre. Clurman's approach to the play was to turn it into a universal statement. He saw the role of Ralph as a spokesman for the middle class. Boris Aronson, who designed the set, accompanied Jules (later John) Garfield, who was playing Ralph, home

31

to the Bronx. "Julie's family could easily be the same family in the play – the same types, the looks of the place, the people, the conversation. . . . I felt the heaviness of the furniture and the whole set-up."[47] Aronson disagreed with Clurman. The way to the universal was through the particular. *Awake and Sing!* was a play about the Depression as reflected in the lives of Jewish Americans living in a Bronx apartment. Sacrifice that particular setting, and the play lost its immediacy. His set kept the strong realistic details of the apartment but managed to reveal several rooms simultaneously.

Spirits ran high. One major difference was that Harold Clurman approached the rehearsals with a joyousness which the Group had never had under the tyrannical Strasberg, who Odets surreptitiously nicknamed General Lee. Kazan served as Clurman's stage manager and the two talents complemented each other; Clurman, as critic and theorist, and Kazan, as stager and craftsman, helped to work out the practical matters of staging. Kazan also focused on turning psychology into behavior, a gift which he would later bring to the direction of his own productions: *Death of a Salesman*, *Streetcar Named Desire*, and *Cat on a Hot Tin Roof* and to his film work: *East of Eden*, *On the Waterfront*, and *Splendor in the Grass*.

Awake and Sing! was extraordinary in that Odets was able to transform and heighten ordinary speech. Although clearly realistic, the dialogue was not simply recorded speech. It had a lyrical lilt and poetic intensity. Yet phrases such as Grandpa Jacob's line, "So life won't be printed on dollar bills" never seem forced or unnatural, although the motif is repeated several times during the evening. Like the melody of a Broadway tune, the words stay with the audience long after the curtain falls. Before Odets, American stage diction had lacked the rugged poetry that seems to be anchored in real emotion. It always seemed like an afterthought embroidered on the character's lips but never emanating from the character's soul. Odets changed all that. It was this quality which became his major contribution to the development of a Broadway style.

Although critics felt that Odets had not mastered some of the technical aspects of playwrighting, they admired his "vitality," "strength," and "fervor." Brooks Atkinson, writing for the *New York Times* (February 20, 1935) recognized that Odets was the Group's "most congenial playwright." *Awake and Sing!* played the Belasco for 137 performances, grossing $10,000 a week.

Why then did the Group fail? Perhaps the Group failed for the very reason it succeeded. It was a theatre of its time. Odets and the Group arrived at precisely that moment in American history when collective action seemed destined to transform American life. Like sister theatres such as the Federal Theatre Project under Hallie Flanagan and the Mercury Theatre under Orson Welles and John Houseman, the Group responded to the current crisis, but could not outlast it. By 1938, something different was happening in America. A new financial recession fueled reactionary forces; collective action no longer seemed to be the answer. The Group reorganized and a part-time business manager, Kermit Bloomgarden, was brought on simply to deal with financial matters. For the first time, Hollywood stars such as Frances Farmer were recruited to play leads, while founding Group members were not only dropped from the production rosters but were omitted from the program. Instead of the cast being listed in alphabetical order, leads were given star billing. Although these changes made good business sense, they violated the nature of the ensemble. Garfield, Odets, and Clurman were among those who followed the golden sun west to Hollywood. Since the Group had always been at its heart an actor's theatre, these changes and defections struck at the core of "groupness." Although Clurman's closing notice would state that there could be "no institutional product without an institutional foundation," the fact was that there could be no institution at all without institutional commitment. But the accomplishments of the Group had not gone for naught. The Group influenced the generation of writers that emerged after the Second World War, including Arthur Miller, Tennessee Williams, William Inge, and William Gibson.

33

2 The Group Theatre's production of Clifford Odets' *Waiting for Lefty* (March 26, 1935) at the Longacre Theatre on Broadway. In the center exhorting the audience to "Strike!" is Elia Kazan (Agate Keller). Courtesy of Culver Pictures, Inc.

3 Donald Oenslager's model for the set for Kaufman and Hart's *You Can't Take It With You*. According to Oenslager, Kaufman didn't know how to use models, but Oenslager obligingly produced one anyway. Courtesy of the Museum of the City of New York Theatre Collection.

4 *You Can't Take It With You* (December 14, 1936) at the Booth Theatre, the unexpected entrance of the Kirbys in Act Two. The Sycamores are caught indulging in their various pastimes. From left to right: George Tobias (Boris Kolenkhov), Paula Trueman (Essie), George Heller (Ed), Henry Travers (Martin Vanderhof), Frank Conlan (Mr De Pinna), Virginia Hammond (Mrs Kirby), William J. Kelly (Mr Kirby), Jeff Barker (Tony Kirby), and Josephine Hull (Penelope Sycamore). Courtesy of the Museum of the City of New York Theatre Collection.

3

YOU CAN'T TAKE IT WITH YOU

> They'll tell you the theatre is dying. I don't believe it. Anything that can bring us together like this, isn't going to die.
>
> Kaufman and Hart

You Can't Take It With You was the comedy hit of the 1936 season. It opened on December 14, 1936, just ten days before Christmas, taking advantage of New Yorkers' desire to find something worthy of celebration in the midst of the Depression. The title *You Can't Take It With You* was meant to console the audience with the bit of philosophy that all glories including success are temporary. However, the success of Kaufman and Hart's play has proved to be anything but temporary. The play took hold immediately and ran for 837 performances, becoming the fifth longest running show of the decade. In terms of critical acclaim, *You Can't Take It With You* won the Pulitzer Prize in 1937, the first farce to negotiate that honor. Its film sale to Columbia Pictures in which Harry Cohen bested the offer of Louis B. Mayer (MGM) was a record-setting $200,000. Frank Capra's film adaptation (starring Lionel Barrymore, Jimmy Stewart, Jean Arthur, and Edward Arnold) won the Academy Award for Best Picture in 1938. And in spite of the success of the film, the Broadway production of *You Can't Take It With You* was able to successfully compete against the motion picture for ten weeks. Today, after two successful Broadway revivals (1965 and 1983), *You Can't Take It With You* has earned the status of a Broadway classic.

By the mid-1930s, writer/director George S. Kaufman had already gained an important place in American theatre. He was responsible for more than twenty-eight productions on Broadway, twenty of which had been successes. No other living American playwright had come anywhere near Kaufman's record of achievement.[1] Kaufman preferred to share the writing responsibilities as a partner in a collaborative team, and then to direct the production. He had worked with nearly a dozen writers. *You Can't Take It With You* was his third collaboration with Moss Hart. The other two had been *Once in a Lifetime* (1930) and *Merrily We Roll Along*

34

(1934).² Kaufman and Hart had been brought together by producer Sam H. Harris (no relation to Jed Harris). Sam Harris was the producer who partnered the famous song-writing playwright George M. Cohan. Following Kaufman and Hart's early successes, Hart had felt that he needed to establish his own career. He did this by collaborating on a series of hit musicals with Irving Berlin (*As Thousands Cheer*, 1933; *Face the Music*, 1932) and with Cole Porter (*Jubilee*, 1935).

Hart's spontaneity provided the perfect foil for Kaufman's oppressive analytical temperament. According to Scott Meredith in *George S. Kaufman and His Friends*, when Kaufman was asked why he preferred Hart as a collaborator, he responded, "It's a case of *gelt* by association."³ The word-play "gelt" for "guilt," where "gelt" is Yiddish for money (from the German "geld"), indicated the value that Kaufman placed on his younger collaborator's abilities, as well as his degree of psychological ambivalence. *Once in a Lifetime* and *Merrily We Roll Along* each ran well over the century mark.

Once in a Lifetime was Kaufman and Hart's devastating spoof of what the "talkies" did to the silent film industry. The plot was simple. Three out-of-work vaudevillians go to Hollywood and teach silent stars how to speak. Their school fails, but they take over the film business. The play is filled with humorous vignettes, including the character of Lawrence Vale, a New York playwright who goes mad from idleness. He spends entire days in a movie mogul's outer office waiting to find out why he was hired. In the Broadway production, the role of Vale was played by Kaufman. Before writing *Once in a Lifetime*, neither Kaufman nor Hart had ever been to Hollywood. However, with the play's success in New York, a Los Angeles production was mounted in which Moss Hart played Vale. Although many studio executives were outraged by the way in which their business was lampooned, the movie rights were quickly sold. Life followed art, and Kaufman and Hart were hired to write the screenplay.

By 1936, Kaufman was again in Hollywood, at the behest of the Marx Brothers. He and Morrie Ryskind were being paid $100,000 to help rewrite *A Night at the Opera*. Although Kaufman hated Hollywood, it was a financial offer that was simply too good to refuse. He knew that the inevitable delays in movie-making would give him plenty of time to work on a new stage play with Moss Hart. Hart, under contract to MGM, was working regularly in Hollywood. He had just been nominated for the Academy Award for his screenplay for *Broadway Melody of 1936*.

In late May, the New Yorkers were reunited. They dined together to celebrate and to talk over possible projects. Hart wanted to adapt Dalton Trumbo's novel *Washington Jitters* for the stage. However, after a few days work, the team found themselves stymied by what they felt were the impossibilities of breathing stage life into Trumbo's political fantasy.⁴

Hart, prone to serious bouts of manic depression, was devastated. He blamed himself for the collapse of what he called the "political thing." In an effort to cheer him up, Kaufman suggested that they go back to a "pip" of an idea that Hart had had two years earlier. Kaufman reminded him that the idea had to do with a lovable, eccentric family "like nothing ever seen on land or sea." "You mean the one about the mad family?" countered Hart. They became enthusiastic in thinking about the various eccentric characters they might draw upon from their own families. They would concentrate their energies on finding an appropriate pastime for each character, leaving the plot to be worked out later. It took only three days to fix the characters in their minds:

> Each member of the household was given his share of special interests snake-collecting for one of them, playing the xylophone for another – and when all were assembled, they were fitted into three episodic acts held together by the thinnest of story lines.[5]

The night before beginning the actual task of writing, they wired Sam Harris: "Dear Sam we start work on new play tomorrow morning (stop) can you tie up at once Josephine Hull, George Tobias, Frank Conlan, Oscar Polk (stop) we are engaging Henry Travers here (stop) Moss and George."

According to Sam Harris, before noon the arrangements had been made. Harris requested the actors to accept no other engagements until Kaufman and Hart had finished writing their play. Later that day, he received a second telegram telling him to book a theatre in Philadelphia for two weeks beginning Monday, November 9. Kaufman and Hart also wanted an "intimate" Broadway theatre, preferably the Booth, for Thanksgiving week. These arrangements were also completed within a matter of hours. "Nothing like this ever happened to me before," remarked Sam Harris. "Engaging a cast before a play is written is something entirely new."[6]

Actually, what Kaufman was doing was not new to the theatre although it was new to Broadway. Kaufman's idea of writing a role for the special talents of a particular actor was centuries old; consider the case of the role of Little Eva in *Uncle Tom's Cabin* for Cordelia Howard. Broadway was not a stock company except for the likes of Kaufman, who was familiar with the talents of many actors, either from working with them on other plays or from his years at the drama desk of the *New York Times*. He knew that for *You Can't Take It With You* to work for a mass audience they had to go beyond the familial Jewish stereotypes. By anchoring the roles on specific actors who were not Jewish, he would readily be able to achieve this universality. Fifty years later, Neil Simon would follow Kaufman's example in casting non-Jews for his typically Jewish family in *Brighton Beach Memoirs*.[7] Kaufman's ability to work a known actor into a role is well illustrated in the role of Mr De Pinna. Frank Conlan was a highly skilled stage pantomimist. In burlesque, he would have been a "rubber-faced" comedian. Kaufman had cast him in the role of the window cleaner in *June Moon* in 1929. As Conlan recalled in his typescript autobiography,

> I played the shortest fat part ever written. . . . I had a most effective pantomime bit alone on the stage which brought down the climactic curtain of the play. I did not get too much notice in the opening reviews but as the run went on I got cumulative attention, pictures in the *Sunday Times* rotogravure section and the *Theatre Magazine*.[8]

Since the role of Mr De Pinna has no particular plot function, it is likely that were Conlan not available to play this part, they would have substantially changed or eliminated it. However, with Conlan available, they knew that they had an actor who could create a hysterical pantomime as he posed bald-headed in a toga for Penny Sycamore's "Discus Thrower." Establishing a place in the play where this scene could be useful helped give Kaufman and Hart a structure for their play. They would build to this scene and rely on Conlan to do the rest. So effective was Conlan's Mr De Pinna that he again garnered feature stories and even newspaper interviews.

With most of the character roles cast, they decided on a tight working schedule. Neither Kaufman nor Hart wished to remain in Hollywood. Kaufman was already set to direct *Stage Door*, his most recent collaboration with novelist Edna Ferber. Sam Harris planned an early October opening at the Music Box.[9] Kaufman and Hart agreed to work five hours a day including lunches. This would make it possible for them to complete an act per week. In reality, the pace went a little slower, and it took them ten days per act.

As early as June 26, Kaufman wrote to his wife Beatrice stating, "I doubt if I can convey the quality of the Hart play in writing." Certainly, this was an indication of just who was dominating the early part of the collaboration. He went on to say:

> You know it's a slightly mad family, and has to do with the daughter of the house, the only sane one. She falls in love with the son of a conventional family, and the play proper concerns her attempts to reconcile the irreconcilable elements. The Tony family comes to dinner – arriving on the wrong night – and finds everything at its most cuckoo. It turns out that the young man himself has a streak of madness in him, and at the finish he converts the girl [to his unconventional views] and they both settle down happily with [her] family. But it has a point, as you see – that the way to live and be happy is just to go ahead and live, and not pay attention to the

37

world. I think the play will have a nice love story and a certain tenderness, in addition to its madness. Does it sound too naive – I don't think it will emerge as such. Of course we have some swell mad things for the family – the father manufactures fireworks in the cellar, the grandfather retired from the world in 1898 and doesn't admit that anything has happened since then, etc. Please let me know how you react.[10]

Beatrice's reactions were favorable.

Obviously, the collaborators were in high spirits. With the "cuckoo" world of Hollywood to serve as a backdrop, they decided to have fun. In the second act, Hart remembered a parlor game which he had played in Palm Springs two years earlier. It was based upon a psychological word association test. The guests, who included Richard Rodgers, Lorenz Hart, Constance Bennett, Robert Taylor, and Barbara Stanwyck, were given key words and then asked to write down the first word that came to mind. The fun came when the associated words were compared to the key words and the identity of the writer was disclosed. Kaufman and Hart thought that would be a wonderful way to probe the defenses of the stuffed-shirt Kirbys. Kaufman and Hart wrote this scene in one day.

Another day, Hart received an unusually heavy envelope at his apartment. Opening it in front of Kaufman, he found an invitation that read, "I'm having my new display of furs at the Beverly-Wilshire. May I have the pleasure of seeing you there?" It was signed "Prince George of Russia." Immediately, Kaufman decided that the pretentious invitation was so ridiculous that they had to put Prince George in the play. Hart pointed out that they already had a male Russian dancing teacher in the play. So, they decided to turn Prince George into a woman, the Grand Duchess Olga, a cousin of the late Czar and now a waitress at Childs' Restaurant. The Grand Duchess would be the last new character to be introduced. The discrepancy between her birth and her present position gives the final episode a delightful air of unreality. When she is called upon to prepare the Czar's favorite dish, "blintzes," a homely Jewish concoction of noodles and cheese, the absurdity of the entire situation immediately prompted laughter.[11]

By July 31, with the revisions of *You Can't Take It With You* not yet completed, Kaufman was forced into hiding in order to avoid a court subpoena. Without Beatrice at his side, Kaufman had found himself in the midst of a very public scandal with movie star Mary Astor. The aloof and unapproachable Kaufman had been named in a child custody suit. Miss Astor's ex-husband was claiming that Astor was an unfit mother. His evidence was a "secret diary" kept by the movie star which detailed her "thrilling ecstasy" with "George." Although the situation was certainly not fun for Kaufman, his name being in tabloid headlines from coast to coast, Kaufman and Hart were able to transform the experience into humor in *You Can't Take It With You*. The "secret diary" became a series of revolutionary messages packaged in candy boxes called "Love Dreams." Quite by accident the "Love Dreams" fall into the hands of the FBI (in life the ex-husband) who have the Sycamore family (the unconventional Kaufman) under surveillance. The FBI suspect a Communist plot and raid the Sycamore home, arresting Wall Street stockbroker Kirby as well as everyone else. When an FBI agent searches the basement, the illegally stored fireworks intended for Independence Day go off – all hell breaks loose.

In real life, the explosion was the public disclosure of the Astor affair. At first, Kaufman hoped to avoid reporters and hid in Hart's apartment. But this soon became too risky, and so he repaired to movie mogul Irving Thalberg's yacht. After a week at sea, studio employees disguised Kaufman and drove him to San Bernardino where he boarded the Santa Fe Chief to New York.

Fortunately, Kaufman and Hart's play was relatively complete. One major problem remained, finding a suitable title. A good title was extremely important for the play, and they had considered several: *Foxy Grandpa*, *Money in the Bank*, *They Loved Each Other*, and *The King Is Naked*. In a letter to his wife Beatrice, Kaufman had even gone so far as to suggest calling the play *Grandpa's Other Snake*. Even before the disclosure of her husband's duplicity, she would have nothing to do with this idea. The final title, *You Can't Take It With You*, seems not to have pleased either Kaufman or Hart, but they decided to go with it on the advice of Sam Harris, their producer.

You Can't Take It With You would have to open on December 14, not immediately before Thanksgiving as originally planned. The delay was due to the disruption in writing time occasioned by the game of hide-and-seek Kaufman had to play with reporters and the county sheriff. By mid-August, the cast received copies of the unrevised draft. Rehearsal scripts would not be completed until after Hart's arrival in New York on the eve of the first rehearsal in mid-October.

Donald Oenslager, a successful designer who worked regularly on Broadway, was hired to do the play's one set. As a teacher of design at Yale University, he defined what he sought from his student designers as "Give me ideas with resonance."[12] In *You Can't Take It With You*, the resonance was provided by an understanding of the way Kaufman worked with his actors. Geoffrey Arundel Whitworth commented, "the director had rehearsed his players as though they were an orchestra and this mad family played a lunatic symphony against a background which served as a staccato accompaniment."[13] Oenslager's realistic set had a poetic flow of receding arches. These arches helped to reinforce a feeling of unity that bound these characters together. Places for rapid entrances and exits were provided by three distinctly different doorways: a conventional door, a swinging kitchen door, and a square corniced open entrance way hung with curtains. Since the emphasis in this play was on character, Oenslager used different areas of the set to reinforce and strengthen Kaufman and Hart's creations. There was Mother's corner with its desk and typewriter. On the sideboard, there were Grandfather's snakes. Father's interest in model boats prompted Oenslager to hang a large model of a man-of-war from the center of one ceiling archway. This decoration was balanced with a plaster cast of the Elgin Marbles set above the room's main entrance. This show would provide special problems for the property man. There were no less than 742 cataloged articles spread over every little nook and corner of the set. For instance, there were eighty-three pictures, large and small, on the walls, from museum quality prints to junk. Selected more or less at random, here are a few of the items: elephant's tusk, tom-toms, stuffed crocodile, stamp album, snake solarium, samovar, ship model, accordion, human skull candy dish, bottle of gin, fifteen manuscripts, sky rockets, pile of candy boxes, statue of Venus, erector ship, and Japanese flower garden bowl. Oenslager had had a comparatively free hand in his work with the set. He described working with Kaufman:

> Despite his extraordinary instinct for the theatre, he had little sense of the visual. He could not read a ground plan. He could not understand a sketch. A scale model confused him. He had full confidence in a few favorite designers and placed complete responsibility for the setting on them.[14]

Even so, Oenslager supplied a paper cut-out model for Kaufman, illustrated in this volume.

Rehearsals began with a cast of skilled character actors. Since Kaufman had cast these actors for their special abilities, he worked closely with them to set stage business. The following account of Kaufman's work with Josephine Hull, given by her understudy, described the process:

> Mr. Kaufman and Mr. Hart are indebted to her [Josephine Hull] for many pieces of stage business. I remember one piece in particular. Miss Wellington (played by that lovely musical comedy actress Mitzi Hajos) had had too much to drink and was asleep on the sofa – had her face turned to the wall – her back to "Penny." Mrs. Hull noticed that "Miss Wellington's" buttocks were not supported by the sofa – were, in fact, suspended in midair, so "Penny" in passing lifted one knee and shoved hard, thereby depositing "Miss Wellington" more securely on the sofa. This invention of Mrs. Hull's was kept in the show and never failed to delight the audience. Such a

dear little lady doing such a practical but "vulgar" piece of business.[15]

Both Kaufman and Hart were directors as well as writers, and they knew that the success of their work depended on timing and detail.[16]

From the very beginning, the one role in the play that gave Kaufman and Hart trouble was the only "sane" member of the family, Alice Sycamore. This ingenue role is crucial to the success of this play since without the love story there is no through narrative line in the play. As Richard Watts, Jr, writing for the *Herald Tribune*[17] (December 15, 1936) commented, it was Alice's duty "to keep the infinitesimal plot alive amid the assorted character studies." To create suspense in the love interest, the Sycamores and the Kirbys had to be irreconcilably at odds. This is what Broadway insiders call a "Romeo and Juliet" story. Kaufman and Hart's major problem arose with the star-crossed lovers; how to prevent these stock figures from appearing like cardboard cut-outs. One way was to bring novelty into the love scenes. But Kaufman despised scenes built on sentimentality so thoroughly that he had a great deal of difficulty writing even minimal love scenes.

Obviously, Kaufman's attitude made it hard to cast the role of Alice. He had brought two actresses from Hollywood to New York to audition. The first one he tried out came across "too snooty" for what was supposed to be a middle-class sort of girl. Instead Kaufman cast Louise Platt, a brunette with angular features and a penetrating gaze. By the time the final dress rehearsal was held at the Ethel Barrymore Theatre in New York, Frank Conlan (Mr De Pinna) remarked that the play was in such bad shape that the stage hands, who were usually fairly accurate about predicting the success of plays, "turned thumbs down." Moss Hart was in deep despair, and so was the entire cast.

While *You Can't Take It With You* tried out at Princeton's McCarter Theatre, Miss Hacket, Kaufman's trusted assistant, had the idea that Margot Stevenson, then playing Kendall Adams in *Stage Door*, might be just right for the part of Alice. There was something about Margot Stevenson that Miss Hackett found "funny." Stevenson was a five foot five blond who had attended the Brearly School in New York and been accepted at Bryn Mawr. Rather than attend that prestigious Pennsylvania women's college, she decided to follow her father's career path and chose the stage. Margot Stevenson's father, Charles Alexander Stevenson, had been a leading man for Mrs Leslie Carter, a perennial favorite of New York theatre-goers.

Margot Stevenson recalled that she was called down to Philadelphia to read for Kaufman while *You Can't Take It With You* was running its final week of out-of-town try-outs. Following the reading, Kaufman asked Stevenson to take a walk around the park while he discussed the matter with Hart. By the time she returned, she had an offer. There was one hitch though; she would have to hide out in the hotel until they could find a job for Louise Platt. Fortunately, it all worked out and Platt accepted a film in time for Stevenson to step into the role for New York. By that time, all minor alterations to the script had been completed. Ticket sales had not been good when the play opened in Philadelphia, but the audience had been slowly building night by night. Moss Hart's mood began to shift from despair to hysteria. To allay his fears, Sam Harris told him that if *You Can't Take It With You* did not run for a year, he would never produce another play. As it turned out, Harris was wrong. The play ran for more than two years.

You Can't Take It With You opened at the Booth Theatre on December 14, 1936. The Booth, named after the American Shakespearean actor Edwin Booth, was Kaufman's first choice. It is a small house by Broadway standards, seating 687, designed for serious drama and intimate comedy.[18] At half hour, Hart was already pacing the back of the theatre. Kaufman was backstage with the actors. Last minute instructions consumed so much of his time that evening that he barely made it to his aisle seat before the lights dimmed.

As the curtain rose, first-nighters watched Penny (Josephine Hull) begin the pantomime that Kaufman had set:

> After a moment her fingers lag on the [typewriter] keys; a thoughtful expression comes over her face. Abstractedly she takes a piece of candy out of the skull, pops it into her mouth. As always, it furnishes the needed inspiration – with a furious burst of speed she finishes a page and whips it out of the machine. Quite mechanically, she picks up one of the kittens, adds the sheet of paper to the pile underneath, replaces the kitten.[19]

The kittens, named Harpo and Groucho, got a big laugh, the first of many that evening. Hull's delightfully daffy demeanor established the play's "contagious lunacy." Just as Penny seems stumped as to what to do about her manuscript, her daughter Essie (Paula Trueman) makes her gawking entrance on toe shoes. Kaufman and Hart had calculated that the odd physical movements of Essie would keep the laughter from "drying up." She is followed in turn by Rheba (Ruth Attaway) who although a servant is frequently consulted for literary advice. Before the audience can fully absorb Rheba and her disarming frankness, Penny's husband Paul comes in with a string of fire-crackers he has just made in the basement. He is followed by the bald-headed Mr De Pinna carrying two good-sized sky rockets. The parade of unusual characters continues. We next meet Ed Carmichael, an Alabama native married to Essie. Carmichael plays the xylophone and prints Trotsky's revolutionary slogans on an old-fashioned hand press. Both xylophone and printing press are located in the living room, as are the hundreds of other props that the characters use in the course of the evening. Next, there is Donald (Oscar Polk), Rheba's boyfriend. His exact function in the household depends on who he is talking to at any given moment. He is buoyant and "uncommonly droll." This series of comic characters is completed by Grandpa Vanderhof, Penny's father, who has just returned from Columbia University's commencement exercises which he attends annually to hear the speeches. He enters addressing his snakes housed in their solarium amidst the living room bric-a-brac. Grandpa, we learn, left the world of business thirty-five years earlier when he discovered that he wasn't having any fun. It is his unorthodox philosophy – do what makes you happy – that guides the Vanderhof/Sycamore family. The only member of the family who holds down a regular nine-to-five job is the youngest granddaughter, Alice. Alice is the last to arrive and announces to the family that she will not be staying for dinner because Tony Kirby, the boss's son, will be taking her to dinner and the ballet.

The family eagerly awaits Tony as Alice goes to dress for the evening. They do not have long to wait before a gentleman arrives at the house. Unfortunately, it is not Tony but a collection agent from the Internal Revenue Service. It seems that Grandpa Vanderhof has never paid any income taxes because he does not "believe" in them. A comic exchange takes place between the agent and Vanderhof who speak to each other at cross purposes. The agent is routed by a combination of snakes and fire-crackers to the relief of Grandpa and all those assembled. It's a scene that might have come from a Marx Brothers film. It is filled with comic bedlam. Moments later Tony arrives. He is followed by the surly and abrasive dancing master Kolenkhov (George Tobias), a character played for an immediate comic effect. Alice and Tony depart for their evening together. The scene ends with Grandpa Vanderhof saying grace:

> Well, Sir, we've been getting along pretty good for quite a while now, and we're certainly much obliged. Remember, all we ask is just to go along and be happy in our own sort of way. Of course we want to keep our health, but as far as anything else is concerned, we'll leave it to You. Thank You.[20]

By this time, the collective craziness of the Sycamore household has been established. In the next scene, we discover that Tony and Alice are considering marriage. This sets up the plot for the rest of the play as Alice realizes that her engagement to Tony occasions a meeting between the bohemian Sycamores and the Wall Street Kirbys. The audience is aware that it is going to witness a train wreck. Just how this will happen is unclear as is what will happen to the budding romance. The first act ends with Alice "almost unable to bear her own happiness," and her father setting off a "red fire" sparkler. Both are aglow, but in different worlds.

The audience reacted with spontaneous applause to the first act curtain. It was clear that if Kaufman and Hart could sustain the pace and novelty of their first act, they would have an extraordinary hit. Shubert Alley, which runs between Forty-fourth and Forty-fifth Street, and the tiny lobby buzzed with excitement and anticipation at the straight-laced Kirbys meeting the unconventional Sycamores.

The second act begins as just a "typical evening" at the Sycamore home. Penny has met Miss Wellington, a down-and-out actress, and invited her for an impromptu play-reading. It turns out that Miss Wellington has a slight drinking problem and passes out on the sofa. Mr De Pinna happens to find an unfinished portrait of himself as a Roman discus thrower. Penny, frustrated with her attempts at play-writing, decides that this is the moment for her to return to painting. Kolenkhov arrives at the height of his artistic temperament, embittered at having found the Grand Duchess Olga Katrina waiting tables at Childs' Restaurant. Essie takes up her dancing, Penny her painting, Grandpa his dart-throwing, and the other family members are preoccupied each with their own pastimes. The living room becomes a three-ring circus of activity, apparently random and chaotic, but in reality carefully orchestrated by director Kaufman. At the fortissimo of these diverse activities, described by one critic "as the weirdest collection of household activities ever assembled on one stage," the Kirbys enter in full formal attire. The recognition of the incongruity of the two cultures was heightened by the Gogolesque pantomime during which each character registers shock. Nowhere else in the play is the contrast between the worlds of the Sycamores and Kirbys more apparent. It is a *coup de théâtre*. On opening night, the audience responded by filling the shocked silence with laughter.

After a short pause for introductions and excuses, the Kirbys have arrived on the wrong night, etc., Kaufman and Hart pick up the pace of activity. Kolenkhov assaults Mr Kirby and then Penny begins a word association game, further probing the Kirbys' defenses. Neither Kolenkhov nor Penny intends any harm, but insult is added to injury. In spite of Tony's pleas, Mr and Mrs Kirby begin to withdraw. Alice, in despair, resigns herself to the impossibility of the marriage. She will give up her job at Kirby and Company. Just when it seems that things could not get any worse, the FBI raid the house and arrest everyone including the Kirbys. The act two curtain is punctuated by the accidental explosion of a basement full of fireworks. The relentless build to this catastrophic moment left the audience breathless. Kaufman and Hart had managed to top their first act.

As the audience caught their breath during intermission, they must have wondered how Kaufman and Hart would manage to bring Tony and Alice together by the end of the third act. The introduction of the FBI, the arrests, and the explosion seemed to have destroyed what was left of civility between the Kirbys and the Sycamores. To pull the audience back in to the play, Kaufman and Hart have the servants, Rheba and Donald, humorously recount the events of the night before. We discover that Alice won't see Tony. She is intent on leaving town. Unpredictably, attention is now diverted by the arrival of the Grand Duchess Olga Katrina. Even in the midst of the current crisis, the Sycamores receive her warmly. In fact, it is the openness of the Sycamores at such moments that reaffirms our belief in the genuineness of their unaffected humanity and wins us over. As the act unfolds, we learn that it is this same quality that appeals to Tony. In front of his father, who has come to retrieve him, Tony reveals that he had deliberately contrived to bring his parents to the Sycamore house on the wrong night so that they could see what a real family was like. It seems that the confrontation between son and father is not as much about Tony marrying Alice as it is about Tony's unwillingness to surrender his idealism to the world of middle-class cor-rectness. To bolster his argument, Tony discloses that the elder Kirby also fought with his father about the same issues. As Kirby tries to deny his son's statement, Grandpa intervenes on Tony's behalf.

> You know, Mr. Kirby, Tony is going through just what you and I did when we were his age. I think, if you listen hard enough, you can hear yourself saying the same things to *your* father twenty-five years ago. We all did it. And we were right. How many of us would be willing to settle when we're young for what we eventually get? All those plans we make . . . what happens to them? It's only a handful of the lucky ones that can look back and say that they even came close.[21]

Grandpa's simple common-sense arguments catch Kirby unprepared. He too is distracted by the Grand Duchess Olga Katrina serving blintzes and genuinely impressed by Grandpa's deception of the Internal Revenue Service. These circumstances notwithstanding, we accept Kirby's capitu-lation as a demonstration of his love for his son. As John Anderson stated in the *New York Evening Journal* (December 15, 1936), the play winds up "in the midst of the dinner table uproar with [Grandpa's] gentle, straight talk to God, which he has simply and sweetly before every meal. He calls God 'Sir.' "

> Well, Sir, here we are again. We want to say thanks once more for everything You've done for us. Things seem to be going along fine. Alice is going to marry Tony, and it looks as if they're going to be very happy. Of course, the fireworks blew up, but that was Mr. De

Pinna's fault, not Yours. We've all got our health and as far as anything else is concerned, we'll leave it to You. Thank You.[22]

Inspite of all of the play's noisy chaos, Kaufman and Hart wisely chose to end *You Can't Take It With You* on a note of quiet philosophy. This change of mode afforded the audience a moment to reflect on the play's sentimental message: that life is too short to not enjoy it and that youthful, romantic love should not be sacrificed for position and wealth. Grandpa's unorthodox ministry did not have to convert, it merely had to restate the obvious.

All the parts that Kaufman and Hart had written for the talents of particular actors: Josephine Hull (Penny), George Tobias (Kolenkhov), Oscar Polk (Donald), and Frank Conlan (Mr De Pinna) were praised for their performances. Even George Heller (Ed Carmichael), an actor who had worked with the Group Theatre (the only actor they could find who could play a xylophone) was praised. About Margot Stevenson in the role of Alice, the verdict was split: John Mason Brown in the *Post* said, "badly played"; but Robert Coleman in the *Mirror* found her "excellent."

Kaufman's direction drew positive comments from most of the reviewers. The pantomime scene at the beginning of the second act where the Kirbys made their surprise entrance was singled out as being particularly memorable. One of the moments that had concerned Henry Travers (Grandpa Vanderhof) were the two occasions when he had to address the Almighty as "Sir." "I was afraid," he told a reporter, "it might offend, but on the contrary it delights the Church people no end."[23] In fact, the final tableau, another memorable stage picture, resembled a traditional American Thanksgiving dinner. This tableau seemed so appropriate that not one critic objected to the improbability of New Yorkers serving a big turkey dinner in the heat of late June.

Brooks Atkinson, reviewing for the *New York Times* (December 15, 1936) recognized *You Can't Take It With You* as "the best comedy these authors have written." He was pleased that Kaufman and Hart did not "bear down on it with wisecracks. Although they plan it like good comedy craftsmen, they do not exploit it like gag-men." In his Sunday piece (December 20, 1936), Atkinson went further, "There is not a wisecracker in the cast. But there are enough props to furnish a madhouse." Richard Lockridge of the *New York Evening Journal* (December 20) raved, "Gargantuan absurdity, hilarious, preposterous antics and the rumble of friendly laughter with madly comic people – it is one of the funniest and heartiest plays to come from the Messrs Hart and Kaufman."

There was no doubt that Henry Travers had been wise to accept Kaufman and Hart's offer to come out of early retirement. Vanderhof was the best role of his stage career.[24] It would be his swansong on the New York stage. Atkinson's verbal picture captures his performance:

In the Shaw plays he was perfect – just ruminative enough to turn the cerebral handsprings of the master satirist. And now he is here again, pottering around placidly in the part of Grandfather, adjusting his glasses, speaking in the dry voice that gives dialogue pawkiness and common sense – withal a little breathless and uneasy as though he could not stand much more of it. Although Mr. Travers gives an impression of slumping down comfortably into a part, he really sets a part firmly on its feet.[25]

Although Hart worried even after the great notices how the "suburban trade, which likes its stuff straight, simple and akin to its own experience,"[26] would take to the play, there was obviously very little to worry about. Ticket sales were brisk. In 1936, in the midst of the Depression, even the title had ready appeal. On stage, there was plenty to keep the eye and the mind engaged. Some in the audience viewed the play as farce, others as a comedy of manners while the sophisticates greeted it as a surreal fantasy. Doneta Ferguson compared the play to the feeling she had in viewing "Salvador Dali's melting clocks."[27] The truth of the matter was there was nothing so profound to *You Can't Take It With You*. The title was not a message, although it did sum up the transitory hilarity of the evening's entertainment. What lingers long after the laughter subsides is the ingratiating warmth of the Sycamores. Ironically, Kaufman, the arch-enemy of sentiment, gave us a wistful portrait of a loving family.

4

DEATH OF A SALESMAN

I could not imagine a theatre worth my time that did not want to change the world.

Arthur Miller

Death of a Salesman (February 10, 1949) is the best-known play by one of America's most prominent playwrights, Arthur Miller. Although not his first successful production on Broadway (*All My Sons* preceded it by nearly two years),[1] *Death of a Salesman* was the play that introduced the author to a wider public. Not only did it win the Pulitzer Prize, the Critics Circle Award, and the Antoinette Perry (Tony) Award, but it was the only play ever chosen at that time for distribution by the Book-of-the-Month Club. Miller emerged as a leader in what appeared to be a renaissance of the Broadway theatre immediately following the Second World War.

Like Tennessee Williams, Miller wrote realistic dialogue that was not afraid to incorporate eloquent poetic diction. Both followed the lead of Clifford Odets in trying to liberate American drama from the limits imposed upon it by the "new realism" of the 1920s. Although most critics were struck by the emotional and thematic content of Miller's drama, his innovations in dramatic form and language in this play may prove to be his most lasting contribution to American drama. Along with Tennessee Williams' *Streetcar Named Desire*,[2] *Death of a Salesman* ranks among the most important dramas not only of the 1940s but of the past half century. Together, they set a certain larger-than-life style rooted in behavior that has remained ineluctably part of Broadway.

Both plays were popular successes appealing to a wide audience. *Death of a Salesman* proved to be so popular that tickets were bought up by speculators who "scalped" them for exorbitant fees. When audiences began to regularly exceed capacity, there was an official investigation into the ticket brokerage business. With tickets in short supply an advance sale of $250,000, two and half times the initial capitalization, built up

48

rapidly. Within a year, the play and its touring companies had grossed over $1,250,000.

However, much more significant than the play's impact on local business conditions was the play's indictment of the American dream of business success. Harold Clurman analyzed the play's thematic implications in *Lies Like Truth*: "The death of Arthur Miller's salesman is symbolic of the breakdown of the whole concept of salesmanship inherent in our society."[3]

Through use of stream-of-consciousness, Miller was able to dramatize Willy Loman's confusion between his failed dreams and the world in which he lives. Willy is someone who is unable to distinguish between reality and fantasy. After a lifetime in sales, he is unable to put his hands on anything real. Even his speech reveals his muddled state of mind. When he makes an impassioned protest to Howard, his boss, not to fire him, he says, "You can't eat the orange and throw the peel away – a man is not a piece of fruit!"[4]

Audiences were either stunned to silence or dissolved in tears over the fate of Willy. They either identified with Willy or felt they knew someone just like him. Critics wrote reams to explain the phenomenon. There were even refuting articles by a supersalesman in *Fortune* (May 1949), a business magazine, as well as psychiatric perspectives in the *New York Times Book Review* (May 15, 1949), and at the New York Psychoanalytic Institute. None of this controversy did anything to deter audiences from attending the play. *Death of a Salesman* played for 742 performances. The incredibly demanding role of Willy Loman went through three cast changes, opening with Lee J. Cobb and being followed by Gene Lockhart, Albert Dekker and Thomas Mitchell. Film and television versions followed, as did Broadway revivals with Willy played by George C. Scott (1975) and, most recently, by Dustin Hoffman (1984).

Although *Death of a Salesman* has become a classic, it was viewed by its author as a social protest play. Arthur Miller was born in 1915 in New York City to well-to-do parents. By the time Miller was 13 years old, his father was forced out of business due to the Great Depression. The family moved from a Manhattan apartment with a view of Central Park to a small frame house which resembled Willy's in Brooklyn. Miller worked his way through the University of Michigan with a series of odd jobs. During this period, he became an avid fan of the Group Theatre, strongly influenced by Clifford Odets. A college play, *They Too Arise*, won the Theatre Guild National Award. Upon graduation, he joined the Works Progress Administration Federal Theatre Project in New York. After the funds were stripped from the Federal Theatre by Congress, he wrote scripts for radio.

All My Sons, Miller's second Broadway outing, won the Drama Critics Circle Award in 1947. It was directed by Elia Kazan of Group Theatre fame. At that time, Kazan was the hottest young director in America. His services were in demand both on stage and in film. Kazan, like Miller, had a strong social consciousness. One of the reasons he was attracted to Miller's Ibsenite *All My Sons* had to do with the play's strong condemnation of capitalist war profiteers. Miller's play depicts what happens to a manufacturer and his family who knowingly sell the armed forces defective engine parts.

The following season Kazan invited Miller to New Haven to see the out-of-town try-out of the new Tennessee Williams' play, *A Streetcar Named Desire*. According to Miller in *Timebends, a Life* "this theatrical experience – opened one specific door for me. Not the story or characters or the direction, but the words and their liberation, the joy of the writer in writing them, the radiant eloquence of its composition, move me more than all its pathos."[5] What also impressed Miller was the powerful effect Williams achieved by mixing expressionistic elements with conventional stage realism. In a sense, Williams' poetic realism challenged Miller to reach deeper than he had ever reached before into his own unconscious sources. Until that moment, Miller's method of composition followed the dramatic structure of the "well-made play" stressing the social context as the primary cause of a character's actions. In *All My Sons*, for instance, Miller decided upon his second act climax and then worked backwards to the beginning of the play, setting up a linear pattern of cause and effect. As Miller wrote in the *Introduction to his Collected Plays*, he was now willing to try something new:

> The first image that occurred to me, which was to result in *Death of a Salesman*, was of an enormous face the height of the proscenium arch which would appear and then open up, and we would see the inside of a man's head. In fact, *The Inside of His Head* was the first title.[6]

Having walled himself away from the world in the cabin he had built in Connecticut, Miller allowed the whole story of Willy to find its own shape as a series of fluid images informed by memories and structured as a confession. Rather than concentrating on cause-and-effect dramaturgy, he began his story near the end. Miller unfolded the drama to his audience very much the way he felt it taking shape:

> The *Salesman* image was from the beginning absorbed with the concept that nothing in life comes "next" but that everything exists together and at the same time within us; that there is no past to be "brought forward" in a human being, but that he is his past at every moment.[7]

In dramatic terms Miller's play had eschewed intrigue and suspense for recognition and shock. He relied on his audience accepting Willy Loman and understanding that from the very beginning that what they had gathered to see was the death of a salesman. This sense of providing witness forms the basis of the first written dialogue in Miller's notebook.[8] In this first version, two guards stand atop the Empire State Building and discuss who will jump today. Although Miller abandoned this externalized vision, he hoped that his audience would accept the inferences of motivation that are embedded in the play. For those who needed an explanation, he decided to supply a "requiem." At the grave site, those closest to Willy would state what for each was the significance of the life. There were two dimensions to Miller's characters. On one level, they would be autonomous while on another, all the characters would exist in Willy's head. Miller saw the play as an extensive dramatic poem. Yet even this idea changed in composition as Miller began to realize how interdependent Willy and his son Biff were as characters. Although no specific actions in the play cause the tragedy of Willy Loman, Miller found that he could not complete the play until he had discovered what was the linkage between Biff's work views and his anti-Willy feelings. As Miller probed this relationship, his perceptions about Biff began to subtly change. In his notebook draft, Miller initially conceived of Biff as a vindictive character driven by the guilt of not being able to live up to Willy's expectations. The initial thrust of his writing had been to precipitate conflict to propel the suicide. There were several crucial issues: the discovery of the woman in the Boston hotel, the display of the gas heater tube apparatus, and the revelation of the stolen pen. When Miller resolved that the stolen pen was the climax of the play, he realized that Biff's motivation was based on a desire to "save Willy." Subsequently, Miller toned down the anger of Biff's rhetoric.

In general, the process of revision entailed sorting out and intensifying the memories in the first act and tightening the structure in the second so that Biff could utterly down Willy's ambitions in a *positive* way. In a marginal note, Miller states:

> Life is formless – its interconnections are concealed by lapses of time, by events occuring in separate places, by the hitches of memory. We live in a world made by man and the past. Art suggests or makes the interconnections palpable. Form is the tension of these interconnections, man with man, man with the past and present environment. The drama at its best is a mass-experience of this tension.[9]

Biff's breakdown and final statement to Willy, "I'll go in the morning,"[10] are interpreted by Willy as a sign of love. It is Willy's desire to reward Biff's love that finally makes the suicide possible. So, although Willy is a man living under the sentence of death as the title suggests, it is not until he finds a positive reason in *his* mind to choose death over life that he elects suicide. The conventions of Greek tragedy are upheld and Willy dies off-stage.

Miller discussed the idea of the play with Kazan in April. In May, he spent one day and the early morning hours of the following day writing the play. Miller claims that he wrote the first two-thirds of the current *Death of a Salesman* script in that one long session. It then took him six weeks to complete the second act. He sent Kazan the completed manuscript in July.[11] In *Timebends*, Miller states that although he did not realize it then, he had actually written a preliminary draft of the play in college.[12] About the new draft, he felt, "It was conceived half in laughter, for the inside of his head was a mass of contradictions." Later, he clarified his feelings: "I realized I had been weeping – my eyes still burned and my throat was sore from talking it all out and shouting and laughing."[13]

Miller had based the character of Willy in part on his Uncle Manny, a salesman who worked the New England territory. He had recently met Manny after a performance of *All My Sons* at the Colonial Theatre in Boston during which time Miller stated that he thought he knew what Manny was thinking; that he, Manny, "had lost the contest in his mind between his sons and me."[14] Miller's feeling of superiority at this meeting helps to explain why he wrote the play with a feeling of triumphant vindication. Perhaps, the play is a work of "psychic journalism," recording not just a time and an event, but the state of mind of the author in observing those times. Perhaps this is why this play seems less limited than *All My Sons* by the attitudes of the late 1940s. The critical perceptions needed to understand this drama are completely integrated into the play's composition.

As Kazan relates in his autobiography, after he read *Death of a Salesman*, "I didn't wait for the next morning to see if I'd have a more 'balanced' judgement . . . but called Art as I turned the back cover and told him his play had 'killed' me."[15] Kazan's enthusiasm was more than momentary. He still maintains *Death of a Salesman* is his "favorite" play. "I am a man who has trained himself to let no pain show," wrote Kazan, "but I felt tears coming as I turned that page."[16] For Kazan, the play revived memories of his father. Yet it was not just the play's unabashed emotionalism that prompted Kazan's interest in 1948. Kazan wrote:

> Here is an antisystem play that is not "agitprop." We are out of the thirties at last – the audience does not have to suffer instruction or correction. The essence of our society, the capitalist system, is being destroyed not by rhetoric but by that unchallengeable vocabulary, action between people, which makes you believe that the terrible things that happen are true, are inevitable, and concern us all.[17]

Although it was not customary for Kazan, the director did not request

Miller to rewrite his script; in fact, he only writes of it happening one other time with Tennessee Williams' *A Streetcar Named Desire*. Kazan states, "Those plays were born sound."[18] Instead, he joined Miller in seeking to find a producer for the play.

Kazan's first choice was Cheryl Crawford. After her Group years, Crawford had gone out on her own and had become a successful Broadway producer. Her relationship with early years of the Group meant that director and producer would have shared experiences and vocabulary. There was no underestimating the importance of these shared values in the frequently divisive process of putting together a Broadway production. However, much to Kazan's surprise, Crawford was dubious about *Salesman*'s "commercial potential." Rather than try to talk her into taking on a project for which she exhibited little enthusiasm, Kazan and Miller decided to approach another Group associate who had now become an independent producer, Kermit Bloomgarden.

Bloomgarden, unlike Crawford, had never been a major force in the Group. In fact, he was brought in after the split with Crawford and Strasberg in the late 1930s as part-time business manager. Since he had begun as an accountant, neither Miller nor Kazan considered him an important artistic associate. Kazan summed up Bloomgarden as "an excellent 'line' producer, who had the ability to see to it that everything necessary for mounting a show arrived on time and in good working order."[19] Miller also was dismissive, "I had last seen [him] poring over Herman Shumlin's account books a couple of years before when Shumlin turned down *All My Sons* . . . Bloomgarden squeezed up his morose version of a smile, or at least a suggestion of one he planned to have next week."[20] However, unlike Crawford, Bloomgarden was enthusiastic about *Death of a Salesman* and with some reluctance the playwright and the director agreed to give the project to him.

Bloomgarden was certainly aware of his outsider status. When a playwright and a director walk into a producer's office together with a play, the producer has already lost a measure of control, if for no other reason, than he no longer has anything to say about who will direct. Kazan's relationship to this project was so central that he was given 7½ percent of the gross box-office receipts as a contractual commitment. This is considerably higher than most directors can command. In fact, it was equal to the then contracted Dramatists Guild minimum given to playwrights. But Kazan was no ordinary director. After *A Streetcar Named Desire* and *All My Sons*, he was already a legend. This meant that Bloomgarden would have to go out of his way to prove his value in this relationship.

After signing contracts, Kazan decided that he needed Miller to rewrite portions of the script in order to smooth out the number of scene changes. At that time, Miller's script specified bare platforms on stage, a kind of no-man's-land setting. There were almost sixty different scenes and Kazan was afraid that the back-and-forth motion of the play would slow the production down considerably in front of a live audience. Kazan asked Miller to put the flashback sequences together. The resulting script was, according to Bloomgarden, so unsatisfactory that he threatened to withdraw. "What I read originally," Bloomgarden stated, "I would be very proud to do, but not this."[21] He then forcefully argued for a return to the original script. This was fortunate at this moment in the relationship because it put a little distance between Miller and Kazan, which Bloomgarden would need if he were to be able to do anything useful as a part of the production team.

According to Miller, one of the ideas discussed during this early period was the possibility of cutting the final scene, "the requiem."[22] This would have placed the entire action inside Willy's head, which might have served as a central visual symbol. However, this would only solve the problem of eliminating one scene, leaving multiple times and locations in the script. Miller felt that it would greatly reduce the scope of his story, which was about a salesman, not just about the Loman family. It was at this point that Bloomgarden made his most important contribution to the production. He suggested that Jo Mielziner be brought in to design the set because he would be able to solve many of the script's problems through the use of stage lighting. Up until that moment, Miller had wanted Boris Aronson, the designer who had created the connected family living quarters for Odets' *Awake and Sing!*

Mielziner met with Bloomgarden on September 24, 1948. Bloomgarden was frank when he characterized the *Death of a Salesman* as a "real toughie." Miller had left the solution of the rapid changes in time and place to be worked out by the designer. Although Mielziner had already been contracted to design Rodgers and Hammerstein's *South Pacific*, he agreed to read the script over the weekend. Bloomgarden wanted to put *Death of a Salesman* into production within two weeks and open in New York before Christmas. By any stretch of the imagination such a time table would have been a rush job. By the time Mielziner had read as far as page seven, he had resolved upon the silhouette of the house that became central to his conception. He made a pencil sketch in the margin of that page.[23] On the morning of September 25, he reviewed his breakdown of the scenes, and he became convinced that the central and most important visual symbol in the play was the image he had drawn of the salesman's house. He envisioned the house as skeletonized, allowing the audience to see the family in their different living areas. Mielziner wrote:

> Therefore, why should that house not be the main set, with all the other scenes – the corner of a graveyard, a hotel room in Boston,

the corner of a business office, a lawyer's consultation room, and so on – played on a forestage?[24]

One of the first sketchs of Mielziner's conception is reproduced in this volume.

Later that day, Mielziner met with Bloomgarden, Miller, and Kazan. He discussed his conceptualization of the production. A long silence followed and then an even longer discussion. "The decision to be made was not just a visual one;" wrote Mielziner, "it would set the style in direction and performance, as well as in design." "Art," said Kazan, "this means a hell of a lot of work for me, and even more for you." At this point, it became clear to Bloomgarden that the idea of going into production in two weeks was simply out of the question. He would need to reschedule theatres both out-of-town and in New York. "It's up to you fellows to make the decision," said Bloomgarden, "I'll go along if you feel you really need the time."[25]

For Bloomgarden, who only produced one show a season, delaying a show was a major setback. There were no stars signed for the production, although several had been approached. *Death of a Salesman* had already been turned down by Ernie Truax, Walter Huston, and Fredric March. Therefore, although the decision to delay the show would mean possible problems in getting a theatre, it did not involve changing obligations already made to signed talent.

Mielziner's solution meant that the play would not have to have multiple realistic sets, nor would a curtain have to be used to interrupt the flow of the action. The play could flow like music from start to finish. However, it did pose certain problems. In this second version of the play, Miller indicated that there were to be both older and younger actors for Biff, Happy, and Bernard. However, with the decision to eliminate the young actors, there were problematic scene changes for the single actors playing both the old and young characters. For instance, if Biff and Happy went up to their rooms to bed in act one in their thirties, how could they then appear within a few minutes on the forestage as teenagers ready to play football? For Miller, this first transition was crucial because it set the tone of the play. On October 4, Mielziner suggested creating trick beds for Biff and Happy, beds with paper mache pillows placed downstage, and drop platforms under the blankets. Once the boys got into the beds, they could be lowered by hidden elevators out of sight of an unsuspecting audience. Moreover, if Miller lengthened Willy's monologue, there would be just enough time to allow the actors to change before they had to appear on the forestage.

By October 8, Bloomgarden had booked Princeton, where he planned on opening the show on January 21. A two-week run in Philadelphia would follow. The Broadway opening would be at the Morosco on

February 10, a playhouse that had gained a reputation for serious drama dating back to O'Neill's *Beyond the Horizon.*

With these matters out of the way, it was possible to address the real problem, casting. During this period, Kazan's energies were divided. He was directing a new musical, *Love Life* and trying out in Boston as well as going back and forth to Hollywood over future film projects. His ideas with regard to casting Willy were different from Miller's. Miller had imagined Willy to be a small, nervous man with a large domineering wife. After auditioning a number of small, nervous actors, Miller began to change his mind. He had been willing to consider Fredric March, an actor who was neither small nor nervous, could he now be interested in Lee J. Cobb?

Miller's image of Cobb dated back to his Group Theatre work: "a mountainous hulk covered with a towel in a Turkish bath in an Irwin Shaw play."[26] His last appearance on Broadway was in Moss Hart's *Winged Victory* (1943).[27] For the past five years, Cobb had been in Hollywood, where he had been cast as a tough guy. As everyone knew, there was nothing small about Cobb. If anything, he was intimidating, larger than life. When he received a copy of the script, he became so absolutely convinced that this part was written for him that he piloted his own twin engine plane cross-country to New York. Upon his arrival in Bloomgarden's office, he announced to a somewhat startled Miller, "This is my part. Nobody else can play this part. I know this man." But Miller was skeptical. Cobb was such a far cry from what he had imagined.[28]

Kazan's decision to cast Cobb as Willy was like Mielziner's use of the house as a central symbol, a major decision that had larger implications. Not only would this have an impact on all other casting decisions, but it set a style for the production. The salesman of the title was no longer a character in a realistic drama, one of life's victims, but a force doing battle with the system. It was consistent with Kazan's basic decision which Mildred Dunnock stated was, "To direct the play on an epic level, and so all the characters he cast were bigger than life."[29] Cobb, who was then 37 years old, was cast against type. He would play a man in his mid-sixties.

Casting Linda Loman proved to be more difficult. At least twenty actresses were read for the part. By mid-October, Kazan had cast Anne Revere for the role, an accomplished actress who had played the role of the reticent Martha Dobie, headmistress in Lillian Hellman's *The Children's Hour* (1934).[30] Within two weeks, Revere had left to take a film role. Mildred Dunnock, who had been passed over earlier, arranged with Bloomgarden to get a copy of the script. She informed the producer that she felt so strongly about this play that she would accept understudy status. On this basis, Kazan and Miller agreed to see her. Neither Kazan nor Miller could imagine her in the role. For Miller, Linda Loman was a woman who "lived in a house dress all her life, even somewhat coarse and certainly less than brilliant."[31] When Dunnock had finished with her first interview, she knew that she had to overcome the image that Kazan had of her as frail, delicate, and cultivated. So she appeared at the next audition wearing padding under a worn housecoat. The disguise was effective and at first neither Kazan nor Miller recognized her. "She was not quite ordinary," Miller states, yet, "she reminded you of women who were."

> But we all agreed, when she was finished reading, that she was not right, and she left. Next day she was there again in another getup, and the next and the next, and each day she agreed with us that she was wrong; and to make a long story short when it came time to make the final selection it had to be Milly, and she turned out to be magnificent.[32]

Dunnock was not signed until December 6. There were a few other casting problems. Casting Winnfred Cushing, from a proper Boston family, as the woman Willy has up to his hotel room again went against type. Cushing would have to concentrate her energies on specific behavioral choices to convey the psychology of the role, rather than on something intrinsic about her as an actress. This was consistent with what Kazan wanted. One role that had given Kazan and Miller no problems was the role of Biff, which would be played by J. Arthur Kennedy. Kennedy had recently played Chris Keller in *All My Sons* and received excellent notices. Brooks Atkinson (*New York Times*, January 30, 1947) wrote, "a superb performance with great power for the climaxes and with insight into the progress of the character." They felt so strongly that Kennedy was "right" that they gave him a contract that required equal billing to any other actor in the production. Later, this concession was to become the source of a bitter conflict between Kennedy and Cobb, when the latter felt his performance warranted name-above-the-title billing.

The physical side of the production was also coming together in early December. Mielziner knew that there would be a lot more lighting instruments used than in most dramas, in fact as many as in most musical productions. But before he could order the equipment, he had to have Bloomgarden and Kazan's approval. As early as November 1, Mielziner had indicated that the lack of stage depth at the Morosco, only twenty-seven feet deep, was going to pose problems with the forestage idea, but Kazan was in Hollywood and the model of the set he received by airmail had not alerted him to the problem. Now, standing in the theatre itself, Kazan became aware that not only were there significant lighting problems, but he needed more space downstage. "Kerm, I'm afraid I'm going to kill at least a row and a half of seats," he announced.[33] Max Allentuck, the general manager, began quickly calculating out what this meant in terms of the show's profitability. After some discussion, a compromise was reached. Only eleven front-row seats in the middle section would have to be sacrificed to create room for a new extended forestage. Bloomgarden agreed even though this meant a loss of $343.40 per week, not an inconsiderable sum over a year. He also agreed to two special follow-spots, lighting instruments generally reserved for musicals. This meant two follow-spot operators would have to be hired for the show, adding to the show's running crew requirements. Covering over the orchestra pit for the new forestage also meant that the musicians would have to be placed in a dressing room with music being piped in over loudspeakers. As it turned out, this decision enabled greater control and better co-ordination with the intricate lighting plot, both of which were desirable for this show.[34] One other thing became clear at this time: the half-week engagement in Princeton would have to be scrapped due to the lighting demands. There would be enough problems playing *Death of a Salesman* in Philadelphia in a theatre that had significantly different dimensions than the Morosco.

Bloomgarden had been able to accommodate these last-minute changes because he had raised twice as much capital as he needed for the production. His original budget had been based on a multiple set show. Mielziner's clever set was saving him a ton of money. A look at the investor's list for the production finds several well-known theatre people investing, such as Lillian Hellman, Leland Haywood, and Joshua Logan. Few had read the play. Bloomgarden refused to circulate scripts because he believed that even knowledgeable theatre people did not know how to read a play. Therefore, those who invested did so out of faith. In the case of Leland Haywood, who badgered Bloomgarden until he received a copy, the initial commitment was reduced by half after reading the script. Obviously, this underscored Bloomgarden's point. Haywood, who produced *South Pacific*, was unable to see the financial potential for *Death of a Salesman*.

Bloomgarden had not returned the excess capitalization. He was aware that with a show that was as "tough" as *Death of a Salesman*, a contingency funding might be necessary. He also knew that from a press standpoint, it would be good to be able to announce that after the road engagement, the production had as much on account as it had cost. Bloomgarden knew how to turn his accountant's education into catchy Broadway headlines.

In fact, headlines were so much on Bloomgarden's mind that he was troubled by the play's title. He talked the matter over at length with his partner, Walter Fried, and could not accept that a play that began with "death" could be a hit. After conducting a poll of other managers and producers which only confirmed his misgivings, he decided to approach Kazan with a new title, *Free and Clear*. These were Linda's last words as she struggled to comprehend Willy's death. Evidently, he won some sort of nodding agreement from Kazan that he would not oppose the name change if Miller could be brought round. However, on the day that Bloomgarden had set to spring his promotional wizardry on the playwright, Miller first saw Kazan, who warned, "They want to talk to you about something I'm dead against. Don't you dare say yes."[35] Miller stood his ground. His Dramatists Guild contract assured him of his rights. Bloomgarden, not to be bested, planted a story about the controversy in *Variety*. It got a headline. He was either a poor loser or a great press agent!

Rehearsals began in New York in the small theatre atop the New Amsterdam Theatre.[36] The larger house had been home to the famed *Ziegfield Follies*. Actors Equity Association agreements allowed producers to dismiss an actor after five days of rehearsal without special compensation. The first actor cast to play Howard was replaced during this period and there were discussions about replacing Cobb. According to Miller, for the first ten days of rehearsals, Cobb stumbled around the stage "in a buffalo's stupefied trance, plodding with deathly slowness from position to position, and behaving like a man who had been punched in the head."[37] While the other actors were nearing performance levels, Cobb seemed hopeless. Miller states that he and Kazan were beginning to question their initial decision and began to refer to him as "the Walrus." It was not until the twelfth day of rehearsal that Cobb caught fire. Miller describes the event brilliantly:

> Lee stood up as usual from the bedroom chair and turned to Mildred Dunnock and bawled, "No, there's more people now. . . . There's more people!" and, gesturing toward the empty upstage where the window was supposed to be, caused a block of apartment houses to spring up in my brain, and the air became sour with the smell of kitchens where once there had been only the odors of earth, and he began to move frighteningly, with such ominous reality that my chest felt pressed down by an immense weight.[38]

From that point on, Cobb began to build one of the most memorable performances in the American theatre. However, there were problems that still needed to be worked out. Kazan requested changes of emphasis in the script. He wanted the Ben scenes strengthened. He felt that they were too shadowy. In the restaurant scene in the second act, he asked Miller to make it clearer that Biff was willing to tell the truth, but his father wouldn't hear it. According to Bloomgarden, Kazan also needed to redirect the end of the first act. The first staging had been highly sentimental which shifted the archetypical proclamation of a failed

American myth back to slice-of-life realism. Although Kazan wanted to turn psychology into behavior, he wanted to control it with a style. Willy Loman wasn't a particular salesman. He was Every-salesman, human yet monumental.

When *Death of a Salesman* opened in Philadelphia, it had less than a $2,000 advance sale. By the time it finished its two-week run, it was playing to packed houses. According to Mildred Dunnock, it was not until Philadelphia that she understood how to do the "attention must be paid" speech in Act One. One afternoon, Kazan asked her to meet him at a concert of Philadelphia's famed symphony orchestra. During the concert, Kazan pointed to the conductor and informed the actress that the next day he would take a baton and conduct her through this difficult section. It was an excellent metaphor for Miller's play. It was in fact a symphonic work and Kazan was its conductor. During the rehearsal the following day, Kazan stood in the auditorium waving a stick and shouting, "Louder, louder, louder." Dunnock states, "I stopped, burst into tears and said, "I can't, I won't do it that way." Kazan replied, "That's exactly the way you will do it." Dunnock protested, "Where are all the nuances?" Kazan rejoined, "We'll come to those in a couple of weeks."[39] The "Attention must be paid" monologue became famous, along with the work of Mildred Dunnock.

During the Philadelphia run celebrities began to arrive from New York. Both *Variety* and the Philadelphia critics had given *Salesman* raves. Fredric March was only one of the many who made the trip down from New York to see what the commotion was about. By the time *Death of a Salesman* was due to open in New York, the word was out. This play was going to be one of the big hits of the decade, another *A Streetcar Named Desire*.

For opening night, the carriage trade was not in evidence – the 1930s had seen their passing – instead there was a celebrity house complete with movie stars. As the curtain rose, audiences were struck by what critic Robert Dash called Mielziner's "compressed" and "huddled" set. The first vision of Willy weighted down by his suitcases was the behavioral stance that became the emblem of the production. Kazan, with Cobb, had found a way of conveying physically, through Willy's form silhouetted in light, the huge burden that Willy was carrying. It was the burden of his life. Everything both began and ended with this vision of the man. The audience quickly took the measure of the man and saw Willy as part of a vanishing breed. John Mason Brown of the *Saturday Review* compared Lee J. Cobb to a "great shaggy bison" and more than one critic commented upon his "grandeur."

Few in the audience perceived the play as Miller had when he wrote it as a vision of Willy's mind. They followed the play as a progression highlighted by flashbacks.[40] The audience marveled at the rapidity of physical movement as the play shifted quickly from climax to climax in breathless leaps over time and space. Unknowingly, William Hawkins in the *New York World Telegram* paid tribute to Mielziner's technical wizardry when he wrote, "One moment the two sons have gone to bed upstairs in plain sight, weary and cynical, and an instant later they are tumbling in youthful exuberance to the tune of their father's delighted flattery." As the first act built to its dramatic climax, the audience felt the play's "heart-wringing reality" (February 11, 1949). They felt the full burden of the moral responsibility that Linda placed on her sons. Ward Morehouse writing for the *New York Sun* (February 11, 1949) observed,

> There is the tremendously moving scene when the patient and loving mother sits down with the boys as they are sardonically considering their father's faults and reminds them that Willy has worked hard, that he was a good provider, and had more good in him than in a lot of other people.

Mary McCarthy, critic for the *Partisan Review*, not only noticed Linda's lines "So attention must be paid,"[41] but she realized their significance; that Linda was "really admonishing the audience that Willy is, as she says, 'a human being.' " "The mother's voice raised in the age-old Jewish rhythms," she wrote, "seems to have drifted in from some other play that was about particular people."[42] And when Linda concluded her remarks with, "Biff, I swear to God! Biff, his life is in your hands!" the audience felt the burden that had been placed on Biff's shoulders. There was no doubt that the audience understood what was expected of the sons of the Loman family.

Before the end of the first act, the cast was aware of the quality of the audience response. As Mildred Dunnock noted, "We felt when we played in it that we could do no less than our best because somehow the audience got so involved in what was happening."[43]

In the second act, critics were struck by Howard's "heartless" (*Post*) treatment of Willy, and *Variety* felt that at that moment "[Willy's] world tumbles around him." By the time Willy had reached Charlie's office, the audience found that "the jesting Charlie" could no longer "aid a shocked and disillusioned old man" (*Herald Tribune*). *Variety* believed Biff when he stated that he was, "a petty-thieving failure" and that Happy was a "lecherous wastrel." Yet, when Biff "catches his father in the midst of a sordid affair" with a "common trollop," the audience etched in its memory the terrifying image of Willy first grabbing for Biff and then falling to the ground shouting, "I gave you an order! Biff, come back here or I'll beat you! Come back here! I'll whip you!"[44] Just as they had registered Biff's "anguish" when he breaks away for home, "broken-hearted."[45]

But there could be little doubt, according to Thomas R. Dash

(*Women's Wear*, February 11, 1949), that first-nighters found "the most stirring scene of the play" to be when Biff "accuses his father of having ruined them all by his effort to make ordinary little people superior beings." The emotionality of the final confrontation so overwhelmed the audience that only one critic saw Willy's suicide as a sacrifice for his son's future. Robert Coleman in the *Mirror* (February 12, 1949), noted that

> [Biff] then determines to salvage something from his wasted life. He has always hated the sham of the big city, the bluster of the go-getter, and decides that his future lies in the clean air of the western outdoors. To make this possible the father, in deep love, takes his own life.

The other reviewers tended to accept Linda's statement made at the end of Act One that Willy's "life is in [Biff's] hands" and judged accordingly. Ward Morehouse's (*Sun*, February 11, 1949) response was typical,

> By this time his two sons, in whom he had taken such pride and who have disappointed him, gravely, are contemptuous of him. His own fault, because he taught them wrong, and when he needed them they turned against him.

No doubt *Death of a Salesman* might have been reduced to a domestic melodrama were it not for Miller's insistence on retaining the "Requiem."[46] With the realistic gravestone stripped away, the characters were better able to put Willy's life into perspective. Linda's tearful speech seemed to haunt the unadorned stage. There was an intense silence when she spoke, and the silence grew when she stopped. The audience needed time to absorb what it had just witnessed. Even after Linda left the stage, the audience was caught up. Finally, after what seemed a long time, there was a great outpouring of emotional applause.

In that long silence, no one was seriously thinking about the play's political implications. This was a human drama, and everyone had been deeply moved. "Only the most fatuous observer could think of *Death of a Salesman* as a propaganda play, and yet, it manages to go deeply enough into contemporary values to be valid and frightening social criticism," wrote Richard Watts, Jr in the *Post* (February 11, 1949),

> Poor Willy Loman, who thought that, for a successful salesman, popularity and fellowship were all and tried to teach his sons what he believed was his wisdom, is a completely credible victim of a prevailing code, as the encroachment of old age destroys its shabby plausibility.

What most struck the critics on opening night was the quality of the acting.[47] There was universal praise for the cast. Atop everyone's list for honors was Lee J. Cobb in the role of Willy Loman. The adjectives that were repeated over and over again by the critics all had to do with the size and depth of the characterization. The word most frequently used was "magnificent." Brooks Atkinson used the word "heroic" in the *Times*. More than one critic compared Willy to Lear, and all stressed the "strength" and "power" of the actor. "Power" was also the word most frequently used to describe the play itself.

Kazan, Miller, and Bloomgarden all commented about Cobb's unstable personality while playing Willy. It was clear that the role was having a profound affect on him both on- and off-stage. Off-stage and on, his relationship with other actors in the cast was as tension-packed. Even though he was the acknowledged centerpiece of the production, he took to berating and jeering other cast members backstage. He provoked a dispute with Kennedy regarding billing. He constantly complained of health problems and sent Miller and Kazan into a panic when he feigned a heart attack. No doubt, Cobb had problems in sustaining the role, but so did Dustin Hoffman. Hoffman not only took several weeks off in the midst of his limited Broadway run, but reduced the playing week by dropping matinée performances. As critics have observed, Loman has as much stage time as any of Shakespeare's major tragic heroes, and whereas the structure of Shakespeare's plays usually provides for a fourth act rest allowing the actor a little time to recover while the consequence of the character's earlier actions catch up with him, Willy is in the thick of it from the moment the lights come up in Act One. Moreover, Miller's marvelously fluid sense of time places incredible demands on an actor's power of concentration. Unlike Shakespeare's plays where time marches forward with inexorable certainty, particularly in the final act, time for Willy functions as an expression of his own confused state of mind. The actor is never carried forward by the force of the play, but must constantly release energy to drive the play forward. Alan Hewitt (Howard) related this telling anecdote about his backstage encounter with Cobb after the first public performance:

> Lee and I met while crossing under the stage, coming from opposite directions to get in place for curtain calls. Lee had just exited to kill himself. You heard the sound of Willy's car starting up and zooming away, and then a moment later, with Jo Mielziner's marvelous transformation of light, you had his funeral on a forestage built out over the orchestra pit. Lee was walking heavily, with his shoulders slumped and mouth hanging open from emotional and physical exhaustion. As I came past him, I said, "Been on yet?" And he looked around in a strangled way and this awful sound came from him. Then he put his hand over his mouth so they wouldn't hear him on stage and fell apart with laughter. He never

forgot this and would often remind me, years later, how I had pulled him out of Willy Loman's misery and back to life as Lee Cobb.[48]

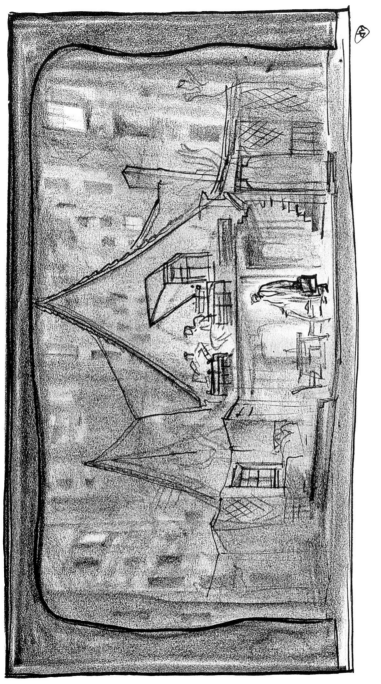

5 Jo Mielziner's sketch for the opening of *Death of a Salesman* with the skrim in place. It was this sketch that convinced producer, director, and author that the play could be anchored around Willy's house. By permission of the Estate of Jo Mielziner, courtesy of W. H. Crain Collection, Harry Ransom Humanities Research Center, University of Texas at Austin.

6 The beginning of Act One, Arthur Miller's *Death of a Salesman* (February 10, 1949) at the Morosco Theatre. Left to right: Lee J. Cobb (Willy Loman), Mildred Dunnock (Linda), J. Arthur Kennedy (Biff), and Cameron Mitchell (Happy). The size of the Morosco stage and the need for rapid escapes required several changes from the initial sketch, but the look and the feel of Mielziner's first sketch remained the same. Photo by Graphics House, Inc., courtesy of the Museum of the City

7 Jo Mielziner's set for Tennessee Williams' *Cat on a Hot Tin Roof* (March 24, 1955) at the Morosco Theatre. The traditional box set is turned on an angle, reflecting the twisted world of the play's characters. This is highly selective realism with only a few essential details. The downstage corner of the room juts into the auditorium allowing Kazan the freedom to ignore realistic convention and deliver the play's poetic language directly to the audience. On the lip of that thrust, one could almost imagine the young Kazan as Agate Keller (*Waiting for Lefty*) raising his hands aloft. Fred Fehl Collection, courtesy of Theatre Collection, Harry Ransom Humanities Research Center, University of Texas at Austin.

8 Ben Gazzara (Brick) obviously in pain and Barbara Bel Geddes (Margaret) as suppliant in *Cat on a Hot Tin Roof*. Bel Geddes' open face registers a plaintive innocence even in this calculated pose. Bob Golby Collection, courtesy of Theatre Collection, Harry Ransom Humanities Research Center, University of Texas at Austin.

5

CAT ON A HOT TIN ROOF

That goal is just somehow to capture the constantly evanescent quality of existence.

Tennessee Williams

Although critics vary as to which of Tennessee Williams' plays they consider his best, *Cat on a Hot Tin Roof* was Williams' favorite. "That play comes closest to being both a work of art and a work of craft," Williams wrote in his *Memoirs*.[1] *Cat on a Hot Tin Roof* opened at the Morosco on March 24, 1955, with Barbara Bel Geddes as Maggie, Ben Gazzara as Brick, Burl Ives as Big Daddy, and Mildred Dunnock as Big Mama. In spite of mixed reviews, *Cat on a Hot Tin Roof* won both the Pulitzer Prize and the New York Drama Critics Circle Award as the best American play of the season. It became Williams' longest running show with 692 performances. At the time that Dore Schary purchased the film rights for MGM (the film starred Elizabeth Taylor, Paul Newman, and Burl Ives), it was one of the biggest film sales ever made. Williams' share, which came off the top, amounted to $750,000. And although *A Streetcar Named Desire* has probably been revived more frequently, *Cat* has also had its share of stellar revivals. The ANTA production in 1974 with Elizabeth Ashley ran for twenty weeks. Most recently, in 1990, Kathleen Turner also did a turn as Maggie the Cat in a production which co-starred Charles Durning as Big Daddy.

The director/designer team for *Cat on a Hot Tin Roof* was Elia Kazan (director) and Jo Mielziner (designer), the same as for *A Streetcar Named Desire* and *Death of a Salesman*. In the two earlier productions, Kazan and Mielziner worked so closely with the playwright that together they produced a seamless work combining the theatrical styles of naturalism and expressionism. This blend of styles was unique to Broadway theatre in this era. All elements of the production worked together to create a new realism, a world that was neither fully real nor fully imaginary. Williams' and Miller's earlier scripts encouraged this kind of production. They contained dialogue that was naturalistic with passages of extended speech that were highly poetic. Kazan cast actors who could anchor the naturalistic conception while enhancing the mythic elements suggested by the play's poetic diction. Marlon Brando, Jessica Tandy, Lee J. Cobb, and Arthur Kennedy were all larger than life. Mielziner's sets for these productions were simultaneously exterior and interior locations using light to permit rapid movement from a naturalistic world to an interior world made of dreams and memories. Not only did these sets unify and contain the action, but each created a central image which embodied the action. The collaborative team of playwright, director, and designer created a popular drama that became readily accessible to Broadway audiences. *Cat on a Hot Tin Roof* appealed to a large, popular audience, larger in fact than *A Streetcar Named Desire*. Yet, in spite of this success, the production marked a turning point in the development of the new Broadway style.

With *Cat* poetic realism reached its limit. Unique in the canon of Broadway plays, *Cat on a Hot Tin Roof* was published with two different third acts: Williams' first version and the Broadway version. The publication of the two third acts indicates that in the playwright's opinion the production failed to merge with the play. In spite of financial and critical success, Williams felt that what he wanted to say had not reached the public because the production had turned his play into something different from his original vision. Although Williams protests in the published version of the play that it was "commercial pressure" that dictated his acquiescence, a careful examination of the playscripts, production, and critical response, indicates that the problem was more complex than Williams' comment suggests.

According to Williams' "Note of explanation" in the published script, the changes he made in Act Three to the Broadway version came about because he valued Kazan's creative input and was afraid that unless he agreed to the requested rewrites, Kazan would lose interest. "The reception of the playing-script has more than justified, in my opinion, the adjustments made to that influence," wrote Williams. "A failure reaches fewer people, and touches fewer, than does a play that succeeds."[2] Certainly there appears to be absolutely no question in Williams' mind that Kazan's suggestions helped to make *Cat on a Hot Tin Roof* a success. Why, then, should Williams seek publication of what amounts to an early draft of the third act, particularly if it would hurt his relationship with Kazan, a director he planned on working with again in the theatre and with whom he was soon to work on the film *Baby Doll*?[3]

With a less well-known playwright and director, requests for rewrites would usually have come from producers like Jed Harris. However, in the mid-1950s, both Williams and Kazan were at the height of their influence. They could easily have fended off such demands. Certainly, the Playwrights Producing Company, Inc. which produced *Cat*, would have been the least likely of Broadway managements to have demanded rewrites for commercial purposes. The Playwrights Company was run by playwrights who championed the rights of authors. The Company was created in 1938 in an attempt to address the problems playwrights were having with the Theatre Guild and other managements. Attorney John F. Wharton helped its founding playwrights – Maxwell Anderson, S. N. Behrman, Sidney Howard, Elmer Rice, and Robert E. Sherwood – create an organization that would produce their plays on terms that would be most favorable and in an atmosphere without commercial pressure. Unlike traditional producing partnerships, the Playwrights Company had a Board of Directors with daily administrative duties handled by a non-voting General Manager, Victor Samrock. Not only was there no pressure from the Playwrights Company to make changes in the script, but Williams was legally protected by his Dramatists Guild contract from having to make changes even if they were demanded.[4]

Why, then, did Williams drastically alter his play? It wasn't because he was compelled to do it by either Kazan or the play's producer. According to Williams' agent, Audrey Wood, when she first read Williams' play in Rome in 1954, the play did not even have a third act. "It can't end with Big Daddy's speech, as it does," Wood remembers telling Williams in *Represented by Audrey Wood*, "You've got to work on the story by sticking with Brick and Maggie."[5] Evidently, Williams disagreed with Wood's criticism, but eventually he complied and wrote the first version of the act now published.

Williams' reasons for writing a Broadway version of *Cat* might have been related to the play's content. In 1955 New York State law officially prohibited the presentation of obscenity on stage. The Wales Padlock Law which was passed by the New York State Legislature in 1927 provided that producers and theatre owners successfully prosecuted for presenting plays that were deemed either fully or partially morally objectionable could find his theatre "padlocked," that is, completely closed, for one year. This draconian law remained on the books until 1967 and had been invoked several times in its forty-year history to prevent the depiction of homosexuality on stage. According to Don Shewey in "Gay theatre grows up,"[6] "When homosexuality did begin to whisper its name onstage, it was usually in melodramatic treatments of false accusation . . . vice . . . or violence." In the mid-1950s, homosexuality was still an "unmentionable" subject on Broadway. Williams was aware that he could not portray Brick as a sympathetic, well-adjusted latent homosexual and also have commercial success on Broadway. It may have been Williams' concern about this issue that made him stop writing *Cat* after reaching the end of the second act. Certainly, the structure of Williams' play up until that point suggests that Brick will deal head-on with his past relationship with Skipper in the play's third act.

Cat closely follows Ibsen's version of the "well-made play" formula. As in *The Wild Duck* and *Ghosts*, there is in *Cat* an act that has been committed in the past which now requires atonement. Brick rejected Skipper, his closest friend and football teammate, after Skipper confessed to having homosexual feelings towards Brick. Following the rejection, Skipper drank himself to death. When the play begins, Brick has also become an alcoholic. He has tried to blame Maggie for Skipper's death, but Big Daddy refuses to allow Brick such an easy out:

BIG DADDY

. . . This disgust with mendacity is disgust with yourself. *You*! – dug the grave of your friend and kicked him in it! – before you'd face truth with him!

BRICK

His truth, not *mine*!

BIG DADDY

His truth, okay! But you wouldn't face it with him![7]

In the interchange following this, Brick tries to get even for having to face his own guilt. Brick reveals to Big Daddy that he is not the only one who has trouble facing the truth, and that in fact Big Daddy is dying of cancer.

BRICK

. . . – And being friends in telling each other the truth . . .

[*there is a pause*]

You told *me*! I told you![8]

Big Daddy will reward Brick's return to sobriety by naming him his heir ("to 28,000 acres of the richest land this side of the valley Nile"), but Brick must pull himself together. This means resolving his relationship with Maggie (even if it means divorce) and giving up the bottle.

Structurally, if the "truth-telling" (the climax of Act Two) is of any consequence, then in Act Three there must be a change (either positive or negative) in Brick's actions or behavior. This is called fulfilling the playwright's "expectations," and every good playwright knows that this practical rule must be taken as seriously as an oath before God. To keep the audience in suspense as long as possible, the final climax should occur as close as possible to the final curtain.

Williams' first version of the third act is weak and the final moments of the play inconclusive. In spite of the powerful impression made by Big Daddy in the second act, Williams managed to keep this character off the stage throughout the entire last act, signifing his continued life by audible off-stage screams. This was not because Williams was unaware of the power of Big Daddy. Williams notes in his *Memoirs* that with Big Daddy he had reached beyond himself "to a kind of crude eloquence of expression . . . that I have managed to give no other character of my creation."[9] With Big Daddy excluded from Act Three, Maggie is forced to announce her pregnancy to Big Mama, a character who has previously shown little sympathy for Maggie and who has little or no influence on Big Daddy's will. Moreover, the final lines of dialogue are deliberately vague. There is no suggestion of an accommodation or a rapprochement between Brick and Maggie:

MARGARET
[*the curtain begins to fall slowly*]
I *do* love you, Brick, I *do*!
BRICK
[*smiling with charming sadness*]
Wouldn't it be funny if that was true?
THE CURTAIN COMES DOWN

THE END[10]

Although Williams suggests in the published text that he felt that his version would do "just as well or nearly, as Cat number two"[11] this has not been the case. The London production with Kim Stanley as Maggie, which was produced after the Broadway version, kept Williams' ending as written and failed.

Kazan's suggestions for rewriting Act Three were given to Williams before *Cat* went into rehearsal (February 7). Williams summarized Kazan's "reservations" in his "Note of explanation" in the published text:

> The gist of his reservations can be listed as three points: one, he felt that Big Daddy was too vivid and important a character to disappear from the play except as an offstage cry after the second act curtain; two, he felt that the character of Brick should undergo some apparent mutation as a result of the virtual vivisection that he undergoes in his interview with his father in Act Two. Three, he felt that the character of Margaret, while he understood that I sympathized with her and liked her myself, should be, if possible, more clearly sympathetic to an audience.[12]

Williams was able to deal with the third of Kazan's suggestions "wholeheartedly" because he felt that Maggie the Cat "had become steadily more charming to me" the more he worked with the characterization. With regard to Big Daddy, as Williams states in his *Memoirs*, "I saw nothing for him to do in that act when he re-entered. . . . Consequently I had him tell "the elephant story."[13] The elephant story proved to be too much for the censors and was eventually removed after the play's Broadway opening.

By far the most significant of Kazan's reservations was the second, the one that had to do with Brick. It was this one that gave Williams the most difficulty. In the "Note of explanation," Williams dismisses the possibility of a realistic change in "heart or even conduct" occurring in Brick's "state of spiritual disrepair."[14] In his *Memoirs*, Williams' tone is combative. He speaks of having his "intuition violated," "Brick was literally forced back to bed by Maggie, when she confiscated his booze."[15] Yet even this revision missed the point. It is Brick's actions, not Maggie's, that are at the dramatic center of the play. Therefore, it is Brick, not Maggie or Big Daddy, who must change.

Certainly, one option open to Williams was to punish Brick further for failing his friend in his hour of need. This would have moved the play further in the direction of tragedy. Brick might have taken a path similar to Blanche's (in *Streetcar*). Blanche is unable to stop her dissipated downward plunge after her rejection of Alan (also a homosexual). Yet, would not such a course of action on Brick's part suggest that Williams was punishing Brick for failing to be an honest homosexual?

At any rate, Williams' initial version of Act Three makes it difficult to know whether Brick was suffering because he rejected his homosexual friend or because he has been untrue to his own feelings. At the very least, Williams needed to clarify this point. In the Broadway version of Act Three, Williams has Brick make a change diametrically opposed to the one he had Blanche make in *Streetcar*. In *Streetcar*, Blanche continues her plunge downward. In *Cat*, Brick and Maggie are together in bed, about to fulfill Big Daddy's wish by the end of the play. This kind of an affirmative, upbeat ending falls into the moral universe of melodrama where virtue (Maggie) is always rewarded. Small wonder that Tennessee Williams, who was outspoken about his own homosexuality, found this particular solution abhorrent.

No doubt Williams had realized his predicament in Rome when he chose to end the play after Act Two. There really was no satisfactory solution to the problem from Williams' perspective that would yield him a successful Broadway play. It was not really Williams' philosophical premise that individuals could not immediately change as the result of a conversation. It was the kind of change that Brick would have to make that violated Williams' dramatic intuition. Yet, as Kazan maintains in *A Life* and as the Broadway version of the play confirms, Williams made the necessary alterations, albeit reluctantly and halfheartedly. As the collection of scripts in the Harry Ransom Library at the University of Texas indicates, he made these changes over several drafts, sometimes by adding or subtracting only a line or two of dialogue on a page.

Because Williams was either unwilling or unable to rethink the character of Brick, he shifted the responsibility for "authorship" to his director. Kazan was required to compensate in the *mise-en-scène* (the director's working script) for those elements that were missing in Williams' play. No longer would Kazan's expressionistic technique serve to expand the naturalism of Williams' script, creating characters with both inner and outer levels of reality. Now that technique would be called upon to mask something that was missing, realistic character development. In *Streetcar* and *Salesman*, characters hovered between different levels of reality. As director, Kazan's task was to anchor the entire conception in real behavior. In *Cat*, his task was different. Brick does not hover, he drifts into an alcoholic stupor. There is nothing heroic about his actions; in fact his is a course of inaction – of acquiescence. To keep the audience sympathetic and interested in Brick, Kazan had to find ways of suggesting change where none existed. Rather than the play working to reveal character through action, Kazan had to find ways of making Brick's inaction appear to be meaningful, even heroic.

This was a director's theatre, not a playwright's theatre. The script now became a pretext for invented stage action. In the cinema, directors were accustomed to functioning as "auteurs." In the theatre, this was fundamentally different. The era when actors redrafted scripts to fit their personalities had passed with the coming of the new realism of Eugene O'Neill. In the late 1920s, with film in its infancy, it was still possible for inventive producers such as Jed Harris to give melodramas bold productions. But since that time, audiences had become far more critical and demanding. Could director, designer, and actors bring back the old wine of melodrama in the new bottles of poetic realism? Would the public accept technical wizardry rather than dramatic truth? Certainly, *Cat* provided a marvelous opportunity to see just how far the director could go in creating theatre on top of a script.

The tension between Kazan's direction and Williams' script existed throughout the original Broadway production, although as one would expect it was most noticeable in the play's final act. Kazan knew that if he was going to make this play work for popular audiences he would need Williams to find a way to bring Brick and Maggie together by the final curtain. Anything short of this embrace would seem to confirm the fact that Brick was an homosexual. In both versions of the published third act, there is a scene in which Dr Baugh informs Big Mama that Big Daddy is "terminal," and in all versions of this act Gooper seizes the moment to present his plan to take over the estate. However, Kazan felt that it was important to have Brick more involved with what is going on in the room than he was in Williams' version of the play. Kazan also needed a change of attitude in Brick towards Maggie. In one of the rewrites, three typewritten pages of dialogue were added, creating action on the gallery (outside the room) simultaneous to the action taking place within the room between Big Mama and Gooper. Brick's irreverent singing of "By the light of the silvery moon"[16] was replaced by a rhetorical address, "Hello, moon, I envy you, you cool son of a bitch."[17] Brick was being reformed with a vengeance.

In the Broadway version, Kazan had convinced Williams that a moment of tenderness between Brick and Maggie out on the gallery was necessary as a harbinger of things to come:

BRICK
How long are you goin' to stand behind me, Maggie?
MARGARET
Forever, if necessary.[18]

It is this statement of her devotion to him that prompts Brick to enter directly into the scene. Even though it is only a two-line addition, the change suggests that Brick and Maggie have made a pact. Brick will allow his disgust with Gooper to surface and risk a confrontation.

Another change in Kazan's Broadway version is the addition of a thunderstorm at the precise moment that Big Mama rejects Gooper's proposal to run the estate. The thunderstorm serves several purposes. As an expressionistic device, it symbolizes the anger of the heavens at Gooper's attempt to take over. On a more practical level, it motivates exits of Gooper and Mae so that Big Mama can have a tender moment alone with Brick and Maggie. During this moment, Big Mama states that Brick "looks like he used to look when he was a little boy."[19] Then she pleads with Brick to give Big Daddy his dream, "You give him a child of yours, a grandson as much like his son as his son is like Big Daddy."[20] Big Mama's sympathetic involvement with Maggie's plight was not apparent in the first draft. Her emotional plea to Brick with references to Big Daddy's death is just the type of heart-rending plea mothers always make to misguided sons in the old melodrama. Were Brick to ignore his mother at this moment, the audience would indeed hate him. With the pressure on Brick mounting from all quarters, it was clear that some kind of a change had to come about before the final curtain.

Following the scene with Big Mama, Big Daddy returns. A moment of comic relief follows which moves the play forward and away from overt sentimentality. As Big Daddy enters, Gooper is attempting to hide the "pregnant" envelope that contains the proposed trust agreement. Big Daddy demands to know what is in the envelope. Gooper responds that it is nothing. In response to Gooper's lie, Big Daddy tells "the elephant story." We know from the way that Big Daddy is talking to Gooper that he has overheard all that has transpired in his absence. And, more to the point, he is angry. We know now that it is his anger that was reflected in the thunderstorm now heard as a distant rumble passing into Arkansas.

The elephant story is significant not only because it is virile and funny, but because it is specifically an advertisement for heterosexuality. It is ironic that this story should have been singled out for censorship. By today's standards, there is nothing offensive about it. No four-letter words are used by Big Daddy in describing the male elephant's erection. The elephant's sexual urge is presented as the natural response of a bull male to a female elephant in heat. The only part of the story that is even slightly off-color is the final line when Big Daddy has the father in the story contradict the mother's dismissal that the elephant's penis is "nothing" by saying that she has been "spoiled."

The controversy caused by this story after the play's opening had less to do with content and more to do with style. Up until this moment in the play, *Cat on a Hot Tin Roof*, though it dealt with sexual issues, was a "clean" play. Sex is presented as an issue, not for humor or titillation. Reference to sexual relations are circumspect. However, Big Daddy's elephant story is a change. Big Daddy is direct, an affront to the prudish. Kazan, rather than hiding this change, had Burl Ives cross down to the center of the stage and take the elephant story straight out into the auditorium in an openly defiant manner. Big Daddy's motivation was his anger, the rage of a man who had just received a death sentence. Burl Ives, an actor of uncommon power, was just the man to make the most of this kind of a situation. Ives, a concert folk singer, had a big voice that could rattle chairs in the last row of the balcony. No doubt, this angry "dirty joke" was the last straw to some in the audience who were already offended by the play, but could not find anything specific about which to lodge a complaint. Their feelings of revulsion at the story only seemed to be reiterated by Big Mama who broke out into hysterical sobbing at the punchline of the joke.

Mildred Dunnock, who played Big Mama, handled the plaintive vein beautifully, the same way she had handled the final shattering moments in the "Requiem" of Arthur Miller's *Death of a Salesman*. Eric Bentley, critic for *The New Leader*, was disturbed by the similarities between these two endings. The similarities were more noticable since they were acted by the same actress, directed by the same director, and even performed in the same theatre. However, others who objected felt a desire to protect Dunnock from the bullying of Burl Ives. Since they were powerless to prevent the spectacle on stage, they took their complaints to the Commissioner of Licenses for the City of New York. The decision to remove the elephant story came so quickly after the Commissioner raised his first objections that one suspects that Williams must have felt secretly pleased that someone else had noticed how different the writing was in this episode. It is clear from what Williams had to say in his *Memoirs* that he never wanted to bring Big Daddy on stage in Act Three. In case anyone in the theatre did not understand that this story was being specifically addressed to Brick as a kind of "put up or shut up" communication, Kazan had Big Daddy cross to Brick and say, "You didn't laugh at that story, Brick," to which Brick responds, "No, sir, I didn't laugh at that story."[21] The quiet response suggests a stoical acceptance by Brick of his obligation.

Certainly, Maggie understood what Big Daddy wanted and expected when she responded by kneeling in front of Big Daddy in what Gooper remarks is an "indecent" position. Critic Eric Bentley pointed out that the position that Maggie assumes was based on Renaissance images of the annunciation. From her kneeling position, she announces to Big Daddy that she is carrying Brick's child. Although Gooper and Mae reject her claim, Big Daddy raises Maggie up, in a sense elevates her, while touching her breasts and abdomen to confirm that there is "life" in her body. The formality of the announcement and the pose were all meant to create closure. However, Bentley found Kazan's use of tableaux here a pretentious evocation, self-consciously forced on to the drama.

Following Big Daddy's exit, Gooper and Mae continue to doubt Maggie's pregnancy, citing reasons why Brick could not have slept with Maggie. In the rewrites prior to the final Broadway version, Williams experimented with various ways of countering these accusations, including having Maggie discuss raping Brick. The final solution has Brick defend Maggie and discuss silent love-making, love-making that goes undetected by the snooping Mae and Gooper. It is the most direct action Brick takes in the course of the play on behalf of his wife. After Mae and Gooper leave, Maggie takes over as mother-protector and discards Brick's bottles, thus forcing him to take her to bed before he can get another drink. In the first version, she locked up the booze. In the Broadway version, she pitches the bottles off the gallery so that the audience can hear them smash below. Maggie is determined to make the lie she told Big Daddy come true.

The new air of militancy was tempered by having Maggie assume a kneeling suppliant position evoking the position she had just struck with Big Daddy. Maggie's final speech underwent considerable changes during rehearsals. At first, Williams was determined to give Brick the last word doubting Maggie's love. This gave the purported union a tentative quality. Williams cut Bricks' line down to a five-word response, "I – I hope so, Maggie," and then totally eliminated Brick's final speech entirely. At the same time, he began to build up Maggie's close by adding, "Oh, you weak people" before finally arriving at the Broadway version, which ties Maggie's determination in to the play's title, "I'm determined to do it–and nothing's more determined than a cat on a tin roof–is there? Is there, baby?" The stage direction indicates that she touches his cheek gently. Brick does not recoil; seated, he looks at Maggie. If the play's final image wasn't quite the hoped-for embrace, it was certainly an unequivocal movement in that direction. Evidently, it was enough for Kazan and too much for Williams.

Although the published Broadway version is relatively complete, it lacks the lyrics to the Spiritual that was being sung under the closing action by the plantation workers in the fields below. In an earlier version of the script, the songs suggested were "Heavenly Grace" and "I Wonder As I Wander." Neither of these suggestions had the soft, tremulous quality of the final choice, "My Buddy." The words of the song used in the Broadway production were:

> My Buddy had a woman
> These are the words she said
> Goin' down the track and never lookin' back
> All: Goin' where my man fell dead (*four times*)
> Well, I asked my buddy
> What are you thinkin' of
> The only thing that's on my mind
> All: Only thinkin' of my love (*four times*)
> (*volume decreases*)
> They had my buddy on the mountain
> Upon the mountain high
> Last words I heard that poor boy say
> All: Gimme a cool drink of water 'fore I die.
> (*continue phrase till curtain*)

The linking of the repeated words "death," "love," and "drink" thematically connect them while the hymn seems to bring a note of finality to both Skipper's and Big Daddy's death. There is also a suggestion of a new role for Maggie, already stated in the script. She will become the libation-bearer. Gesture, lighting, and hymn underscored the idea of a resolution that made all right with the world. The ghosts were put to rest and virtue was triumphant. It was affirmative, moralistic, and clean.

Jo Mielziner's design consisted of a square platform turned on a forty-five degree axis so that one of its corners became a forestage thrust into the auditorium. The turned stage made it clear to the audience that what they were seeing was something out of kilter, not just with the room but by extension with the people in the room. The forestage was a refinement of the idea that Mielziner had used in *Death of a Salesman*. In *Cat*, the idea was bolder.

Mielziner based his room on actual rooms he had seen on old Southern plantations. He made a trip to the South while working on the design concept. The rooms he had seen provided for a variety of entrances from outdoor galleries. Open rooms off galleries met the practical necessity for cooling during the hot Southern summer. However, what was most useful to Mielziner was that the open room put an end to the need for a multiple setting. It also did away with explanations about how the family knew what happened in the privacy of Brick and Maggie's bedroom. Quite simply, there was no privacy in Big Daddy's house. The walls of the room were made up of slatted blinds or curtains so that the entire stage could be animated with light in changing hues and intensities. The use of light to enhance mood was one of the innovations that Kazan and Mielziner had used with great success in both *Streetcar* and *Salesman*. What Mielziner wanted to do in *Cat* was to use the light even more self-consciously to express the psychology of character, accentuating it as an expressionistic element. Since the walls never had solidity, the room would always seem to be an island adrift, mirroring the sexual ambivalence of Brick's character.

The idea of sex was kept firmly in the audience's mind by placing a large raked bed upstage center. The bed served as the central iconographic image, much as Willy's house had served in *Salesman*. Since Brick was on crutches, he had to navigate, as best he could, around the bed to get to the bar, upstage left, and his couch and pillow, downstage right. This design maximized Brick's discomfort and helped to build the tension to that final moment when the man on crutches would come comfortably to rest in Maggie's large bed.

The set for *Cat* had less realistic detail than either *Streetcar* or *Salesman*. In *Salesman*, Mielziner had given us two floors of a house. The neutral forestage was an afterthought. Willy's house not only provided a central image but added a sociological dimension. In *Cat*, the dynamic between character and environment was much more muted. Brick alludes to the two male lovers who had inhabited the room earlier, but there is nothing left to connect them to the room except memory and architectural details such as the ceiling relief and moldings. No doubt the decision to eliminate realistic detail was made in order to emphasize the psychological dimension. The hard-edged borders of the platform stage created something of a boxing arena for the pitched battles between wife and husband and between father and son.

More importantly, the absence of detail focused audience attention on actor and text. The room was always a platform stage, a stage that the director might use to present actors directly to the audience. This was a bold innovation, for it suggested that Kazan had tired of the realistic contrivance of having his actors act in ignorance of the audience. This change indicated that the actors were going to address the audience directly, which is exactly what Burl Ives did when he told the elephant story in Act Three. As stated above, the bold staging of this sequence accentuated the importance of the elephant story and contributed to the problems the play had with the censor. Kazan viewed his use of direct address in *Cat* as a return to the theatre of Shakespeare. Yet he did not forsake such modern enhancements as the follow-spot as a way of focusing audience attention. The fact is that the mood lighting, the follow-spots, and use of the thrust had more in common with the Hollywood movie close-up than it did with the Shakespearean soliloquy.

Kazan's importance to *Cat on a Hot Tin Roof* is obvious not only in terms of the Broadway third act but in the entire conception of the play. Four major casting decisions – Big Daddy, Maggie, Brick, Big Mama – each taken for very specific directorial reasons, indicate how he controlled the production. For Big Daddy, Kazan cast Burl Ives. In Kazan's mind this gave the play size, it made it something more than domestic drama, a realistic slice-of-life. Although Ives had appeared as an actor on stage as well as in Kazan's film of Steinbeck's *East of Eden*; he was known as a folk singer. Ives, like Big Daddy, was larger than life: a man of huge appetites, an admirer of women, food, and full living. He was a country person, a person of frank expression. This was his natural quality on stage and there was nothing about the character of Big Daddy he had to act; in fact, he was probably incapable of suppressing these aspects of his personality on- or off-stage.

Kazan, as he relates in his memoirs, *A Life*, had been drawn to Ives when he faced the problem of Big Daddy's long speeches in the second act. Again, as in *Death of a Salesman*, Kazan's metaphor was musical. He proposed to use Ives as a singer, having him perform these speeches, "Straight out, as if it were a concert."[22] To cover Ives' lack of stage acting experience he arranged the other actors around Ives. Williams protested that this was a realistic play and that people in the South did, in fact, speak the way he had written Big Daddy, but Kazan won the day. "So I went against the grain," wrote Kazan, "for I knew it was the only way Burl could play the part, straight out . . . that was the style of performing that he – and I – enjoyed."[23]

The decision to cast Barbara Bel Geddes as Maggie also went "against the grain," but for different reasons. Barbara Bel Geddes, now famous as the matriarch in the *Dallas* television series, was a warm and appealing young actress. She had made quite a reputation for herself in the 1951 comedy hit by F. Hugh Herbert, *The Moon is Blue*, in which she played the role of Patty O'Neill. In that play, Bel Geddes managed the unlikely accomplishment of being both naive and worldly at the same time. At the end of this "sophisticated" comedy virtue and love triumphed and Patty was vindicated. Bel Geddes not only created a coherent character out of a series of attitudes but enchanted audiences by being "radiantly beautiful." It was exactly her sexy clean quality, the professional virgin, that Kazan wanted in the role of Maggie.

Unlike Elizabeth Ashley, who would play the part two decades later, Bel Geddes was not a sex goddess nor did she have Kathleen Turner's hard-edge, almost masculine quality. Bel Geddes had the ability to convey sexual passion in a manner that was warm and sympathetic to audiences. Her attacks on Mae and Gooper never appeared to be wanton or bitchy. Even when faced with the radical insecurity of constant rejection from her husband, Bel Geddes could choke back tears and manage a wry smile of faith. Some critics complained that all this well-bred composure was not the lower-class alley-cat that could claw her way to the top of the heap. But this was not the image that Kazan wanted. Bel Geddes had no need to be the Cotton Carnival Queen. She was natural royalty. No wonder that when MGM purchased the rights for *Cat* it was for their young star Grace Kelly, the screen equivalent of Barbara Bel Geddes. Eventually, the movie studio decided not to go with blond innocence and chose to emphasize the sultry qualities of the role by casting Elizabeth Taylor. The movie also removed all but the most innocuous references to Brick's sexual ambivalence and focused the conflict on the son's need for a father's sustaining love.

In Kazan's working script he listed three actors for Brick. Ben Gazzara was the third. Gazzara was very young when he played this role and was known to Kazan through their mutual involvement with the Actors Studio. Gazzara had followed in Kazan's own footsteps as an actor and had trained with Lee Strasberg. Both Kazan and Gazzara had a certain ethnic quality, the sons of first-generation Americans. Gazzara had already attracted critical attention for his portrayal of the calculating sadistic Jocko de Paris in the Off-Broadway production of *End as a Man*, a project which began as a series of improvisations at the Actors Studio. In fact, there were a number of similarities between Kazan and Gazzara as actors although they were a generation apart. Gazzara had been accepted into the Studio with an audition from one of Odets' Group Theatre plays. But although these qualities may have held an unconscious appeal for Kazan, his decision to cast was based on the Gazzara's rough masculinity. Strasberg thought of Gazzara as a young Marlon Brando, an idea that Gazzara sought to discourage. He thought those who tried to imitate Marlon were "punks." However, his acting had a similar earthy realism, a tough up-from-the-streets quality which Kazan could use to make Brick attractive, boyish, physical, but above all, masculine. It was this quality in particular that Kazan needed to undercut Brick's sexual ambiguity.

The original character description for Big Mama has nothing in it that would suggest Mildred Dunnock for this role and indeed several critics felt that she was miscast. Kazan had written Jo van Fleet on a script. He had recently directed van Fleet in the film *East of Eden*.[24] In the film, van Fleet played James Dean's mother, believed by Dean to be dead, but whom it turns out runs a nearby brothel. However, van Fleet was not available. Again, Dunnock persisted. She wanted the part very badly and as the choice narrowed, she reminded Kazan that she was from the South. Vocally, she contrived an entirely new way of speaking for the role. She came into auditions with what she called her "whisky voice." As she had proven with the role of Linda Loman in *Salesman*, she could look the role by making certain physical adjustments. Kazan did not insist that she look fat and dumpy like a Japanese wrestler. He saw her as an important instrument in his ensemble, someone who could give the role variety and depth, shifting it away from a stereotypical characterization. He relied on Dunnock to find qualities that might arrest the audiences' attempt to dismiss her as an unimportant character. Kazan also needed an actress bright enough to compensate for Burl Ives' lack of stage experience in those scenes where the director needed Big Daddy to play to the other actors and not to the audience. For all these reasons, he made another decision that went against the grain and cast Dunnock.

Cat on a Hot Tin Roof arrived on Broadway after two successful try-out weeks in Philadelphia. It was in Philadelphia that Kazan froze the show, giving Williams up to the last moment to make changes such as removing the elephant story, a subject that was actually discussed before the play came to New York. Williams seemed content although he remained quite uneasy, not just about that story. Kazan's major concern was to avoid having the play dismissed as a play about confused sexuality or worse yet a play about a latent homosexual. Therefore, the critical response was extremely important in attracting an audience to what was in essence a clean version of a dirty show. Out of fifteen contemporary critical reviews, more than half referred to homosexuality but without using the word "homosexual." In other words, the critics in these reviews chose to use words such as "unnatural" or "abnormal." Four critics specifically used the word homosexual in one context or another, and three reviewers did not mention it at all. Most significantly, Brooks Atkinson of the *New York Times*, the all-important "money" review, was one of those reviewers who did not discuss Brick's sexuality at all. No doubt Atkinson, who wrote a rave notice of the show, felt that mentioning this issue might harm the box office for what he felt was an "important" play.[25]

Of the more thoughtful critics, John Gassner, writing in *Theatre at the Crossroads*, observed that "if Williams had anything of consequence to say in his family drama he did not manage to get it across." Gassner also praised Williams' "vivid characterizing power."[26] Eric Bentley was so disturbed by the play that he went to see it several times before writing his review entitled, "Tennessee Williams and New York Kazan," reprinted in *What is Theatre*. Bentley praised Williams for "dialogue at its best: it is supple, sinuous, hard-hitting." He found Kazan's direction "formalized." He disliked this quality and felt that it gave the play a false grandeur. Although one can disagree with Bentley's conclusions, one cannot seriously take issue with his analysis.[27] There was no doubt that Kazan had forced his vision on the play, willfully distorting its real message to make it a hit.

Our discussion of *Cat on a Hot Tin Roof* would not be complete were we to omit Tennessee Williams' reaction to the opening night. Clearly, it was a traumatic and harrowing experience for him. Although one could easily dismiss the playwright's emotional reactions, as Kazan has in his *A Life*, as due to nerves, alcohol, or the influence of sycophantic friends, none of these reasons are necessary. Williams' near-psychotic state of mind could just as easily be explained by how he felt about what he saw on stage happening to *his* play. Immediately following the play he interpreted Audrey Wood's statement that she was not accompanying him to Kazan's private party – to which she had not been invited – as "Rats! Rats! Leaving a sinking ship!" At that moment, Williams was absolutely convinced that his play had been a failure. He imagined that he had heard an unusual amount of coughing from the audience through-out the evening, a sure indication that the audience was bored. Moreover, during intermission he had encountered two close friends who had said nothing to him. In his opening night panic, he had forgotten that he had instructed these friends earlier specifically *not* to say anything to him. However, their silence seemed to be proof that the play had failed.

No doubt some of this tension had been created by the spectacle of the opening itself, which almost dwarfed the play it purported to honor. According to Williams' brother Dakin, "Everybody was there, including honeymooning Debbie Reynolds and Eddie Fisher, Walter Winchell, and Marilyn Monroe."[28] In addition to Kazan's party, there was a big party at Gracie Mansion, the official residence of the Mayor of New York, given by the first lady of the American theatre, Helen Hayes, in celebra-tion of the play's costume designer Lucinda Ballard. Politicians and cel-ebrities were in abundance, and eventually Audrey Wood managed to catch up with an outraged Williams. "He behaved as if he were a deserted child," Wood related in her memoirs, "who'd been abandoned in a snowstorm by untrustworthy relatives, or hurtful friends."[29] Wood and Williams repaired to Toffenetti's restaurant, an all-night place on Times Square, where they read the predominantly favorable newspaper reviews in silence. It wasn't until long after three in the morning that they parted. Wood writes that in spite of the evening's obvious success, "There was no conversation, barely a good night."[30]

Williams states in his *Memoirs* that the opening was "particularly dread-ful. I thought it was a failure, a distortion of what I had intended."[31] Although Williams and Wood did not permanently part company after this occasion, Williams juxtaposes the events of his opening night jitters with this statement:

> After that, I went to Italy. . . . I was unable to write. Strong coffee no longer sufficed to get the creative juices to flow. For several weeks I endured creative sterility, then I started to wash down a Seconal with a martini. And then I was "hooked" on that practice.[32]

Williams blamed his "creative sterility" and resulting drug dependency directly on the opening of *Cat on a Hot Tin Roof*. Imagine the frustration and disappointment that Williams must have felt at realizing that his most successful play was largely due to Kazan's impositions. In 1973 Williams tried his hand at creating a new combined version of his and Kazan's third acts. Although it was an improvement over the first version, it did not have the audience appeal of the Broadway version. However, since times had changed, particularly the audience attitude towards homosexuality, the newly adapted version did not inhibit a successful revival.

6

WHO'S AFRAID OF VIRGINIA WOOLF?

> I write for me. For the audience of me. If other people come along for the ride then it's great.
>
> Edward Albee

With the arrival of Edward Albee's *Who's Afraid of Virginia Woolf?* at the Billy Rose Theatre on October 13, 1962, Broadway entered a new era. "Edward Albee is clearly the most compelling American playwright to explode upon the Broadway stage since Tennessee Williams and Arthur Miller in the mid-forties," wrote Mel Gussow (*Newsweek*, February 4, 1963: 49). At least part of the excitement created by Albee had to do with a shift away from the psychological realism of Miller and Williams and towards a more abstract mode of expression identified by Martin Esslin as "the theatre of the absurd." Prior to *Who's Afraid of Virginia Woolf?*, Albee had been identified as the chief American exponent of this European theatrical style.

Albee's first produced play, *The Zoo Story*, had received its world première production at the Schiller Theatre Werkstatt in Berlin (September 28, 1959). Although the play had had a reading at the Actors Studio in New York prior to the Berlin production, it was not to be produced in the United States until January 14, 1960 (Provincetown Playhouse, Greenwich Village). The association with the Provincetown immediately suggested comparisons to Eugene O'Neill. However, Albee's reception on Broadway, both with *Who's Afraid of Virginia Woolf?* and with the plays that followed, has been quite different from O'Neill. Richard Amacher wrote:

> His new plays are awaited always with anticipation of something strange, fascinating, exciting, or alarming – just as were the works of O'Neill during the 1920's, although O'Neill seemingly encountered less hostility from his audience and his critics than has Albee.[1]

The "hostility" that Amacher mentions had to do with Albee's opposition to what he perceived as the Broadway establishment. Prior to

Who's Afraid of Virginia Woolf?, Albee's work had been done largely Off Broadway. During that period Albee wrote a widely-read polemic attacking Broadway for the *New York Times Magazine* entitled, "Which Theatre is the Absurd One?" (February 25, 1962: 30). Again, in a satirical one-act, *Fam and Yam*, he attacked famous American playwrights for acquiescing to establishment values. In fact, during the 1960s, Albee cast himself in the role of *enfant terrible* and provocateur. Albee's feeling of alienation from Broadway is expressed directly in his choice of subject matter and his unwillingness to compromise his work to gain acceptance in the commercial arena. Fortunately for Albee, his early partnership with producer Richard Barr protected the playwright's right to experiment and insulated him from many of the pressures of Broadway commercialism.

Richard Barr was one of those extraordinary producers who felt that the playwright, not the star or the director, was of central importance in the theatre. Perhaps these feelings originated in his concern for the text. Barr's early training was as a director. He became friendly with playwright William Inge. Through this friendship, he came to realize that the financial stakes on Broadway had become so great by the mid-1950s that playwrights even of Inge's stature were forced to make changes in their scripts in order to get produced. "I have just won the Pulitzer prize," Inge remarked to Barr, "I have a major hit on Broadway; I am going to be very rich; and I am miserably unhappy!"[2] Inge's unhappiness could be traced to director Joshua Logan, who together with management, had given the playwright an ultimatum: either change the last act of *Picnic* so that it was "less sad and less frightening" or they would not produce it. Rather than lose the opportunity to see his work before an audience, Inge made the required changes. Barr was so outraged by what he had heard that he decided to enter a new producing arena called "Off Broadway." He was convinced that Off Broadway, where the financial stakes were relatively small, there were opportunities to produce a "playwright's theatre," and that this kind of theatre would attract sufficient audience to be profitable.

In 1959, at the age of 41, Barr was able to turn his dream into a reality by optioning Albee's *The Zoo Story*. The play was brought to his attention by Edward Parone, a William Morris agent who handled younger writers. By the time Barr communicated his interest to Parone, Albee was already in Berlin to attend the opening of his play there. In Berlin *The Zoo Story*, a one-act play, was produced with a companion piece, Samuel Beckett's *Krapp's Last Tape*. Barr felt that the two plays made an evening and set out trying to acquire the rights to the Beckett play for New York. He soon found that not only was the Beckett play under option, but the playwright had stated that the New York production had to be directed by Alan Schneider. When Albee returned, Barr told him that he wanted to produce the two one-acts together Off Broadway as the first step in launching a permanent company devoted to new plays. Albee was agreeable.

There were several bridges to be crossed before *The Zoo Story* and *Krapp's Last Tape* arrived before a New York audience. Barr found it necessary to take on a producing partner, Harry Joe Brown, Jr, because Brown refused to part with the rights for *Krapp's Last Tape*. Although this reduced the money he had to raise, which he estimated for both plays to be $9,000, by half, it also meant a loss of control. Further complications arose in that Albee had made a commitment to have Milton Katselas direct *The Zoo Story*. Katselas had handled the reading at the Actors Studio. This meant that the evening would go forth with two producers, two playwrights, and two directors. This was far from an ideal arrangement for the beginning of a new venture. Economic necessity dictated one set for both plays. In this instance, Barr was successful at finding one designer to handle both plays, William Ritman. As Ritman explained to Barr, he thought more in terms of designing a space rather than individual sets. This was precisely the right solution since both plays take place in very different locations but share a sense of being internal monologues. The last major hurdle had to do with the fact that Alan Schneider was directing at Washington's Arena Stage at precisely the time he was needed in New York to mount the Beckett play. Fortunately, Barr's mother lived in Washington, DC, so he was able to send actor Donald Davis, who had been cast to play Krapp, to live in his mother's apartment. It was there that rehearsals were held for *Krapp's Last Tape* during Schneider's spare time.

In New York, there were also complications. George Maharis, Jerry in *The Zoo Story*, learned that the TV pilot he had done, *Route 66*, had been picked up by network television. This meant that he would have to leave the cast shortly after *The Zoo Story* opened. Tension between Maharis and Katselas flared up over "interpretive issues."[3] Since the theatre was set and the date announced, Barr found there was no other course available to him but to ask Katselas to step aside from his directing duties. Obviously, Barr was within his rights as producer to fire the director had Katselas refused to comply, but such public disagreements always have a habit of reaching the press and creating major problems. Moreover, Albee did not feel Barr was justified. Fortunately, a settlement was reached in which Katselas received directing credit in the program, even though Barr stepped in to handle the final rehearsals.

In spite of these difficulties, the double bill of *Krapp's Last Tape* and *The Zoo Story* turned out to be a major success. Barr's production company, which he now called Theatre 1960, was off to a good start. Following the opening of *The Zoo Story*, Barr met with Albee and stated:

I realize that it is customary for the author of a first successful play to offer the producer – if he does not already have an advance option – the author's next play. I'll make a deal with you. I want your next work and all your future work as long as you seriously believe that I am the best person to produce it. Further, *I will promise to present anything you write.*[4]

This was extraordinary. Like many famous theatrical agreements, it was never put down on paper, but it served as a stabilizing force for both producer and writer for a period of twenty-nine years. As Barr states, it was "the longest association of author and producer in modern theatre history."[5] This informal agreement made possible the continued production of Albee's shorter works Off Broadway, for instance, in the six years after its opening, *The Zoo Story* was revived eight times. Barr's commitment to young writers later resulted in Barr and Albee founding the Playwright's Unit with profits earned from the successful production of *Who's Afraid of Virginia Woolf?*. The Playwright's Unit gave many young writers a chance to see their plays in production. It also encouraged young writers to look beyond the aesthetic and economic limitations of Broadway. In a sense, because the funding for the Playwright's Unit came from Albee's own *Who's Afraid of Virginia Woolf?*, both Albee and his play had a tremendous influence on the theatre. Unit writers John Guare, Lanford Wilson, and Sam Shepard, to name only three among many, turned out to be America's next generation of leading playwrights.

Even before the Playwright's Unit, Albee with a handful of short plays – *The Zoo Story*, *The American Dream*, and *The Death of Bessie Smith* – had become the leading American playwright working Off Broadway. His blistering attack on middle-class sensibilities was considered shocking. Audiences were literally caught off guard by Albee's verbal wit, which mixed realism with absurdity. The one-act plays quickly divided the audience into two camps: the insiders, who found Albee's attacks wickedly humorous, and the outsiders, who were either insulted or baffled by it all. Each of Albee's Off Broadway successes can be seen as taking a step towards Albee's first full-length play. In *The Zoo Story*, Albee experimented with story-telling. In *The American Dream*, he probed the theme of the lost child. In *The Death of Bessie Smith*, he dramatized a sexual power struggle. And in the fragment play, *The Merry Month of May*,[6] he tried his hand at giving life to prototypes of *Woolf?* characters George and Martha. Albee was a new "heavyweight" contender and Off Broadway was his training camp. Albee's following viewed him not only as an artist but as a cultural leader. Albee relished the role. He yearned to be in the Broadway arena, on the barricades, the "great white hope" of the intelligentsia.

Albee obviously knew from his close study of Williams' success that plays with highly sexualized female characters were the key to attracting controversy on Broadway. As he began working on *Who's Afraid of Virginia Woolf?*, his concern was to find a vehicle for the hard-driving character he heard in his head. Albee greatly admired Williams, particularly such works as *Suddenly Last Summer*. He actually attempted (and later abandoned) a play built around the same kind of frustrated female character that Williams had used so effectively in *Summer and Smoke*.[7] This fragment shows how Albee intended to build the play by linking together disclosure stories told by individual characters. This method of composition follows what Albee has described in several published interviews as his primary way of working; that is, he listens to his characters and when he becomes convinced of their need to speak publically, he writes a play. What is unusual about this method of composition in terms of Broadway is that it departs significantly from the pattern of the "well-made" play, which aims at working out a central intrigue. In Albee's plays, the central intrigue is secondary to the exploration of characters. In Albee, character, not plot, becomes the driving force.

Who's Afraid of Virginia Woolf? is about an unhappy, middle-aged couple and their struggle to free themselves from illusion. The central intrigue involves both Martha's desire to have an adulterous affair and George's desire to punish Martha. George's revenge is his decision to eliminate what he describes as "the bit," the fantasy son that Martha and he have concocted. Immediately prior to the entrance of the visitors, Nick and Honey, George delivers a stern warning to Martha not to start in on "the bit" or else he will take a countermeasure which she will regret. Martha is defiant about George's prohibition. In fact, as soon as she and Honey are off stage, where George cannot hear them talking, Martha defies George and tells Honey about their son. In one of the early drafts of *Who's Afraid of Virginia Woolf?*, George does not deliver his prohibition about "the bit." Instead, Albee has Nick (called "Dear" in this version) and Honey enter as George and Martha argue over who should open the door. The entrance is just as effective, but no central intrigue is developed to be worked out in the play's third act. Evidently, this particular problem of finding a central intrigue to link the entire play together occupied Albee for quite some time, for the first two acts were completed during the summer of 1961. The play's final act took a little longer and was not completed until the spring of 1962, long enough for Barr to have undertaken other production projects while waiting for Albee to find a suitable ending. Once Albee decided on "the bit," he then went back and rewrote his first act to add the fantasy child. This method of composition is diametrically opposed to the kind of "well-made" play that has remained the mainstay of the commercial theatre where the climactic scene or "obligatory scene" in the third act with all its attendant discoveries and reversals is the *raison d'être* for the work.

But Albee was not interested in that type of play. He did not feel that it was his obligation to work out a specific problem for his audience. He was determined to deal with complex subject matter in a manner that was consistent with its complexity. He would not reduce his play to a formula. He did not begin with a premise that the play's actions would either prove or disprove anything. For Albee that way of looking at a play was reductionist. It suggested that the play was about something that the author could just as easily restate as a narrative. For Albee, the play was a dynamic form that did not have meaning until it was enacted. He actively fought the tendency of critics to summarize his works, because by necessity they left out the element of interaction among characters and between play and audience. If the audience wanted to know what the play was about, they had to be willing to "suffer the play." Otherwise, he would just as soon aver that the play was about nothing. This was a radical view for an audience that has been brought up with a penchant to pigeonhole not only works of art but the most intimate experiences of their daily lives.

Albee's point of attack with *Woolf?* begins with Martha's sexual appetite. The central conundrum, "the bit," neither explains nor excuses her behavior. The loss of the fantasy child may have a profound effect on her relationship with George or it may merely be the end of one game. Although the emotional intensity at the end of the play seems to suggest a purgation we can never be quite certain. Certainly, the killing off of the fantasy child by itself will not make George and Martha "happy" or even honest, or ready to begin another day without illusions. At best, the fantasy child is a symptom or manifestation of the problems that Martha and George are having in their marriage. The reality of the couple's problems lies buried in the various and conflicting mythologies of their marriage. The task of figuring all this out, if in fact it can be figured out, is left with the audience. The playwright's refusal to solve the puzzle of George and Martha's complex relationship in simple unequivocal terms that would be acceptable to a Broadway audience increased the controversy created by the play's already provocative depiction of female sexuality. Because Albee's exceptional gift at capturing real speech suggested so much that was actually not said, only implied, reaction against the play *focused* on the tip of the iceberg, the play's language.

Actually, there are many graphic images in the play, but comparatively few "four-letter words." This was not the case in an early draft of the first two acts which was read by Richard Barr. Barr was nervous about breaking what he termed the "word-barrier" because he felt too much dirty language might prejudice the entire audience against the rest of the play. Therefore, he informed Albee, "I'll take one 'fuck' uptown!"[8] Playwright and producer discussed the matter. In the end, Albee decided to remove all of the four-letter words so as not to have critics and audiences dismiss it as a play that only dealt with sensationalistic issues of language. Albee felt that this would have been letting the critics off too easily. However, in spite of his effort, the protest over the play's language would persist.

In spite of Albee's advocacy for the theatre of the absurd in the press, the original production of *Who's Afraid of Virginia Woolf?* was thoroughly naturalistic. This was epitomized by a clock that kept real time and chimed at appropriate intervals during the evening.[9] As with *Cat on a Hot Tin Roof*, *Woolf?* had a unity of time and place that allowed for continuous action. In spite of the closeness of his relationship with commercial producers Richard Barr and Clinton Wilder, Albee decided to seek a production by the Actors Studio. The Studio had brought on board veteran producer Cheryl Crawford (formerly with the Group Theatre) and Roger Stevens (eventually the producer for the Kennedy Center in Washington, DC). With a Ford Foundation Grant of $250,000 dollars, the Studio was about to embark on a new activity and become its own Broadway producer. Like Tennessee Williams, Albee was attracted to the naturalistic acting practiced by Studio members. He was particularly interested in having Geraldine Page play Martha. Page was well known for her Williams' heroines.[10] She was at the height of her career and universally praised for the intense inner reality she created on stage. Problems immediately began to surface with Lee Strasberg, the Studio's Artistic Director. Since its founding, Strasberg had become the Studio's guiding force. In this role, he was not simply an acting teacher but, for his disciples, *the* authority on all things theatrical. It was his self-appointed mission to protect the Studio from anything that might hint at scandal. Obviously, this meant safeguarding the Studio's name and the reputation of its members. Page was easily influenced by Strasberg and the former Director of the Group who had turned thumbs down to Odets had absolutely no use for *Who's Afraid of Virginia Woolf?*. Roger Stevens also opposed Albee's play. As he so succinctly put it in speaking for the Studio, he would not "help subsidize the speaking of dirty words on the stage." Cheryl Crawford (who turned down *Death of a Salesman*) opposed the play's bitterness and brutality. By early July of 1962, negotiations with the Actors Studio reached an impasse. They remained that way until O'Neill's widow, Carlotta (Monterey), gave the rights to the Studio to produce *Strange Interlude*.[11] The Studio leaped at this opportunity to get out of a potentially embarrassing situation with Albee, who had an advisory position to the Studio akin to playwright-in-residence. It is ironic that O'Neill's play, considered so daring for its sexuality in the late 1920s, should have become the Studio's "safe choice" in the early 1960s.

Since producing on Broadway was much too costly for Barr and Wilder to undertake on their own, they sought out a producing partner. In 1958, Billy Rose, one of show-business's legendary personalities, purchased the National Theatre on Forty-first Street and renamed it after himself.[12] Rose was associated with "girlee" shows. His artistic efforts included the Aquacade, nymphs in swimsuits kicking and splashing in unison. The Aquacade did for the live theatre what Esther Williams did for the screen. Rose's interest in owning a theatre (without a pool) had little to do with art and a lot to do with money. At the time, he had plenty of it, but he hated to see any of it go to the Internal Revenue Service. He could easily claim to IRS that owning the theatre was a constant cash drain. Ownership expenses could be used to justify all kinds of expenses. But, if by chance, every five years he could find one hit show he knew that the returns of that one show would be more than enough to make up for all his losses, real and fictionalized. Barr and Wilder having been unsuccessful in generating sufficient interest from any other theatre owners, reluctantly brought *Who's Afraid of Virginia Woolf?* to Billy Rose. Rose did not read the script, but accepted the recommendation of Malcolm Wells, a young man working in his office. What Rose liked was the humor in the play's title. He felt that if the play could be marketed as something "dirty," there was a chance he could make a buck. However, Rose did not like to take chances with art. He considered it absolutely mandatory that the play have at least one star.

Scripts were sent to Katharine Hepburn and Henry Fonda. Hepburn declined, saying she wasn't good enough and Fonda's agent sent the script back unread.[13] Several other famous stars of stage and screen were also contacted to appease Billy Rose. At this point, Barr suggested what he thought of as a great publicity stunt. Since Broadway was obviously prejudiced against Albee's play, why not have two productions of the play and two openings on the same night: one Off Broadway and one on Broadway. Show the public the double standard and embarrass the hell out of the Broadway crowd when the Off Broadway show turned up a winner. Rose was furious. He wanted nothing to do with such a cheap trick and threatened to withdraw his theatre if Barr and Wilder made any attempt to go ahead with such a scheme. The idea was immediately dropped.

It was at this point that Uta Hagen, who had not appeared on Broadway for six years, began to be seriously discussed for the role of Martha. Hagen, who had played Blanche DuBois in *A Streetcar Named Desire*,[14] the title role in *Saint Joan*, Desdemona in *Othello*, and Georgie Elgin in Odets' *The Country Girl*, made her stage debut as Nina with the Lunts in *The Seagull* in 1938. She was considered to be one of the first ladies of the American theatre, although her standards for both play and director were so idealistic that few producers dared to hope that she would return to the stage from her self-imposed exile. Fortunately, after reading only four pages of Albee's script, she had made up her mind that she really wanted to play Martha. Once she made up her mind her commitment to the project was unswerving.

Both Alan Schneider and Uta Hagen knew and approved of George Grizzard for the part of Nick. Ironically George Segal, who was to play the role in the film, was mentioned by Barr, but dismissed as being "too ethnic." For the critical role of George, Richard Burton was considered, as was Robert Flemyng. Eventually, the role went to Arthur Hill, a Canadian actor who had gained recognition in two Pulitzer prize-winning plays on Broadway, *Look Homeward, Angel* and *All the Way Home.* Hill received the script from his agent while he was working on a film in England, *In the Cool of the Day*, for John Houseman. Because the filming was held up, he was late in starting rehearsals, and it took him a long time to catch up to the others.

The role of Honey, which in many ways seems the least challenging role to play actually caused the most difficulty in casting. Albee had been impressed by Lane Bradbury, one of the Actors Studio members he had in mind when he thought the entire production would be done by them. According to Alan Schneider in *Entrances*, Lane had the wrong quality for the role and came across as being completely "colorless."[15] Schneider, who had discovered Melinda Dillon and cast her as Grusha in *The Caucasian Chalk Circle* at the Arena Stage in Washington, decided to replace Lane with Dillon. However, he neglected to inform Grizzard of this change. The result was that Grizzard arrived at rehearsal one day to find out that he had a new wife several inches taller than he was. Since Grizzard was supposed to be a kind of "he-man" in the play, he was very upset and threatened to quit. Schneider spent several hours talking him back into the play.

Unlike most Broadway productions of the period, *Who's Afraid of Virginia Woolf?* did not have an out of town try-out. The producers felt that they would have been risking a considerable loss touring such an unconventional play. Instead it was rehearsed the way most Off Broadway productions were rehearsed, on the stage of the theatre in which it would open. This meant that the set was built on the stage of the Billy Rose Theatre and all props and most of the costumes were available for the actors to work with almost from the first day of rehearsals. The show was blocked on the set, eliminating the need for the reblocking that generally occurs when a play shifts from rehearsal studio to the theatre. The only drawback was having to pay the three required union crew members for doing nothing. Since *Woolf?* takes place on a unit set, it did not require scene shifts. Still, the union crew was far less costly than any other arrangement. Three weeks were allotted for rehearsal, followed by five invitational previews and five low-cost previews.

Because of these economies the production came in at $75,000. Since more than $20,000 had to be put up as refundable bonds, the actual cost of the production was only $45,000. This meant that the entire investment could be recouped in a matter of weeks. Anticipating that the show would make money, and knowing that a good percentage of that would go to the government for taxes, Barr and Wilder decided to make Albee a partner in the production company giving him 25 percent of the weekly operating profits on a weekly basis in lieu of the 10 percent due him under the Dramatists Guild's Minimum Basic Contract. Considering that *Who's Afraid of Virginia Woolf?* would eventually return thirty times its original investment to its backers, Albee was in line for a windfall.

The constricted rehearsal time allowed little or no time for rewrites on *Who's Afraid of Virginia Woolf?*. Albee had heard the play read by actors and colleagues prior to going into rehearsal and had already made his adjustments. During the actual rehearsals at the Billy Rose, most cuts were made to bring the running time of the play down to three and half hours, a very long time for a Broadway show. Because of the length of the show, the producers decided to save the strength of the cast and do away with the two matinée performances. However, this decision did not appeal to Billy Rose who counted on receiving the same rent for the theatre whether or not the play ran for six or eight performances a week. Since Rose was unwilling to reduce his rent, the producers decided to cast a matinée company. This separate company would not only play the matinées but would be available on a limited basis to tour college and university campuses which it was deemed would provide an excellent audience for this play. The matinée company was cast with as much care as the evening company. Kate Reid, a Canadian actress, with a slightly coarser quality than Hagen played Martha and Shepperd Strudwick, who had participated in one of the early readings, played George. Ben Piazza (Nick) and Ava Petrides (Honey) rounded out this company.

Although Schneider and Albee disagreed about how realistic the set should be, Ritman was able to satisfy both by providing a living room that still created the feeling of womb or cave.[16] Schneider, who disapproved of the typical spine-only books that appeared in Broadway libraries, stocked the shelves with real books. A slight problem materialized with regard to the song "Who's Afraid of the Big Bad Wolf?" which had been used in the Walt Disney film *The Three Little Pigs*. It turned out that the song was still under copyright and the woman who had written the song wanted an inordinate amount of money to permit the use of it in the show. At the last minute Clinton Wilder realized that the tune of the old nursery rhyme "Here We Go Round the Mulberry Bush" would do just as well, and it was substituted for the Disney ditty.

Throughout the rehearsals, Albee, who kept in daily contact with Schneider, attended only those rehearsals when the director was ready to present a run-through of an act. After seeing the first act, Albee suggested to Schneider that Nick and Honey sat down too soon. Schneider restaged it so that Nick spent more time admiring the abstract painting of the state of Martha's mind. In the second act, Albee felt that the "Bergin story" seemed a bit too long. Hill was still having difficulties filling his role emotionally. Unlike Hagen, who worked out all of her motivations before beginning rehearsal, Hill worked by building motivation once he had the outer frame of his character. Schneider, who felt that the "Bergin story" held the play together by providing George with much-needed motivation for his actions against Martha, suggested that they keep the speech as written. To compensate, George's speech late in the third act was cut. Also, a short scene was cut at the beginning of the third act and a compensating change made at the end of the second. In the third act, Albee was unhappy with the way that Hagen was romanticizing the story in which she described the activities of her imaginary son. Although Barr and Wilder felt it was improper to have the playwright rather than the director speak to an actor, they decided in this instance to encourage Albee to speak to Hagen outside of the rehearsal on the phone. Hagen it turned out had once lost a child, and had great difficulty in opening herself up emotionally to the real vulnerability she felt about this issue. Schneider reports that she only let herself completely go once in preview with the full intensity she was capable of giving to the role.

As the production moved towards its first "free" preview, the company started to feel that they had "something interesting and original." Rather than follow the theatre custom of not inviting "theatre people" to see the show, the producers decided to make a special point of encouraging fellow professionals to share the excitement of the occasion. With a show in trouble, the word from "theatre people" can be the kiss of death. They are notorious for being one of the most difficult audiences to please. But in this instance, "theatre people" began to talk up the show. With each preview, audiences became more and more enthusiastic. After the first paid preview, Billy Rose decided to hire two more cashiers. He reasoned that "Any playwright who can get that many laughs with that much venom and invents a game like 'Hump the Hostess' is my kind of writer. I've got the hit I was looking for." To assure the proper return on his enthusiasm, Rose decided to take out a series of ads in the newspapers telling secretaries that they would understand the play, but the boss wouldn't. He signed his own name. The five low-priced previews sold out. In fact, the company was actually beginning to make money.

By the time Who's Afraid of Virginia Woolf? opened on Saturday night, October 13, the play already had two audiences: those who came to the theatre ready to understand every inside joke and catch every innuendo and those who were more or less uninitiated. For those in the latter group they had two choices: either to join up with the theatre "in crowd" (many of whom had been carefully planted in the house by management) and enjoy the savagery or to take their hats and coats and leave. Alan Schneider states:

> Even before the curtain went up, there was a buzz and hum through-out the audience that had nothing to do with friend or relatives. The audience seemed to have a sixth sense that they were in for something special. Even the "regulars," jaded and cynical as they tend to be about anything short of an atomic explosion in the adjoining seat, seemed to be actually alive. With Uta's "Jesus H. Christ" entrance, I felt the audience fused into rapt attention, punc-tuated by machine-gun bursts of New York laughter. And two minutes into the performance . . . nothing could stop us.[17]

At the final curtain call, the entire audience was up, and cries were heard of "Author! Author!" but Albee, though he had spent three-and-a-half hours pacing the back of the house with producers and director, refused to acknowledge the call. "This is the actors' night," he said, and refused to go to the stage.[18] There was no company opening night party to celebrate, although Uta Hagen held a gathering at Sardi's for fellow cast members.

The problem with opening on Saturday in New York is that reviews do not appear until Monday morning in the early editions. Therefore, instead of the usual five or six hours wait, Barr, Wilder, and Albee had to wait until mid-afternoon Sunday when the professional press agent's spies in various newspaper printing plants could be coaxed into reading the reviews over the phone to those nervously awaiting the verdict. Unfortunately, the most easily coaxed pressmen work for the least repu-table papers, the tabloids, the *Daily News* and the *Mirror*. The critics of both of these papers felt obligated to protect their readers from a play of which *News* critic John Chapman said, "It is three and half hours long, four characters wide and a cesspool deep" (October 15, 1962). Robert Coleman of the *Mirror* also hated the play and everything it stood for, "*Who's Afraid of Virginia Woolf?* . . . is a sick play about sick people." His review concluded, "Many in the first night audience loved it. There were salvos of bravos. We loathed it. But we do not enjoy watching the wings being torn from human flies" (October 15, 1962). This critical reaction hardly did much to brighten the atmosphere at producer Clinton Wilder's East-side home on a dreary October Sunday. The general malaise that set in after hearing Billy Rose read his shorthand transcrip-tions sent Barr reeling from the room.

It wasn't until late afternoon that Walter Kerr's review in the *Herald Tribune* lightened the atmosphere. Although the *Herald Tribune* was on the decline by the early 1960s, Walter Kerr was highly respected and widely read by theatre-goers. Kerr stated, "It is a brilliant piece of writing with a sizeable hole in its head. It need not be liked, but it must be seen." The last four words are the words that producers and playwrights dream about reading in reviews. The value of opinion "pro" and "con" can be helpful, flattering, useful, maybe even enlightening, but what keeps plays open are reviews that tell readers "it must be seen." Kerr warned his readers that Albee's play "spells everything out," while at the same time vividly describing it as "horror with guffaws." However, what really bothered Kerr was the device of the imaginary child. "It is both thin and familiar," he wrote, "neither vigorous enough nor inventive enough to account for the size of the scab" (October 15, 1962). Although Kerr would eventually make the journey to the *Times* when the *Herald Tribune* folded, the critic of record for that all-powerful newspaper was Howard Taubman. Taubman had the misfortune of following Brooks Atkinson, a figure much beloved by the theatre community. Coming from the music desk, he was viewed as an outsider. His reviews so angered producer David Merrick that he threatened to seat the *Times* critic in a row immediately behind the New York Knickerbockers, the City's professional basketball team. Merrick maintained that he would see no less than he ordinarily saw, but now at least he would have an excuse. However, Taubman's review of *Who's Afraid of Virginia Woolf?*, although cautious, was perceptive. Like Kerr, he objected to the "too flimsy" climax. But he compensated for his statements about the play's structure by recognizing most of its virtues. "Mr. Albee's dialogue is dipped in acid, yet ripples with a relish of the ludicrous. His controlled, allusive style grows in mastery." He concluded, "His new work, flawed though it is, towers over the common run of contemporary plays. It marks a further gain for a young writer becoming a major figure of our stage." Most importantly, he uttered those magic words so important to every reader of New York newspapers, "You are urged to hasten to the Billy Rose Theatre" (October 15, 1962). The other reviewers, including Albee-booster Richard Watts, Jr, of the *Post*, concurred.

By ten o'clock Monday morning, there was a line of about one hundred people at the Billy Rose box office. On the first day, *Who's Afraid of Virginia Woolf?* took in $13,000 at the box office, more than doubling the total advance sale for the production. This was impressive for a straight play. Billy Rose's gamble in the play was handsomely rewarded. He admitted publicly to making almost $3,000,000 on the run of *Who's Afraid of Virginia Woolf?*. However, under the table he made considerably more money by selling the prime house seats at exorbitant prices to ticket brokers. Since taking "ice" was, strictly speaking, illegal, this was money that Billy Rose did not bother to declare on his income tax returns. It was a gift. According to producer Barr, "The money was carried to [Rose] nightly in a suitcase filled with cash by one of his minions after the treasurers and managers had received their split."[19]

By Tuesday, October 16, Albee was the overnight hero of all New York. Whitney Bolton, writing for the *Morning Telegraph*, New York's most expensive newspaper and bible to racetrack touts, was laying odds,

> Albee may well come to the end of this season in possession of all the prizes and awards at hand. I cannot imagine a better-written, more demanding, more stimulating play. All concerned, in and out of New York, are urged, begged and solicited to see *Who's Afraid of Virginia Woolf?*.

By the weekend, the Sunday retrospectives even of the strongly negative reviewers mellowed slightly. John Chapman's headline in the *News* (October 21, 1962), "For dirty-minded females only," probably helped boost sales although clearly this was not his intention. Even the stodgy *Christian Science Monitor* got on the bandwagon as critic Melvin Maddocks noted with remorse, "He has managed for inadequate reasons to make half our Broadway theatre seem imbecile and the other half hypocritical" (October 20, 1962); this from the newspaper that crowned Tennessee Williams "the poet laureate of degredation, decadence, and despair" for *Cat on a Hot Tin Roof*.

Yet, in spite of Bolton's prediction, *Who's Afraid of Virginia Woolf?* did not win all the awards. It was denied the Pulitzer, causing a furor when the expert panel split with the Trustees of Columbia University who award the prize. This falling-out had the heat and intensity of a George-and-Martha spat. Ultimately, this dispute changed the way the prizes were awarded by giving greater power to the judges and less to bankers, landlords, and corporate executives who are the trustees of the University. But for Albee, it was a grim reminder that his play, though it moved some to laughter and others to tears, left a large segment of the Broadway audience angry, even hostile. In the years following, Albee would receive two Pulitzers: one for *A Delicate Balance* (1966)[20] and another for *Seascape* (1975).[21] The award for *A Delicate Balance* was merited; however many viewed it as a belated recognition, and perhaps an apology for the denial of *Who's Afraid of Virginia Woolf?*. Many had considered this denial a form of censorship. Without question, the Pulitzer controversy fueled interest in the play giving it the allure of forbidden fruit.

Under the auspices of Donald Albery, *Who's Afraid of Virginia Woolf?* reached London with Uta Hagen and Arthur Hill in the leading roles. However, the Lord Chamberlain found a great deal of Albee's language offensive. After a series of discussions several offending phrases were changed. The nature of these changes irked and amused the American cast who thought changing "scrotum" for "privacies" was absolutely terrible as well as unspeakable. But since the Lord Chamberlain at that time still had the ultimate authority, the changes were made. In Boston,

Albee agreed to change "Jesus H. Christ" to "Mary H. Magdalene." Unfortunately, Nancy Kelly, who was playing Martha, slipped on opening night and blurted out "Jesus H. Magdalene." There were no repercussions, but Barr states that "the public reaction to the attempted changes effectively ended censorship in Boston."[22]

Who's Afraid of Virginia Woolf? has received several notable productions including a Broadway revival in 1976 with Colleen Dewhurst as Martha and Ben Gazzara as George. Since the word-barrier had been broken by such shows as *Hair* (1968),[23] Albee decided to insert "fuck" for "screw" in Act One and directed the play himself, proving his capability in this area as well. In 1989 Albee directed another major revival in Los Angeles with Glenda Jackson as Martha and John Lithgow as George. Since *Who's Afraid of Virginia Woolf?* is justifiably one of the most powerful and gripping works of recent Broadway, it will be repeatedly revived with stellar casts. For the actress who goes beneath the surface, Martha is a compelling study of female sexuality. No doubt much of the furor that greeted the play's initial production was shock and denial of this acid-etched portrait. From similar feelings, a few revisionists[24] promulgated a theory that Martha is really a man (in drag) and that the play is really about homosexual couples. There is absolutely no basis in fact for these assertions. If one needs a theory, it would seem more likely that the play can be traced to the author's strained relationship with his adoptive parents. During the period of composition, they were completely estranged. What better way to account for the parental whim that eliminates the "fictional" child. However, a work of art needs no explanation. It stands on its own merits and deserves to be evaluated for what it actually reveals to us about the human condition.

9 Edward Albee's *Who's Afraid of Virginia Woolf?* (October 13, 1962) at the Billy Rose Theatre. From left to right: Uta Hagen (Martha), Arthur Hill (George), Melinda Dillon (Honey), and George Grizzard (Nick). Martha in her party dress performs for Nick in Act One. Photograph © Alix Jeffry, courtesy of the Billy Rose Theatre Collection, New York Public Library.

10 The Broadway production of *American Buffalo* (February 16, 1977) at the Ethel Barrymore. Left to right: Robert Duvall (Teach), Jon Savage (Bobby), and Kenneth McMillan (Donny). Duvall in one of his rare reflective moments. Courtesy of the Chicago Public Library, Special Collections Division.

7

AMERICAN BUFFALO

My *profession* of artistic vision arose, I think, not so much to express whatever "individual" ideas I may have had or may have, but, rather, to accommodate and embrace a deviant personality which was not going to be employed elsewhere.

David Mamet

While *Who's Afraid of Virginia Woolf?* was playing on Broadway, David Mamet was working in theatres that were Chicago's equivalent to Off Broadway. Born and raised in Chicago, Mamet's first exposure to theatre occurred as a teenager while working as a waiter at Second City, an improvisational troupe. Mamet learned a great deal about the economy of the topical blackout skits which were the basis of the Second City format. Unlike the legitimate theatre, there was little fear of censorship in Chicago's nightclubs.[1] At Chicago's Hull House Theatre (Jane Addams Center), Mamet became aware of plays by such writers as Bertolt Brecht, Harold Pinter, and Edward Albee. The program of this amateur theatre was decidedly experimental. The "absurdist" dramas Hull House produced were dark and menacing. Such plays as Harold Pinter's *The Birthday Party* and Jack Gelber's *The Connection* depicted the violence and alienation of a world devoid of humanity and warmth. Plays were presented starkly on the small thrust stage. Actor and audience shared the same space in an intimate auditorium. David Mamet, who then aspired to become an actor, became fascinated with the idea of finding an acting technique that would somehow combine the spontaneity of the improvisational work of Second City with the kind of detailed realism required to make performance in this intimate theatre whole and convincing. In 1968, through a Junior Year Abroad program at Goddard College, Mamet discovered master teacher Sanford Meisner at the Neighborhood Playhouse in New York.

Meisner was an original member of the Group Theatre in the 1930s. He co-directed the original production of Clifford Odets' *Waiting for Lefty* and had acted successfully on stage and screen. Although Meisner

97

utilized many of the ideas of Stanislavski, he did not directly follow the teaching of his colleague, Lee Strasberg, with regard to emotional memory. He maintained that it was important to avoid teaching a technical approach that might be applied too self-consciously when an actor worked on a play. Meisner's method was to challenge his students through action-based objective exercises. The emphasis was on achieving a spontaneous flow of imagination and energy. He was opposed to Strasberg's reliance on analysis. Meisner had a profound impact on Mamet's way of seeing theatre. His ideational work complemented the improvisational approach that Mamet had observed at Second City while helping the actor lay the groundwork for developing a character's inner life.

In the years that followed, Mamet acted as well as taught acting at his alma mater, Goddard College in Vermont. He wrote his first play, *Duck Variations*, for students in his acting classes. Several of these students became the nucleus of Mamet's theatre, the St Nicholas Theater Company, including Steven Schacter and Bill (W. H.) Macy. With a small grant from the Vermont Arts Council, Mamet took his company with two of his one-act plays, *Duck Variations* and *Clark Street: or, Perversity in Chicago* (later *Sexual Perversity in Chicago*), on tour throughout New England in 1972. Bonnie Jacob, writing for *Boston After Dark* (July 25, 1972) reviewed the plays, finding them "original and refreshing." She stated succinctly what many other critics later discovered: "Mamet understands conversation well: his use of language is powerfully accurate and, at times, almost musical. Linguistically and theatrically, Mamet's characters can trace their ancestors to Pinter and Beckett – but their insights are their own."

By 1975, David Mamet and the St Nicholas Theater had settled in Chicago. According to the theatre's mission statement, its aim was "to explore the art of the stage, presenting works which exemplify care and thought in every phase of production based on a shared understanding of the technique of creating on a stage."[2] The program of this fledgling theatre echoed the reformist founders of the Little Theatre Movement fifty years earlier. Coincidentally, the first production of the St Nicholas Theater mounted at the Grace Lutheran Church was Eugene O'Neill's *Beyond the Horizon*. It was directed by David Mamet, then the Artistic Director of the theatre.

American Buffalo (1975) was David Mamet's first major success. Although he had gained critical recognition for early works *Duck Variations* (1972) and *Sexual Perversity in Chicago* (1974), it was not until *American Buffalo* that Mamet came to the attention of a wider audience, not just on Broadway, but throughout the world, with productions in London (at the Cottesloe, June 28, 1978), Berlin, Tokyo, Stockholm, Paris, and several other cities. Since its initial run on Broadway, *American Buffalo* has been revived with Al Pacino (as Teach) on and Off Broadway.

It is the only American play written in the 1970s to be given such major revivals. However, in contradiction to these accolades, the initial Broadway run of *American Buffalo* received only mixed notices. Hailed by some critics and dismissed by others, *American Buffalo* ran for only 135 performances. However, when the play was revived four years later with Al Pacino, it was proclaimed by the *New York Times* as "the best American play of the decade" and had a combined New York run at the Circle-in-the-Square (Downtown) and the Booth Theatre (Broadway) of 378 performances. The changing fortunes of *American Buffalo* have much to tell us, not just about the play and its productions, but also about what had happened to Broadway in the 1970s, as it shifted from being the premier theatrical venue to being a showcase for the best work created elsewhere in the American theatre.

American Buffalo concerns the planning of a failed robbery of American buffalo-head nickles. The idea for the robbery originates with Donny Dubrow, the owner of a Chicago junk shop in which the scene is laid. The entire action of the play is concentrated on a day and evening in April when Donny, together with his one employee, Bobby, a young drug addict, decide to rob a customer's apartment on the theory that the customer has a rare coin collection. The play begins with Donny teaching Bobby about the finer points of underworld life. He is interrupted by Walter "Teach" Cole, Donny's poker-playing pal. Teach convinces Donny that Bobby is too much of a risk to involve in a break-in. Donny reluctantly agrees and betrays the youngster upon whom he has recently lavished his paternal protection. However, rather than accepting Teach's two-man operation, Donny insists on involving a mutual friend named Fletcher. Although Teach is angry, he reluctantly goes along with Donny. In the second act of the play, Donny and Teach wait for Fletcher to arrive. As midnight approaches, Bobby arrives with a story that Fletcher has been mugged and taken to the hospital. Bobby has one of the coveted buffalo-head nickles with him which he wants to trade for immediate cash. Teach and then Donny become suspicious of a double cross. When Bobby fails to correctly respond to questions asked by the two older men, Teach hits Bobby in the head with a blunt object. The boy begins to bleed from his ear. As the two men discuss what to do, a phone call corroborates that the boy was telling the truth. Teach leaves to get a car to drive Bobby to the hospital while Donny cradles Bobby in his arms, and the two share a moment of reconciliation.

In *American Buffalo* the characters of the play are members of a subculture working within society but against that society's socially accepted goals. Unlike the characters of Odets' social protest plays of the 1930s, Mamet's characters do not question materialism or envision a life outside the current struggle. What comes first and foremost is winning, and to win they will utilize whatever means they can. There is almost no room in their psyches for reflection or thought. In fact, reflective responses seem to be dismissed by the characters as either unwelcome weaknesses or distractions. This limits opportunities for the kind of lyricism found in Odets, Williams, and Miller. The artistic focus of the play mirrors the characters' own absorption in the on-stage action. Like the improvised Second City blackout sketch, the plays go forth in a constant-time present with little or no reference to past events that are not directly a part of the play's inciting action. In *American Buffalo*, we are totally engaged in planning a robbery. There are references to an habitual set of relationships and incidents outside the shop. Beyond this, there is apparently nothing.

The first production of *American Buffalo* was directed by Gregory Mosher in his second season at the Goodman Theatre as assistant to Artistic Director William Woodman. The Goodman had become Chicago's established regional theatre after its separation from the Chicago Art Institute in 1969. One of Mosher's duties was to organize the Stage Two project, an experimental program. During its first season show-time was eleven thirty, following regular performances, and productions were staged in the lobby of the stately main auditorium. In planning the second season, Mosher had approached Mamet and asked him to direct a play. Mamet responded by bringing Mosher his own script, *American Buffalo*. "Do this play," Mamet implored, "Just do this play."[3] It was decided that a joint production of the play would be mounted that would involve both the Goodman and Mamet's St Nicholas Theater.

The first version of *American Buffalo*[4] was called a "work in progress" even though it was reviewed by the first-string Chicago theatre critics. A grant from the Illinois Arts Council had enabled the Goodman Theatre to present Stage Two attractions at the Ruth Page Center, a converted Elks Club used for dances located on North Dearborn. Michael Merritt received his first paid commission to do the set. His entire budget for the show was $500. "I decided that the primary scenic element would be chairs," Merritt stated in an interview with the author (June 7, 1992), "we had those in abundance in the basement. I put the chairs on wagons and stacked them. I also hung some of them from the ceiling to create the environment of the junk shop. I had the chairs going in all different directions kind of swirling about the stage." When Mosher arrived to look at the set, he commented to Merritt, "Don't you think the chairs are *a little too lyrical?*" Merritt restacked the chairs so they were more orderly and the set was approved.

Although the joint Goodman Theatre and St Nicholas Theater production (October 23, 1975) proved to be highly successful, a review of the criticism indicates that there were problems with this production, due to the casting of the role of Teach. Bernard Erhard, an actor new to Chicago, had strong credentials in musical theatre but was unable to internalize the role. Claudia Cassidy, for Radio Station WFMT (October 26, 1975), suggested a cartoon characterization – "the reptilian visitor with the fanged smile loaded with poison" while the Bury St Edmund, writing for the *Chicago Reader* (October 24, 1975) noted that "Erhard seems to manipulate his character rather than feel it." Mosher and Mamet gave the roles of Donny and Bobby to actors with whom Mamet had a special affinity, J. J. Johnston and William H. Macy. Macy had worked with Mamet for more than five years, first as a student at Goddard College and then as an original member of the St Nicholas Theater Company. Johnston and Mamet went back even further. The two had worked together as actors in summer stock in 1969[5] and recently in a children's theatre company. Mamet was familiar with Johnston's career as a boxer and the time the actor had spent living on the wrong side of the law.[6] Therefore, it came as no surprise that when the production was transferred for an extended run at the St Nicholas Theater (December 21, 1975), Mike Nussbaum, an experienced Chicago actor, was brought in to play the role of Teach. Mamet had known Nussbaum from his days at Hull House. According to Mosher, "Nussbaum found something in the character of Teach that nobody else ever figured out about him – namely, that he is a poet, not a thug."[7]

Acting values seemed to be crucial in this three-character play, particularly with regard to the role of Teach. According to Mamet, the entire meaning of the play could be jeopardized by changing the balance in the acting ensemble. In an interview for the *New Theatre Quarterly* (February 1988) Mamet states that it is Donny, the junk store owner, who is the "protagonist" of the play:

> *American Buffalo* is classical tragedy, the protagonist of which is the junk store owner, who is trying to teach a lesson in how to behave like the excellent man to his young ward. And he is tempted by the devil into betraying all his principles. Once he does that, he is incapable of even differentiating between simple lessons of fact, and betrays himself into allowing Teach to beat up this young fellow whom he loves. He then undergoes recognition in reversal – realizing that all this comes out of his vanity, that because he abdicated a moral position for one moment in favour of some momentary gain, he had let anarchy into his life and has come close to killing the thing he loves. And he realizes at the end of the play that he has made a huge mistake, that rather than his young ward needing lessons in being an excellent man, it is he himself who needs those lessons.[8]

No doubt, this statement is what Mamet intended the audience to perceive in his drama, but it is not what the audience *did* perceive. Reviewers and critics, starting with this early Chicago version of the play, perceived this as Teach's play. It was Teach as intruder that naturally offered an actor the best opportunities for a bravura performance while critics found the victim, Bobby, the most sympathetic. Although Mamet insists that Donny is the "protagonist," the "recognition in reversal" comes about when Donny receives a phone call from Ruthie. Donny does not truly "undergo" it. He registers and responds to new information. Although Mamet does dramatize this response which builds the strength of Donny, it is too little too late to shift the focus away from the violent confrontation the audience has recently witnessed.

However, if there were any production in which the Donny and Bobby relationship should have emerged as central, it was in this early Chicago production before the Broadway rewrites. In the first version of the script, Donny was a stronger character. Moreover, in casting Johnston, whose "moose-like" qualities gave him a hulking presence on stage, director Mosher physically compensated for the role's lack of dramatic development. Macy, who played opposite Johnston, felt that the actor's identification was so complete with the role of Donny that he "owned the part."[9] Opening night critic St Edmund understood this dynamic when she wrote that "Donny is the touchstone" of the play, which meant that he "anchors the others and keeps them from just blowing away."[10]

Following the Chicago production, an Off Broadway production was mounted at St Clement's Church in January 1976. Gregory Mosher directed a cast of New York actors which consisted of J. T. Walsh (Bobby), Michael Egan (Donny), and Mike Kellin (Teach). Sets were by Akira Yoshimura. The play won an Obie Award for Best New Play (Off Broadway's equivalent of the Tony Award), and Mike Kellin received an Obie for his distinguished performance as Teach. It is important to note that even without the subsequent changes in the role of Teach created for Broadway, that it was Kellin's performance that garnered all of the praise.

By early 1976, David Mamet was attracting considerable attention both in Chicago and New York. While *American Buffalo* was still playing in Chicago, his earlier one-acts *Sexual Perversity* and *Duck Variations* opened Off Broadway at the St Clement's Theatre. The double bill proved to be so successful that a commercial Off Broadway production followed at the Cherry Lane Theatre, a theatre that a decade earlier had become identified with Barr–Albee–Wilder productions. At 28, Mamet had enough significant regional and Off Broadway credentials to attract the interest of veteran producers Edgar Lansbury and Joseph Beruh. In spite of the production momentum of *American Buffalo*, it would take it almost a year to reach Broadway. The reason for this delay ultimately had to do with finances.

Although Lansbury and Beruh were established both on and Off Broadway, they were not flush. Of their Broadway successes, Frank D. Gilroy's

The Subject Was Roses (1964) was the most acclaimed. *Godspell* (1971), an Off Broadway effort, had easily been their most successful. Beruh, who optioned *American Buffalo* during the summer after the Obie awards, stated that what passed before his eyes in reading the play was, "America as it is today – Watergate, ITT, the Lockheed scandals – someone had really captured what the country is about, sadly."[11] Although Lansbury and Beruh appreciated that the play had already been critically successful both in Chicago (where it won a Joseph Jefferson Award) and Off Broadway in New York, they left the question of rewrites open pending decisions by the director, Ulu Grosbard. Grosbard had worked previously with the team on Gilroy's *Subject Was Roses*. Grosbard had already earned valuable film credits. He had worked with Elia Kazan in 1961 as the assistant director on the Academy Award-winning film of William Inge's *Splendor in the Grass*.[12] After directing Lansbury and Beruh's Broadway production, Grosbard went on to direct the film version of *The Subject Was Roses*.[13] He was enthusiastic about Mamet's play:

> "I felt I was in the presence of an original voice in the American theatre with a unique vision, intelligence, an extraordinary ear for translating real behavior, who could capture in dialogue what is not being said, and who could do that with a class of people that is never represented in the American theatre. I couldn't believe that he was twenty-eight and not from a lower-class background."[14]

Over the years Grosbard had gained a reputation for being a "perfectionist." He would not undertake a project unless he felt absolute confidence in his script. Although he was obviously impressed with Mamet's play, he told Beruh that he still felt it needed work. However, in his first telephone conversation to Mamet from Hollywood Grosbard talked about casting and not the script. Grosbard placed one condition upon his acceptance of the project: if Robert Duvall was available then the role of Teach would be his. This condition posed no problem for the playwright, who was an avid "Duvall fan."[15]

In spite of Mamet's present reputation for being incredibly loyal to those actors and designers who worked with him on early productions, the playwright was in no position at age 28 to resist Grosbard's demand. Moreover, there was no reason for Mamet to object to the director's proposal. When Mamet studied with Sanford Meisner, Duvall's name had been frequently mentioned. Meisner considered Duvall one of America's greatest actors. According to Mamet, "Sanford Meisner would tell us, 'There are only two actors in America. One is Brando, who's done his best work, and the other is Robert Duvall.' "[16] If this statement seems somewhat biased, it was. Brando was a product of Strasberg's Actors Studio while Duvall was a product of Meisner's Neighborhood Playhouse.

Grosbard was not typical of most theatrical directors. He did not take on a series of projects and hop from one to another for simple financial gain. He made strong commitments to the few projects he believed in and then nursed them along until they reached fruition. As a result, his career had paid the price. He had directed only seven professional productions in New York and two movies. Two of the productions had been done with one actor in a principle part, Robert Duvall (*The Days and Nights of Beebee Fenstermaker* (1962)[17] and *A View from the Bridge* (1965)). In fact, *A View from the Bridge* typified Grosbard's sustained commitment to a project. He had first directed Miller's play at the Gateway Playhouse in Bellport, Long Island in 1959 with Duvall unconventionally cast as the swarthy, Sicilian longshoreman Eddie Carbone. Both director and actor were in their twenties, and it had been the first stepping-stone in both their careers. It took Grosbard six years to realize *A View from the Bridge* Off Broadway. Nearly seventeen years had gone by since Duvall and Grosbard first worked together and the director was still thinking about projects for the two of them.

With playwright, director, and producers now in agreement, the major question was the availability of the star. Lansbury and Beruh knew that they needed a star of Duvall's reputation to be able to raise the $190,000 to produce this three-character one-set play on Broadway. As incredible as it may seem, the cost of production had so inflated in the labor-intensive theatre business from the 1960s to the late 1970s that *American Buffalo* would capitalize at an amount that was four times greater than *Who's Afraid of Virginia Woolf?*. Without a star of Duvall's reputation, it would have been impossible to attract financing of that magnitude for an unknown play by a virtually unknown writer.

Duvall's reasons for taking the part of Teach in *American Buffalo* indicate the way Hollywood had come to regard Broadway. Duvall was interested in Broadway because he found his Hollywood career temporarily stalled. Not that he wasn't making movies; starting with *To Kill A Mockingbird* (1963), Duvall had been working steadily. But the kind of roles he was getting were those in which he had to show "practiced restraint." The role of Tom Hagen, the trusted *consiglieri* in *The Godfather* (I and II) was typical. Although Duvall had been nominated for an Academy Award for best supporting actor, he was still being cast in background roles. By contrast, Al Pacino, the young actor who appeared with him in *The Godfather* (1971), was being offered leading roles in films such as *Serpico* (1973).

Because he trusted Grosbard, Duvall accepted the role of Teach even though he confessed he did not understand the play the first time he read it. Duvall was less bothered by working for one-third of what he made for a far less demanding film role than he was about the time commitment. He wanted a six-week time contract. When it was communicated to Duvall that this was simply impossible, he did reconsider and accept, even though this meant going against the advice of friends such as Dustin Hoffman who thought Duvall was crazy for not devoting himself to building his film career. Duvall defended his decision, countering that doing a play would make him a better actor. He wanted the opportunity to do tight ensemble playing, a hallmark of a Grosbard production. He also wanted to see if he could meet the challenge of keeping a role such as Teach fresh night after night. At the back of his mind was the thought that if he could do all this, he might also succeed in getting better film roles.

Grosbard and Mamet worked together on rewrites for four months before rehearsals began. In all, there were six drafts of the play. Beruh states that there was no thought of trying to make *American Buffalo* into a "well-made" play. While this may have been the case, there was a feeling that a Broadway production required more consistent characterization. This meant eliminating ambiguities and anchoring every significant detail of the action in psychological motivation. For instance, Grosbard wanted to know why Bobby showed up in the second act with a nickle wrapped in a cloth? What was the significance of that detail, not just in terms of the plot, but in terms of Bobby's overall psychological development? This meant totally rethinking the play from the inside out and establishing a root action for this choice early in the play.

With Duvall now cast in the role of Teach, Grosbard wanted Mamet to refocus the play on Teach. Since the play naturally moved in this direction, this was more a task of refining and readjusting. For Mamet, this kind of tinkering with a work he had thought finished in Chicago did not come easily. When asked by an interviewer about the rewrite process, he likened the new commercial pressures on his writing to "a furlough in hell."[18]

In order to illustrate the kinds of changes that Mamet worked into his script, I will give a few specific illustrations from the beginning of the play and a crucial scene in the play's second act. In the opening moments of the Chicago version of the play,[19] Donny and Bobby entered the junk shop and then began a conversation. In the Broadway rewrite, the action began in the midst of a conversation between Donny and Bobby already seated in the junk shop. Instead of a long rambling monologue by Donny, Mamet changed the play so that Bobby interrupted Donny, turning Donny's introspective monologue into dialogue. This subtle change undercut the character of Donny while strengthening the character of Bobby. Starting the play in the middle of a conversation helped to shift both characters to the background since the play's first major entrance now belonged to Teach.

The pattern of changes became even more obvious in the second act when a critical line in the development of the play's plot shifted from Donny to Teach. In the Chicago version of the play, it was Donny, not

Teach, who delivered the crucial ultimatum to Bobby, "I want you to tell us here and now – and for your own protection – what is going *on*, what is set *up* . . . where Fletcher is . . . and everything you know."[20] This change made the play's most violent confrontation directly between Teach and Bobby. On Broadway, Teach completely took over the play while in Chicago he erratically followed and occasionally led. The action of striking Bobby crystallized the changes in the dynamic within Teach's character. In Chicago, Teach pistol-whipped Bobby in response to Donny's questions. This was a predictable and deliberate piece of stage violence. On Broadway, Teach explosively grabbed the nearest object and bashed Bobby in the head. The difference in audience response between the explosive violence and the planned violence was phenomenal. In the first script, Teach was deliberate, slow, and ultimately less threatening. In the rewritten script, Teach was unpredictable, uncontrollable, and psychotic. He was a threat not only to the characters on stage, but to the audience, a reality that would subsequently be made clear when Teach tore apart the junk shop and hurled pieces of it into the auditorium.

Duvall's method of preparation for Teach consisted of total immersion. He took himself to Miami where once he had met a teamster who was also an ex-con. To get inside Teach, he modeled himself on this acquaintance. He not only talked about the life of a small-time hoodlum but he spent time observing the man's every mannerism. He learned among other things the trick of tucking a revolver in a belt above his genitals to avoid a frisk search by cops. Freshly schooled after his crash course in the ways of the underworld, Duvall arrived in New York ready for rehearsals.

Finding the required $190,000 to produce this three-character one-set show was another issue. According to Grosbard, "All commercial investors turned us down flat. Deaf ears! Deaf ears!"[21] Fortunately, there were people in Chicago outside the traditional circle of theatrical investors who were willing to stake the young playwright. For these investors, it was not just a matter of their faith in Mamet's play as a money-making venture but a desire to see the nation's second city triumph over New York's Broadway. Even so, there was still not enough to go forth with a production. Finally, the money could only be raised by the artistic staff, such as Grosbard, investing their fees in the production partnership. For an artist, this is an extremely risky business since it means that months of work could go uncompensated if the production fails. However, as a show of faith in the project such a sacrifice does help to build a "close-knit" family. For Mamet, it meant that the director was willing to engage at the same level as he was. Mamet's respect for Grosbard grew: "He created in all of us the most fantastic feeling of competence. He's one of three or four people I've ever met who has any idea how to direct a play."[22]

Yet Grosbard's view of the play was quite different from Mamet's: "The play is about conflicts of values – friendship, loyalty, business. All three characters have to confront their own weaknesses. They are dependent on each other for survival." About the issue of language, Grosbard was also clear. In an interview with Mel Gussow of the *New York Times*,[23] he indicated that he did not feel that Mamet had written naturalistically: "If you turned on a tape recorder in a junk shop and let it run for a week, most of it would be very boring. The artistry is in distilling the essence of that experience." He saw the evening as a composition of both humor and emotion. His task: to charge the play with intensity and enlarge it. With the limited physical action provided by the script, interior and verbal action had to be taken out front, performance needed to be larger than life. Ultimately, this meant relying more and more on Robert Duvall. For his part, Duvall was keenly aware of this pressure and utilized it to build his performance. On and off stage, he spoke like a "thug." Although on other occasions he liked to relax by singing country songs, he foreswore the pleasure out of fear it would "violate" the inner rhythms of his clipped Chicago accent. Duvall's internal self-criticism was merciless. Following a first preview before an audience made up of theatre professionals, he confessed that he felt depressed: "It was almost like a reverse kind of intimidation having a lot of actors in the audience. I mean, I wanted it to be terrific. I wanted it to soar. Maybe it can't soar all the time."[24]

On February 16, 1977, *American Buffalo* opened at the Ethel Barrymore Theatre. Clive Barnes, then writing for the *New York Times*[25] (February 17, 1977), felt that it was a "comedy about violence, and a play about action that is curiously inactive." The idea of inactivity seemed to be particularly unsettling to his highly influential colleague Walter Kerr who had moved from daily critic to a Sunday column. Kerr stated, "Nothing at all happens in *American Buffalo*, which is what finally but firmly kills it as a possible evening in the theatre" (*New York Times*, March 6, 1977). Both Kerr and Barnes took exception to Mamet's language; Barnes for its obscenity, "one of the foulest mouthed plays ever staged" and Kerr for "logorrhea, out of the compulsive, circular, run-on and irrelevant flow of words that tend to spill from folk when they're otherwise impotent." Michael Feingold, writing for the alternative *Village Voice* (February 28, 1977), took exception to Barnes' review. In defending Mamet, he made a cogent "post-Watergate" argument that not only did President Nixon's speech seem similar to the speech of Mamet's characters but that like the characters in the play the nation's former chief executive was also consumed in planning a "third-rate burglary." Feingold saw the play as a kind of political drama which did not seek to directly reference particular past events but which made the audience "think . . . in itself the mark of a good play." This controversy between the establishment *Times* and the upstart *Voice* was joined by the *Voice*'s Julius Novick. In a review headed, "It's not supposed to be eloquent" (February 28, 1977), Novick drew an important distinction between making poetry, a characteristic once attributed to Clifford Odets in the 1930s, and making music:

> That is, [Mamet] has not tried to work up his crummy lowlifes to the point where they are inspired to give eloquent descriptions of their experiences and beliefs, but he has developed the *rhythms* of their lassitude, their bitching, their rising excitement, their fear, their negotiating, quarreling, cross-examining, with a subtle, beautiful dexterity that has to be heard to be fully enjoyed.

The controversy between the *Times* and the *Voice* over the play's language was echoed by the rest of the critical establishment. Gordon Rogoff (*Saturday Review*), John Simon (*New Leader*), Brendan Gill (*New Yorker*), Douglas Watt (*Daily News*), Hobe (*Variety*), and Rosalyn Regelson (*Soho Weekly News*) attacked while Alan Rich (*New York Magazine*), Martin Gottfried (*Post*), Howard Kissel (*Women's Wear*), and Alan Havis (*Our Town*) defended.[26] In comparing the critical reception given *American Buffalo* to those given either Albee's *Who's Afraid of Virginia Woolf?* or Williams' *Cat on a Hot Tin Roof* one would have to say that the condemnation heaped on Mamet's play far outweighed the negative criticism leveled at either of the other two. The difference had to do with Mamet's free-flowing use of obscenity, an issue about which all the critics felt obliged to warn their readership.

In Chicago, one critic out of five had agreed with Mamet that Donny was the protagonist. In New York, following the revisions and Robert Duvall's performance, there was no discussion of Donny except as a secondary character. The critics were mesmerized by Duvall's performance. Gottfried in the *Post* (February 17, 1979) stated: "One of the funniest and most striking characters ever to walk an American stage . . . a dazzling virtuoso performance." "Duvall, in the showiest part," wrote Feingold in the *Voice* (February 28, 1977), "is the most memorable of the three, playing with a monomaniac intensity and galloping rhythm that make Teach both threatening and fascinating to the audience." Specific moments of the performance drew very strong responses. Teach's assault on Bobby shocked the audience into silence and when Teach destroyed the junk shop critics Walter Kerr and Michael Feingold admitted ducking for cover. Duvall's years of restrained acting were clearly at an end with what Barnes described as his "wild gusts of paranoid fury" (*New York Times*, February 17, 1977).

Kenneth McMillan, who had given a masterful performance as one of the boozy sergeants in David Rabe's *Streamers* (April 21, 1976) a season before, left a clear afterimage in the mind of Clive Barnes, who praised the actor for being "luminously stupid as the junk-shop owner." Michael Feingold called him the "fixed star in contrast to Duvall's comet . . . witty enough to give Donny . . . the solidity and mildness of a John Bull innkeeper." Kissel found that McMillan suggested "authority in spite of apparent wheeziness." About John Savage's Bobby, Kissel said, "In some ways, the most impressive performance . . . his is the most cryptic role and Savage's choices are marvelous; he has one of the most expressive, nuanced deadpans in the business." Feingold also admired the young actor "for making the junkie interesting without falling into the trap of sentimentality and making him lovable."[27] Most of the critics agreed that Savage made the role vulnerable and sympathetic. Two critics thought that there might have been the suggestion of an unexplored homosexual relationship between Donny and Bobby.

Santo Loquasto's set received a great deal of attention, not all of it positive. Unlike Michael Merritt's suggestive interpretation of a junk shop, Loquasto created what Rex Reed writing in the *Sunday News* described as:

> A magnificent labyrinth of used appliances, electrical wiring, rubber hosing, broken toys, discarded Pepsi cans, wheels, pots, ladders, and scrap iron. How would you describe this? I asked the woman sitting next to me. "A mess?" she replied, baffled. Well, yes. But too sumptuous a mess for the tiny play that unravels in its Kafka-esque maze.[28]

Gottfried likened it to a "massive sculpture" and Kissel thought it "ought to be signed and framed." Whether or not it overwhelmed the play is open to question. One reviewer stated that he would have liked time during intermission to go on stage and shop.

Novick's perceptive review (*Voice*) averred that the directing and the writing made it clear that "realism" was not finished in the theatre. "What the epitaph-mongers neglected was the possibility that the realistic tradition might be reinvigorated by the influence of the very playwrights who led the reactions against it." Novick was observing a pattern. Young writers who started their careers Off Broadway or in the regions changed styles as they approached working on Broadway. Whether this came from maturity or whether writing for larger theatres dictated simplification, Albee and now Mamet had shifted subtly to the realist camp.

American Buffalo's mixed critical reception only intensified the problem of finding an audience for the play. With a four-month commitment to Robert Duvall and the hopes that business might improve, the play moved from the Ethel Barrymore to another Shubert theatre, the Belasco. The construction of the Belasco is such that orchestra-seat holders are less aware when the balcony is empty. At one performance of the play, Duvall told *Cosmopolitan*[29] Ted Morgan, there was no applause at the curtain call. Duvall was obviously upset, but he responded in character and gave the audience the finger. At such moments, he drew a certain amount of comfort from knowing that no lesser person than Elia Kazan has seen the play and praised it. It was clear that people were finding the language of the play offensive. When Duvall's parents indicated that they wished to come to New York to see the play, even the lead actor felt obliged to discourage them from attending since he knew they would find the language offensive. When it was announced that in spite of the awards the play was closing, audiences materialized, but by this time it was too late and *American Buffalo* closed, completely losing its investment. Mamet was not surprised. It reaffirmed what he thought of Broadway.[30]

Al Pacino's revival of *American Buffalo* less than three years after the initial Broadway production was a very different experience for an audience. There was no guesswork about who was the main character. The audience knew who they were supposed to watch and why. Audiences were coming to see Pacino, not necessarily Mamet's play. The interpretations were different, too. Whereas Duvall had epitomized the businessman seen as a criminal, a theme that Mamet has later developed in a different way in *Glengarry Glen Ross*,[31] Pacino played Teach as a disturbed outsider. Pacino's street-smart Teach entered looking disheveled and acting restless. Like a caged animal, Pacino paced the junk shop, rummaging through merchandise as if he was searching for clues. His explosive thrust towards Bobby seemed almost accidental as if some wild fury suddenly escaped from a level beneath consciousness. Pacino used the vulnerabilities of his fellow actors and played a game of cat and mouse with them in much the same way his character did in the film *Dog Day Afternoon* (1975). This was a performance designed for a more intimate theatrical playing space than the Ethel Barrymore, which is why Pacino had initially opened the play Off Broadway on the thrust stage at the Downtown Circle in the Square. When his *American Buffalo* finally did come to Broadway it played the Booth Theatre, the same intimate house selected by Kaufman half a century earlier for the premierè of *You Can't Take It With You*.

Pacino's Broadway run began on a note of tragedy when the actor playing Bobby, James Hayden, a young man who had been struggling with drug dependency, died of an overdose. It gave a level grim reality to the production as press coverage of the play shifted from the drama page to page one and lead stories on television's nightly news. Pacino's presence on Broadway now became known to a whole new potential audience. Hayden, who was playing a drug addict at the time of his death, seemed to epitomize all of those disquieting questions that always seem to lurk just beneath the surface about what is real to life and what is an imitation. Background stories on Hayden dramatized his romantic relationship with Amanda Plummer. They stressed his promise, his possible stardom. He was cast in the mold of James Dean, an actor whose early death in an auto accident continued to create myth years after the event. The mythology of Broadway and Hollywood intrigued Mamet. A few years later, he would deliberately exploit these issues by casting Madonna in *Speed the Plow* (1989), a drama which probed the duplicity of Hollywood's intersecting worlds of ego and sexual gratification. Following the news stories, Pacino's *American Buffalo* settled in for a long comfortable run. The play had undergone a sea change from a work-in-progress in a north Chicago lodge hall to a recognized star vehicle, just as Mamet had climbed from relative obscurity to be the best-known American dramatist of his generation.

8

BROADWAY BOUND

To pry and probe and eventually to leave the remains of his victims spread out on a typewritten page with their names disguised, but their identities known to the world, exposed for all to see . . .

Neil Simon

No discussion of Broadway could be complete without a consideration of Broadway's quintessential playwright, Neil Simon. In the past thirty-one years, he has had twenty-eight plays on Broadway. More than once, he has had four plays running simultaneously. His string of successes surpasses anything in the history of the American theatre. In fact, in financial terms, his successes have surpassed the combined career totals of all the other playwrights in this volume. In spite of this, it was not until the 1980s, with the appearance of what has been called the "Brighton Beach Trilogy" – *Brighton Beach Memoirs*, *Biloxi Blues*, and *Broadway Bound* – that Simon has been taken seriously as a writer. *Broadway Bound*, in particular, struck many critics as a departure. Up until that point Simon was politely, but firmly dismissed as a writer of "gag-infested" comedies.

The tendency to view Simon as a passing phenomenon is reflected in the noticeably few Broadway revivals of his work. With the exception of the female version of *The Odd Couple* (and musicals), Simon's plays have only played the White Way once. Perhaps, this is because the original productions by directors such as Gene Saks and Mike Nichols appeared to be definitive or because the subsequent exploitation of the plays in film and television seemed to have exhausted their box-office appeal. Or maybe the lack of revivals seems so startling because there is clearly a need for Simon on Broadway. As recently as 1992 he had two productions running: *Lost in Yonkers* and *Jake's Women*. There were reliable rumors that two additional plays were in the works. One title that has been recently produced is *The Goodbye Girl*. In the case of *The Goodbye Girl*, a 1977 film,[1] the Broadway version is a musical. It may be that Simon intends musical versions of all his plays and films. If this is the case, Broadway will be stocked with Simon well into the next millennium.

When Neil Simon began his rise to fame and fortune on Broadway, he neither looked for nor did he receive the blessings of the critical establishment. Critics looked askance at a successful television writer having the nerve to seek entrance into the pantheon of playwrights. They referred to him as a writer of "sitcoms," suggesting that the "situation" and not his manipulation of it was responsible for the play's success. The reality that Simon was writing a new kind of "domesticated farce" simply escaped critical observation. If critics had compared Simon to Kaufman and Hart, they would have found several important similarities. Both Simon and Kaufman and Hart wrote contrived comic lines. But critics seemed to object much more strenuously to Simon's "gags" than they did to Kaufman and Hart's "wisecracks." Although it may be said that there is an element of contemporary social commentary in *You Can't Take It With You*, it is chiefly confined to the play's title. It could be argued that *You Can't Take It With You* goes beyond farce and becomes a comedy of character. Yet, for all of these distinctions, there can be little doubt that Simon and Kaufman and Hart have more that binds them together than most critics have acknowledged. Why then has Neil Simon been ignored by the critical establishment while Kaufman and Hart have been welcomed by them?

The answer to this question is complex, but it has a great deal to do with unstated canons of theatrical criticism. Certainly, there is an historical prejudice against the writers of comedy. Comedy has traditionally been given a lower standing. This point of view begins with Aristotle, who omitted comedy from his *Poetics* and who talked slightingly of the subjects of comedy, men who are less than we are. Whether this second observation was meant to apply only to social station or to moral integrity and native intelligence is debatable. There have been occasional instances in the history of the theatre where comic authors have been praised. Molière has certainly been lauded by the critics. And yet, the critical commentary on Molière is thin and insubstantial, a mere fraction of what we find on Shakespeare as a tragic author. There seems to be a persistent critical complaint that comedy is by its nature tied to a particular time and place.

But the prejudice goes much deeper. It has to do with an implied moral quality in the writing. Comic artists practice a form of "deception." There is the sense that comedy requires craft but seldom genius. Comedies seem to be constructed out of comic conventions and the writing of them, therefore, displays merely a technical virtuosity. Viewing comedy in the theatre belies this point. Audiences do not question how a playwright gets the happy result of laughter, while the critics feel cheated if they cannot attach some kind of greater significance as to why the laughter appears. If the critic cannot even justify or explain what produces the laughter, then both the laughter and the cause, the play, are simply hokum. There is a reaction that sets in against a play being playful. A play must have substance.

Broadway reviewers put the same issue in a slightly different manner. What seemed to trouble them was that Neil Simon lacked a consistent "voice." The idea that a playwright should even have a "voice" can be traced to the critical writings of Walter Pater who stated more than a century ago that "All art constantly aspires towards the condition of music."[2] Although clearly Pater was not writing about the theatre, he was highly influential on a whole generation of writers. His ideas strengthened the romantic notion that artistic composition sought an abstract purity, a "natural" form. Since comic writing in the theatre relies on artifice, rhetoric, and convention, the practical attainment of an ideal of purity was impossible. Moreover, the more perceptive the critic, the more artifice he found in composition and performance. Eric Bentley, who heatedly objected to *Death of a Salesman* and *Cat on a Hot Tin Roof*, is a clear example of this point. Because he saw Kazan's craft as director, he objected to it as manipulative. But audiences who were taken in ("duped") by Kazan never shared Bentley's misgivings.[3] To avoid the *sin* of theatrical manipulation, it has become useful not to disassociate artists from their work but rather to view them through the work, a form of biographical criticism. Thus, artist and work become one, and the critic can now discuss the artist's voice. If we apply this doctrine directly, the greatest artist of the theatre should be striving for total self-expression, the realization of him or herself on stage.[4] In this model, the success of the artist would no longer depend upon the audience, since writing *for* the audience would indicate an inartistic lack of self-sufficiency. Although such theories may prove valuable in studying playwrights who rose to critical prominence posthumously, such as Georg Buchner, it is of little value in evaluating a contemporary comic writer such as Neil Simon. Writers such as Simon are not self-sufficient. Comedy needs an audience. Moreover, it is of little, if any, value for a comic writer to view his work as an expression of his voice. If he is successful, the comic author speaks for his audience, not just himself.

Perhaps the closest that Simon might come to the critics' ideal would be to write a play similar to Kaufman and Hart's *You Can't Take It With You*, in which laughter arises more from character than from circumstance. For this kind of play to be effective, the characters have to be more than recognizable types. They have to appear to be rounded. Kaufman and Hart succeeded with their audiences by creating an extended family held together by mutual affection. Their characters were keyed to the specific talents of actors. Grandpa Vanderhof was created for Henry Travers. In their writing for that actor, they would automatically make adjustments from their own familial model, adapting the character so that the role would fit the actor like a glove. They would allow enough typification so that their audiences could project into the character giving the role in performance the appearance of roundness. Sentiment would blunt the edge of satire and gentle humor would replace derisive laughter. For Neil Simon to write such a play, he would have to find a subject matter which would forcibly restrain his tendency to make his characters more extreme, hence more ridiculous. Moreover, Simon would have to convince his audience that he was no longer aiming at comic exaggeration. The audience would have to see his characters as based on real people.

Since Clifford Odets' *Awake and Sing!*, Broadway audiences have become accustomed to accepting autobiographical plays as "authentic." Audiences believe that the playwright has been compelled to dramatize his rite-of-passage to win their allegiance. It has become almost an unstated rule on Broadway that if an author wishes to be taken seriously, he has to write a play which shares his guilt in exposing his disturbed family with the audience. Critics are mindful that guilt is an "authentic" feeling. In their reviews they state that the playwright has spoken passionately, and most importantly, with his own voice. No doubt, as Simon reviewed his career in the early 1980s, he must have realized that he had avoided writing this kind of a play. Perhaps, since the audience that appreciated his earlier plays had stopped coming as frequently to the theatre or since Simon had grown tired of being denied such literary distinctions as the Pulitzer Prize, he belatedly decided to write a "first" play and try his hand at a rite-of-passage play. Either way, Simon needed to prove to the world that he could be emotionally vulnerable.[5] Paradoxically, he had to forsake the notion of writing a comedy in order to earn the respect he deserved as a writer of comedies.

What Broadway loves about plays like Odets' *Awake and Sing!* is that no one has to puzzle over the play's meaning. The playwright tells the audience directly what he is thinking through his on-stage persona. All we have to know about Ralph Berger, and by extension Clifford Odets, is that he believes that life shouldn't be printed on dollar bills. Ralph Berger's "epiphany," his confrontation with materialism, would have pleased James Joyce, the father of the portrait-of-the-artist form. Yet successful as Odets' efforts at self discovery were, they pale beside those of Eugene O'Neill, who wrote an unabashedly autobiographical drama, *Long Day's Journey Into Night*.[6] O'Neill's posthumously produced play has been hailed as his greatest and is becoming the playwright's best-known work. No wonder, then, that Simon, America's most successful playwright, should have taken to adapting both O'Neill's and Odets' work when he set about to write his own autobiographical play, *Broadway Bound*.

In his dedication to his wife Carlotta at the beginning of *Long Day's*

Journey Into Night, Eugene O'Neill states that the script was "written in tears and blood" out of a need "to face my dead at last."[7] The play depicts one day in the life of the Tyrone family as they struggle to deny the inevitable passage of Mary Tyrone (Mary Ellen "Ella" O'Neill) into the night of drug addiction. Counterpoised to this struggle is Mary's own unwillingness to believe that her son, Edmund (Eugene O'Neill) has a case of tuberculosis serious enough to warrant his confinement to a sanatorium. The linking of the two stories of denial suggests the underlying connections between mother and son, both of whom have serious illnesses and both of whom are drifting perilously close to death-like night. Although the drama suggests that nothing can be done to save Mary, there is hope for Edmund if the father will forgo his usual miserliness and spend the money necessary to send his son to a private sanatorium. The change in the father comes about after a scene of confrontation and confession in which the father sees for the first time that Edmund, the afflicted son, has the "makings of a poet."[8] This results in the renewed commitment to save his son. Yet the closing moments of O'Neill's drama focus on Mary as she drifts into a drug-induced reminiscence of times long past. In her death-like state, Mary seems full of reproach for those around her who are still amongst the living.

The Brighton Beach Trilogy – *Brighton Beach Memoirs*, *Biloxi Blues*, and *Broadway Bound* – deals with the growth and development of Eugene Morris Jerome (Neil Simon), the author as a young man. Simon utilizes Eugene in all three plays as a narrator and shows his development from age 15 to 23. The trilogy shows a growth in Simon's willingness to go beyond what is comfortable and familiar. In the first play, Eugene is a wry commentator on his family and his own fascination with sex. In *Brighton Beach Memoirs*, Eugene is outside the on-stage action. Unfortunately, this allows Simon to completely bypass whatever real drama might exist. Instead of struggle, we get nostalgic reminiscences. With the writing of *Biloxi Blues*, Simon came closer to having his hero deal with real feelings. The play displayed a growth in dramatic intensity as well as personal awareness in dealing with such societal concerns as anti-Semitism, the need for personal integrity, and social justice. By the third play, *Broadway Bound*, the playwright's shift in thought and tone is so profound that we actually experience a drama of personal remembrance. For the first time, we are made to believe that the playwright is dealing with issues that seem crucial to the author's sense of self.

The change in the playwriting is paralleled by the evolution of Simon's *alter ego*, Eugene Jerome, the engine that drives each of these plays. In *Brighton Beach Memoirs*, Eugene as narrator provides a running comic commentary on the events happening around him. He simply bobs and weaves through the play without a blow landing on his smug face. In *Biloxi Blues*, Eugene's attempt to continue this pattern is foiled by a counterforce within the drama, the character of Arnold Epstein, who calls Eugene to account. At the conclusion of Act One, Arnold accurately describes Eugene, "You're a witness. You're always standing around watching what's happening. . . . You have to get in the middle of it. You have to take sides. Make a contribution to the fight."[9] In the second act, Arnold courageously demonstrates the consequences of such a commitment by confronting a drunken and crazed Sergeant Toomey. Although the happy outcome of Arnold's confrontation probably undercuts its dramatic effectiveness, it does give us one of the few moments of high drama in the Simon trilogy.

With *Broadway Bound*, Simon decided to find reason and cause to engage Eugene in a dramatic confrontation which does have personal consequences. Rather than depicting a secure relationship between Eugene's parents such as we find in *Brighton Beach Memoirs*, Simon chose to set his third play at the precise moment when Eugene's parents' marriage dissolves. To make certain that there is enough personal conflict to create a genuine impression on his hero, Simon has Eugene and his brother (Stanley) get their first "break" in show business at the moment their father decides to leave the family. The dichotomy between the troubled home and the opportunities of show business is dramatized in the first scene of the second act when the young writers watch their family listening to the team's first radio play. The family response to the boys' efforts is ice cold. Only Jack, the philandering father, realizes that the humor in the radio broadcast thinly veils the family's own private problems. Deeply embarrassed and hurt, he lashes out at Stanley and then Eugene for betraying the family. In spite of their feelings of guilt, the boys are successful. Their new radio careers provide the occasion for their exodus. The young writers are now literally Broadway bound.

Eugene, who acknowledges exploiting family secrets for show business success, understands that he now must choose between the fast-paced world of the entertainment industry or life in Brighton Beach with his abandoned mother. Although Simon avoids having Eugene deal directly with the feelings of guilt raised by this issue, he does create a dance for mother and son. The memory Kate Jerome recounts during her dance with Eugene is of a dance thirty years earlier with the future movie star George Raft. Not surprisingly, this is a memory that has show business implications. Just as Mary Tyrone and Edmund are linked in *Long Day's Journey Into Night* by the father's denial, so are Kate and Eugene by the father's abandonment. The result is that Eugene loses his narrative neutrality:

I'll be honest about one thing. Dancing with my mother was very scary. I was doing what my father should have been doing with her but wasn't. And holding her like that and seeing her smile was too intimate for me to enjoy. Intimacy is a complex thing. You had to be careful who you shared it with.[10]

Since the commentary comes after the dance, the audience has an opportunity to see and feel exactly the kind of moment that Eugene is describing. Moreover, Simon has brought the audience along with Kate's narrative of the event at the Primrose Ballroom. The audience can feel this moment with her. With this sepia tone portrait of Kate Jerome's, the Brighton Beach Memoirs trilogy comes to a close.

In both O'Neill's and Simon's plays, we have the portrait of the artist as a young man. Edmund Tyrone has just started to write. He receives the begrudging recognition of his father. Edmund has the "makings of a poet," while Eugene Jerome receives his father's condemnation for revealing family secrets. Coincidentally, both young men are 23 years old. Both men are alienated from their fathers and share a primary identification with their mothers. Both mothers are alive only in a remote past memory. Both memories have to do with screen images. Kate's memory has to do with the dance she danced with George Raft. In the case of Mary Tyrone, her strongest memory is linked to the young romantic actor James Tyrone. Like Kate Jerome's memory, it is associated with music. Mary begins her reminiscence by playing the piano. She is considering a life devoted to the Blessed Virgin: "That was the winter of senior year. Then in the spring something happened to me. Yes, I remember. I fell in love with James Tyrone and was so happy for a time."[11]

Both women express through memory a desire to be rescued in order to transcend the sadness of their current lives. They feel abandoned by their husbands and get their sons to share their desire for a lost time . . . a time in which mother is free from the father. In a sense the sons are trying to exorcize their mothers through their own writing. How else are they to be free of the guilt they feel for wishing the father dead?[12]

Simon's connections with Odets are less profound. He borrowed the character of Jacob, the socialist grandfather, from *Awake and Sing!*. In both plays, the grandfather is used to recall the idealistic faith the older generation felt for the New World. Not only age, but a loss of respect for labor (workers' alliances), has robbed these once powerful men of the leadership roles they held in the family. Both grandfathers are ridiculous throwbacks to a bygone era. In Odets' play, Ralph is actually rescued by the grandfather's suicide. His faith in social activism is kindled by Jacob's books, not his insurance benefits. In Simon's play, Ben's sacrifice, spending the winters in Brighton Beach to protect his needy daughter, makes the character seem even more inconsequential.

The critical reception of Neil Simon's *Broadway Bound* was both positive and perceptive. Gordon Rogoff, writing for the *Village Voice*

(December 16, 1986: 126), was one of several critics who recognized how closely this play was tied to twentieth-century Broadway history. "*Broadway Bound*," he wrote, "is the obligatory first play [Simon] never wrote, the one in which the dramatist celebrates his presumed talent by showing us his roots." Simon had finally come full circle and was writing the kind of serious personal play that was expected of Broadway play-wrights. Jack Kroll, in *Newsweek* (December 15, 1986: 76), extended the list of influences to include not only Eugene O'Neill and Clifford Odets but Arthur Miller. He viewed the contributions of these authors as a "legacy," indicating that it was Simon's obligation to add something uniquely his own to it. Brendan Gill of the *New Yorker* (December 15, 1986: 114) added another half a dozen working-class Jewish authors to the list and praised Simon for making diligent use of his forebears.[13] Critics appreciated knowing that Eugene in *Broadway Bound* was clearly related to Buddy in Simon's actual first play *Come Blow Your Horn*, as the earlier play seemed to take place immediately following the events in *Broadway Bound*. Edwin Wilson's retrospective piece in the *Wall Street Journal* (December 8, 1986) provided the context for evaluation:

> *Broadway Bound* . . . is Mr. Simon's *Death of a Salesman, The Glass Menagerie,* or *Long Day's Journey Into Night* – an honest, incisive account of the author growing up in a troubled family. And because it comes from Mr. Simon, it is also funny.

Simon has defined his own problem as an inability to commit himself emotionally to a deeply felt position. In the introduction to his first volume of plays entitled, "The portrait of the writer as a schizophrenic," Simon describes the problem through an anecdote about a marital spat:

> I could not contain myself, and a faint flicker of a smile crossed my face. Suddenly the anger and hostility drained from me and I found myself outside the situation looking in, no longer involved as a man in conflict, but as an observer.[14]

With the final scene in *Broadway Bound*, this neutrality of observation had somehow been bridged. Simon arrived at this particular juncture after serving a three-decade-long apprenticeship on Broadway.

If Simon's journey to self-discovery invites comparison with Eugene O'Neill's journey four decades earlier, it is not because the two are comparable literary figures. O'Neill's achievement goes beyond self-actualization. The image of O'Neill as a tormented artist spilling his guts on the page as a relief from his early traumas[15] is, as Judith E. Barlow has stated, "a romantic fiction."[16] *Long Day's Journey Into Night* is a work of meticulous craftsmanship that has tragic inevitability, three-dimensional characters, and tremendous power. Moreover, the quality of thought and diction surpasses anything that Simon has achieved. One senses the difference between the two in the glaring dissimilarity of the autobiographical disclosure. O'Neill prohibited Carlotta from bringing *Long Day's Journey Into Night* to Broadway until twenty-five years after his death. Simon did not have to levy any such restrictions on his work as the revelations were at best sentimental. Perhaps this is the difference between tragedy and comedy.

In both Eugene O'Neill's and Neil Simon's plays, the son/author character is left to consider what role he played in the family saga. Although O'Neill and Simon create their family dramas very differently, the audience in both instances has been gathered not only to witness, but to offer absolution. On some level both son/authors feel guilty. Psychic separation and self-sufficiency has been won, but at the expense of the failed family. For O'Neill, for Simon, and yes, for so many Broadway playwrights, the intimate personal disclosure fulfills the purposes of confession. The audience, through its shared feelings and applause, offers absolution for the truth no matter how painful it may be. If there is such a thing as the author's voice, it is heard most clearly at that moment of pure emotional contact when hopefully the two, speaker and audience, come together.

With *Broadway Bound* behind him, Simon wrote *Lost in Yonkers*.[17] Whether or not it is destined to become an American classic, as one critic averred,[18] it did win the Pulitzer Prize. Cast in the mold of the most unforgettable character story, Simon again probed the experiences of his youth in a play that mixed laughter with tears. The critics who had dismissed Simon's bittersweet tone in such plays as *The Gingerbread Lady*[19] were now inclined to accept him. He had proven himself, not simply by a showing of technical craftsmanship, but by writing with "emotional truth."

11 Al Hirschfeld's drawing of Neil Simon's *Broadway Bound* (December 4, 1986). From left to right: Linda Lavin (Kate), Jonathan Silverman (Eugene), Jason Alexander (Stan), Phyllis Newman (Blanche), John Randolph (Ben), and Philip Sterling (Jack). Hirschfeld drawings which appear in the *New York Times* have almost become synonymous with Broadway theatre. In this extraordinary grouping the focus is on the comic team of the quarreling brothers. © Al Hirschfeld. Drawing reproduced by special arrangement with Hirschfeld's exclusive representative, The Margo Feiden Galleries, Ltd, New York.

12 Ensemble photograph of Robert Schenkkan's *The Kentucky Cycle*, the 1992 winner of the Pulitzer Prize. Directed by Warner Shook and produced by the Intiman Theatre Company (Seattle, Washington) and the Mark Taper Forum (Los Angeles, California). *The Kentucky Cycle* is the only one of the Pulitzer Prize-winners not to have played New York. Photograph © 1991 Chris Bennion, courtesy of the Intiman Theatre, Gary Tucker, Public Relations Manager.

9

ANOTHER OPENING

The theatre is fluid: it assumes the shape of the society that contains it.

Elmer Rice

This is an extraordinary time in American theatre. This is a time of incredible revitalization, political thinking, structural pushing.

Jon Robin Baitz[1]

Since the 1930s when Kaufman and Hart wrote their play *The Fabulous Invalid*, prophets of doom and gloom have been predicting the demise of Broadway. What these Jeremiahs and Cassandras do is to look at the numbers. Not surprisingly, they find that the numbers of working weeks, theatres operating, and productions staged have moved progressively downward. What they fail to tell the reader is that the numbers follow national trends. Business and population have been moving away from the north-east towards the south-western part of the country. They also fail to mention that starting in the late 1950s hundreds of not-for-profit institutional theatres have sprung up, making the theatre a national industry.[2] In fact, as early as 1966, *Variety* stated, "Hinterland legits top Broadway," indicating that for the first time in modern history, there were more professional actors working in regional theatres than on Broadway or in touring Broadway productions.[3] Since that time, playwrights have found that although there are much smaller financial rewards in not-for-profit theatres, subscription bases and foundation support offer them greater opportunity for experimentation. Many not-for-profit theatres have become something akin to play laboratories. Funding to enable research and development now comes from a host of different foundations such as the Fund for New American Plays at the John F. Kennedy Center (Washington, DC) and the W. Alton Jones Foundation as well as from corporate sponsors such as: American Telegraph and Telephone and American Express.[4]

In 1985, Broadway's old line producers and theatre owners gave belated recognition to the fact that Broadway theatre was truly a national

121

business. Their trade organization, for years known as the League of Broadway Producers, became the American League of Theatres and Producers.[5] The constitutents of this organization include presenters and theatres as well as producers from all over the United States and Canada. Shows presented on the road, outside New York, as "for profit" ventures, in 1992 grossed $500,000,000, an all-time high. Shows produced on Broadway grossed over $290,000,000, also an all-time high. What this means is that professional theatre, once confined to the ten-block radius around Times Square, now happens all over the American continent. Since most of the touring shows presented outside of New York originate in New York, the City has retained its place as the theatrical production capital of America. In fact, for all of the doom and gloom, Broadway is in no danger of losing this distinction.

In recent years, the differences between for profit and not-for-profit have become less and less meaningful. For profits pay taxes on earnings while not-for-profits do not. Perhaps Gerald Schoenfeld, Chairman of the Shubert Organizaton, is right: theatres should be relabeled as the taxed and the non-taxed.[6] Not only are the incomes of the for profits taxed but so is the real estate. A healthy rivalry between the "fors" and the "not-fors" exists for new scripts. But today, the nature of the business requires interdependence. There are too many issues of national concern that require both arms of the business to work together. President Clinton's proposal to cut the deduction for business entertainment from 80 to 50 percent not only affects Broadway but Off Broadway, Off Off Broadway, and all not-for-profit theatres throughout the nation. If the tax code is changed, it is estimated that *all* theatres will loose 10 percent of their patrons. This could well spell the difference to certain marginal operations. Senator Strom Thurman's attempt to eliminate the funds for the National Endowment of the Arts and the growing influence of reactionary forces during the Reagan and Bush administrations also affected all theatres. The thunder on the "right" was a wake-up call to theatres who discovered that although the US Constitution grants First Amendment rights (freedom of speech), it does not protect them. And then there has been the continuing health-care crisis due to AIDS and the loss or denial of health insurance for many theatre workers. Because of the temporary nature of theatrical employment, this crisis, more than any other, has tended to unite rather than divide the industry.[7] Fund-raising events such as "Broadway Cares/Equity Fights AIDS" make no distinction between for profit and not-for-profit. In fact, with each day that passes these distinctions seem more and more artificial and ridiculous. At one time or another, the same individuals who work on Broadway work Off Broadway or in the regions. Whether they are in one venue or another, their artistic ability does not go through a miraculous change. What does change is their paycheck.

The reason that fewer dramatic plays are now mounted on Broadway (75 percent of the activity is musical[8]) than in the not-for-profit theatres is that many of the not-for-profit theatres are year-round operations. They have permanent staffs that can supply many of the services that are needed by developmental projects. Moreover, for the most part, these theatres do not have to pay separately for rehearsal space, offices, etc. All of these items (and many more) are part of an annual budget, the cost of which can be spread across several shows. In the 1920s, Broadway productions cost in the $20,000 range. Today, the same kind of a production would cost well over $1,000,000. Contrary to popular opinion, organized labor is not the issue. Some of the major cost factors on Broadway are non-theatrical. Items such as publicity, advertising,[9] insurance, and legal work are all extremely expensive but necessary budget items. Add to these costs real-estate taxes and the cost of maintaining a stock of theatres most of which were built prior to 1928 and one begins to understand the complexity of the business. Changes in public laws requiring access for the handicapped (Americans with Disabilities Act), for instance, require special capital expenditures as well as a reduction in seating capacity. So, even though dollar grosses on Broadway continue to grow, these figures do not necessarily reflect increased income. There are simply more horses at the trough. The key figure of attendance remains relatively constant. If one takes into account inflation and the high cost of production, capital outlays, and expenses, there is little enough left over to divide with investors, and even less to invest in play development.

At least part of the increased costs of production is due to the "more and better" syndrome. Thirty years ago, three hundred lighting instruments were sufficient to light a Broadway musical. Today the number is near a thousand. What can be said of lighting goes for all aspects of the physical production, the largest single expense in a Broadway production.[10] Today's audiences simply demand "bigger and better" productions. They have become accustomed to seeing film and television where the illusion is total and complete. And so they expect to see a comparable level of "showmanship" on Broadway. They are led to expect "miracles" because of ticket prices which at $50 a seat give even the most devoted theatre-goer second thoughts. Still, theatre ticket prices have not inflated as much as tickets to other attractions, particularly sporting events. Unfortunately, for the theatre there are no large television contracts for broadcasting rights nor are there the same kinds of corporate sponsorship arrangements available as there are for professional sports. There is no Nike Sportswear factor. Broadway's flirtations with television, cable television, and now pay-per-view have to date never gotten beyond the kiss-and-tell stage. One thing is for certain; gone are the days when Miguel de Cervantes could claim that all that one needed for live theatre was "four boards and a passion." Today, the passion must be designed by Robin Wagner, costumed by Pat Ziprodt, lit by Jules Fisher, and insured by Lloyds.

Yet Broadway persists. In fact, contrary to myth, there are actually more theatres in operation today than there were thirty years ago, albeit for a shorter season. Several older theatres have returned to legitimate production after the broadcast industry moved production out to the west coast. There are also several new theatres in the district: the Gershwin, the Minskoff, and the Marquis. Unfortunately, there is no production jam as there was in 1980 when productions were forced to play longer runs in theatres outside of New York with the hope that a Broadway show might close. But then again there have been some changes in the income tax codes which make it more difficult (but not impossible) for non-professionals to invest in Broadway shows. If the Clinton administration wishes to spur employment growth and help the arts while investing in the renewal of the inner cities, they should restore investment tax credits in the entertainment industry. Income from increased production activity in this area will more than offset any losses in collected revenues from investors. Since one out of every two theatre-goers is a tourist, the 24.5 percent hotel tax alone might well make up the difference. In fact, what marketing studies have shown is that the theatre business in midtown Manhattan not only provides jobs in the theatre but in a wide range of service industries. As New York City's number one tourist attraction, it is estimated that the theatre contributes at least three billion dollars annually to the economy. In New York, Broadway is still big business.

In the six decades we have surveyed, Broadway's ticket for success has been challenging the many, not pleasing the few. Sometimes the plays that have won large audiences have been damned by the critics, while the critical darlings have been greeted by thunderous silence. As important as the *New York Times* critic is for Broadway, shows such as *Pippin* and *Evita* run without ever receiving full critical endorsement.[11] Moreover, critical attitudes seem to change after the public votes their support at the box office. Suddenly, the critic who damned the show finds something that merits a follow-up story. A reversal, if not a retraction, is printed. Today, print ads and print criticism no longer have the same kind of credibility or pulling power. In the last twenty years, the number of daily newspapers in New York has sharply decreased. The intense competition among the print media that used to help to create stories and readership has all but vanished. Newspapers have been replaced by television and television commercials. Viewers have shorter attention spans than readers, a factor that has had a very definite impact on Broadway. Unfortunately, the high cost of doing business over the airwaves also has an impact on the theatre. Big shows, and even small shows, have found that the television commercial has become crucial for their survival on the

Great White Way. To support these high ticket items, Broadway is constantly on the lookout for its own outside sponsors; major corporations either foreign or domestic, who want their name associated with a Broadway hit.[12]

Broadway's concern with market share means that the role of the Broadway producer has changed. No longer is the producer's time and energy focused primarily on the development of product. He is no longer the source of the idea who hires the creative team. Like all marketeers, his emphasis is on the market. He deals with investors who can commit hundreds of thousands of dollars, not two or five or even ten thousand dollars. Although the Office of the Attorney General of New York State stipulates that offerings that go to over thirty investors must go through an elaborate filing procedure, many of the biggest and most expensive shows have fewer than ten investors. A few phone calls are made to the top executives of major media and film firms. If the big money does not come quickly into place, it is extremely unlikely that the project can be mounted on Broadway. The time and effort necessary to assemble a comparable army of small investors is a task for Hercules. Producers like Jed Harris who have the time and the ability to go in and reshape the product are the subject of myth. Not that Broadway is free from megalomaniacs. Far from it. There are probably more per square foot than anywhere else in America. But they probably have little of Jed Harris' theatrical knowhow and talent. With Jed Harris, there was little doubt that he was the primary creator who offered the opportunity of employment to others. There was never any question that he was ready and able to step into the production. He maintained direct control. He was at one and the same time, writer, director, designer, acting coach, general manager, and actor (the last for the world at large). Jed Harris was not a specialist, except in putting on a show. He was followed by the likes of Kermit Bloomgarden, Herman Shumlin, Richard Barr, Morton Gottlieb, Roger L. Stevens, David Merrick, Hal Prince, and, most recently, Joseph Papp. All of these individuals were committed to the plays they produced because in one way or another they felt that the play reflected them. Perhaps it is best to call them "creative producers." In the case of Joseph Papp,[13] he built his own not-for-profit institutional theatre Off Broadway and used it as a staging area for his Broadway-bound projects such as *Hair*, *A Chorus Line*, and *That Championship Season*. The Broadway hits not only helped to underwrite the work in his not-for-profit theatres, but also lured mainstream audiences and potential investors into underwriting the experimental work he also produced. Joseph Papp made it appealing for investors to become donors. When Papp found a commercially viable project, he knew he could call upon the same individuals to invest in the Broadway production. The donors/investors knew that they would not only make money for themselves but they would also be making money for their favorite charity. Financing from the Shuberts was usually available for the asking. With *A Chorus Line*, the returns were handsome and the entire theatre community benefited to the tune of well over half a billion dollars.[14] With Joseph Papp, there were no committee decisions. He personally stood behind the work he did, a fact he let the critics and the public know through poster and pronouncement. However, his goal was not personal enrichment. What he sought was to impose his taste and politics on New York audiences. The institutional theatre that now carries his name has six stages and a summer-long free Shakespeare Festival in New York's Central Park.

It is too early to speculate on who will replace Joseph Papp on the New York theatre scene. There are several candidates. His hand-picked successor JoAnne Akalaitis at the Festival established her reputation as an avant-garde director. Her short tenure at the helm indicated that her artistic sensibilities were incompatible with the terrors of big-time producing. Lynne Meadow at the Manhattan Theatre Club and André Bishop at Lincoln Center have both had their share of successful Broadway transfers, yet have shunned the role of Broadway showman in favor of maintaining tighter control over their individual institutional theatres. Neither one of these individuals seems to crave the mantle of Joseph Papp. Outside of New York, there are artistic directors of major theatre companies who have the vision and the talent. There is Zelda Fischandler (Arena Stage, in Washington, DC) of the Acting Company; Mark Lamos at the Hartford Stage Company; Robert Brustein at the American Repertory Theatre in Cambridge, Massachusetts; Michael Maggio at the Goodman Theatre in Chicago; Garland Wright at the Tyrone Guthrie Theatre in Minneapolis; Lloyd Richards at the National Playwrights Conference, and Gordon Davidson at the Mark Taper Forum in Los Angeles. So far, Lloyd Richards and Gordon Davidson have come the closest to succeeding Joseph Papp in supplying plays for Broadway.

Lloyd Richards began his career as an actor but made his reputation as a director before securing positions as Dean of the Yale Drama School, the Artistic Director of the Yale Repertory Theatre (New Haven, Connecticut), and Director of Eugene O'Neill National Playwrights Conference (Waterford, Connecticut). Richards has been devoted to the emergence of African American mainstream writers ever since he directed Lorraine Hansberry's *A Raisin in the Sun*. His manner is totally different from that of Joseph Papp, who had little trouble in gaining acceptance among the predominantly Jewish power structure of Broadway. Papp, although he sometimes claimed to be the new Messiah, had plenty of merchandizing skill. He was truly a supersalesman. He never appeared squeamish when he was asked to switch hats and to literally become a song-and-dance man. Richards' demeanor is closer to that of a Baptist minister. His fanaticism seems more tightly controlled and rooted in a sense of his mission as an African American cultural leader. Recently, his focus has been restricted to the development of plays by August Wilson. The Pultizer Prize-winning *Fences* is a clear example of how Richards approaches the developmental process.

Fences was first produced as a work-in-progress at the O'Neill Center. It was an extremely long work at that time. Richards allowed the playwright to explore his subject matter, a generational dispute within a working-class African American family on the eve of the Vietnam War. A heavily revised play was then mounted at the Yale Repertory Company, the Goodman Theatre, and the Seattle Repertory Company before it finally emerged on Broadway. The Seattle production was independent and utilized that theatre's talent pool. The Chicago production was the first one held in a city where there was a sizable racially mixed audience. Each venue resulted in play modifications that codified and strengthened the play's dramatic center, the larger-than-life role of Troy Maxson (James Earl Jones). Even the name suggests the character's overwhelming impact on his son. *Fences* ran on Broadway for a total of 526 performances.[15] The Richards–Wilson team has been responsible for several Broadway productions since *Fences* (1986), including *The Piano Lesson* (1990), *Joe Turner's Come and Gone* (1988), and *Two Trains Running* (1992). Each play has journeyed to Broadway, following a process of refinement in not-for-profit institutional theatres. As was the case with the writers of an earlier era, August Wilson has a fairly good idea of his actors. Actors such as James Earl Jones, Roscoe Lee Brown, and Mary Alice have become models for his imaginative constructs. The plays themselves are intricate exercises in realism, but not of the kitchen sink variety. August Wilson's work utilizes transcendant symbols as emblems. Although the objects are everyday parts of the realistic environment, fences or pianos, they also have an abstract quality. August Wilson takes up where Ibsen left off in such plays as *Rosmersholm* or *John Gabriel Borkman*. Therefore, although the stage performances are rooted in closely observed behavioral choices, the environment that the characters inhabit is created through the character's imagination. In the Pultizer Prize-winning *The Piano Lesson*, the audience didn't need to believe in spiritual possession to understand that a brother and sister can be haunted by a spirit that appears to emanate from the ancestral piano. Although some may complain that too much depends on a literal evocation of the supernatural, August Wilson relies on his actors to keep the growing symbolism in check. Young and racially mixed audiences flock to see the latest August Wilson play, not only to revel in his continuing cycle of people's history plays, but to hear language which captures the essential truth of their own daily existence. August Wilson's language is beautifully crafted. There are many memorable evocative images. He is to the African American experience what Clifford Odets was to Jewish American generations earlier. The audience registers their recognition with bursts of knowing laughter.

On the west coast, Gordon Davidson has distinguished himself with numerous landmark productions. For twenty-five years he has been the motivating force behind Los Angeles theatre. The Mark Taper Forum, an open thrust stage built at the height of Tyrone Guthrie's influence, is his theatre. Davidson, originally from New York, comes from the same Jewish liberal tradition that now dominates the Broadway theatre. His father Jo Davidson was an actor and teacher who taught generations of students about the Group Theatre and the emergence of the American version of Stanislavski's method. Gordon Davidson's interests have continued that sense of passionate liberal intellectualism that marked the work of that earlier era. As the director of a not-for-profit institutional theatre, he has sought to expand the audience base of his theatre. *Children of a Lesser God* (1980) by Mark Medoff was a Davidson production that brought deaf audiences not only to his theatre but also to Broadway where it ran for 887 performances. With regard to multiculturalism, Davidson has sought to anchor his theatre in Los Angeles' own ethnically diverse community. He has been an early champion of Chicano theatre, particularly Luis Valdez's El Teatro Campasino. The Center Theatre Group of Los Angeles' production of *Zoot Suit*, a play which challenged Anglo audience's ideas about Hispanic and Latino stereotypes, journeyed to Broadway. With the assistance of the Shubert Organization, *Zoot Suit*[16] attempted to draw New York Hispanic audiences. What neither Davidson nor the Shuberts counted upon was the strong nationalist division among Hispanics. The kind of English laced with Mexican slang spoken by the zoot suiters was unintelligible to Puerto Rican New Yorkers. The result was that a production that was supposed to bring a new audience to Broadway put off as many as it turned on. Even the incredible larger-than-life portrayal by the then unknown actor Ed Olmos went for nought in the confusion. This brave effort lasted only forty-one performances.

Davidson, like Papp and Richards, has created his own play development workshop, the Taper Too. His interest in social problems has led him to take on large controversial works, two of which were destined to make it to Broadway. *The Kentucky Cycle* by Robert Schenkkan has already won a Pulitzer Prize without being produced in New York City, one of the orginal requirements established by Pulitzer for the award. *The Kentucky Cycle* was developed over several summers at the Taper Too and the Sundance Playwrights Institute. The cost of the project was underwritten by grants from the Fund for New American Plays, the American Express Company, the Arthur Foundation, and the Vogelstein Foundation. Schenkkan's cycle of plays probes the relationship between the people and the land in the coal-mining area of eastern Kentucky.

The full cycle is a two-evening-long plea for a conservation of human and natural resouces. It challenges the American myth of a boundless, renewable frontier. By exploring three interlocking families – the Rowans, the Talberts, and the Biggs – Schenkkan traced the history of the Cumberland region back two hundred years to the appearance of the first white man on the land. From the very beginning the land itself functions in the role of an independent character. The scenes are short and the dialogue terse and jaunty. As with August Wilson's cycle plays, this is people's history. But Schenkkan's technique is less realistic and more agitprop. Under Warner Shook's direction in Los Angeles the actors' arms were outstretched in evocation of Odets' earlier *Waiting for Lefty*. Because the ensemble members play several different roles, none of the characters emerged as distinct individuals. Rather they communicated in a kind of Greek chorus the anguish, outrage, and pain of life in the Cumberland. Whether this kind of "docu-drama" has enough audience appeal to make a Broadway run remains to be seen. Having started at the small Intiman Theatre in Seattle and then moved to the Taper in Los Angeles, The Kentucky Cycle is now scheduled to make the next leg of its journey to the Kennedy Center.

If *The Kentucky Cycle* does go to Broadway, it will be running against another Davidson production, Tony Kushner's *Angels in America*. As was the case with *The Kentucky Cycle*, Davidson's involvement came about at the workshop level. Oskar Eustis, who later co-directed the mainstage production at the Taper with Tony Taccone, mounted the work in 1990. The world première of the first part, *Millennium Approaches*,[17] took place the following May at the small Eureka Theatre Company in San Francisco with funding from the Kennedy Center's Fund for New American Plays. The Eureka Theatre had initially commissioned Kushner to write a much smaller work. Declan Donellan then brought the first part of *Angels in America* to the Royal National Theatre in London where it ran for a season and captured the *Evening Standard* award for best new play. At that point, there were many interested in the project but only Davidson was in the right position to latch on to the work through Taper director Eustis. Kushner's subtitle "A gay fantasia on national themes" is certainly at one with Clurman's statement that "a true theatre creates from its Idea . . . born of an impulse in the society in which the theatre's artists live and is directed towards that society."[18] Although the play is a look backwards at the history of the 1980s and Reaganism, it transforms that history through fantasy into myth. If *The Kentucky Cycle* seems to be a TV mini-series, Kushner's work is truly operatic in its baroque embellishments. Kushner's attitudes about political theatre come from Bertolt Brecht and such English writers as David Hare, Caryl Churchill, and David Edgar. *Angels in America*, an AIDS play like William M. Hoffman's *As Is* and Larry Kramer's *The Normal*

Heart, is much bigger than its progenitors. It is neither rant nor melodrama. It is the work of an impassioned intellect familiar with the political issues that lurked underneath the Reagan and Bush administrations' willful ignorance about the plight of those infected with the AIDS virus. The theatrical heart of the drama is not the suffering of a sympathetic victim, but the iron-clad denials of one of modern history's most incredible villains Roy Cohn. Kushner has captured the essence of this destructive genius. Ron Leibman chews yards and yards of canvas in what for him may well be the role of a lifetime. Using a technique that is anything but Brechtian, this actor presents theatre-goers with a character that comes close to their vision of the anti-Christ. Roy Cohn, an advisor to Presidents, counsel for Senator Joseph McCarthy, and infamous Red-baiter, is a character filled with self-loathing, contradiction, and denial. At one point, he sneers at a doctor that he cannot be a homosexual because, "Homosexuals are men who in fifteen years of trying cannot get a pissant anti-discrimination bill through City Council. . . . Homosexuals are men who know nobody and who nobody knows, men who have zero clout. Does this sound like me, Henry?"[19]

The fact that old Broadway still exists can be seen in the bidding war *Angels in America* touched off between Bernard Jacobs, President of the Shubert Organization, Broadway's Goliath, and Rocco Landesman,[20] the head of Jujamcyn Theatre, the street's David. The Shuberts who often view Broadway as if it were their fiefdom, were angered when their offer of the Booth Theatre in the heart of the theatre district (the theatre which Kaufman and Hart had sought for *You Can't Take It With You*) was turned down in favor of Jujamcyn's Walter Kerr Theatre located on the district's fringe.[21] Evidently, the decision came down to a one on one between the grandfatherly Jacobs and the outspoken 36-year-old Kushner. As the contents of the final deal emerged, it was clear that what Kushner wanted was not simply Broadway's best theatre or its oldest and best established theatrical firm. Jujamcyn put together a package that was novel, perhaps revolutionary. To secure *Angels*, they promised to honor the heavily discounted subscription list of the New York Shakespeare Festival which had originally been the next slated venue for the two-play event. They also agreed to donate one dollar from every purchased ticket to a group of AIDS organizations. But this was not enough for Kushner, who sensed that he was in the driver's seat, and so he pushed for and received assurances that a certain number of day-of-performance tickets would be sold only at the box office. These tickets would be sold at a price that was two-thirds off. Wednesday matinée tickets would be selling for $7.50, a price that was last seen on Broadway several years prior to Kushner's birth. For Rocco Landesman, who trained at Yale and in America's regional theatre, presenting *Angels in America* was a bid for the allegiance of the disenfranchised homosexual.

Even though it would cost $2,000,000 to mount just the first play, *Millennium Approaches*, he calculated that the play and the notoriety of producing it was worth the effort. In his discussion with the press, he was willing to call his investors "donors." *Angels* would take a minimum of thirty-six weeks to recoup with royalty participants holding off until the investors recouped. "We're absolutely committed to making this play available not simply to the Broadway audience, which will seek it out, but to the audiences that might not initially think of coming to Broadway," stated Landesman,

> We'll be marketing the play with the Shakespeare Festival, and with close links to the downtown arts world and the Gay and Lesbian community through various organizations . . . it's a chance to widen the horizons of what Broadway can do, both artistically and in terms of reaching an audience that we must get to come back to the theatre.[22]

To assure that the *Angels* production was everything it could be, George C. Wolfe was brought in to direct. Wolfe, who had scripted and directed the musical *Jelly's Last Jam* for Jujamcyn, was on his way to becoming one of America's most sought-after young directors and now the new Artistic Director of Joseph Papp's New York Shakespeare Festival. It is off to a good start, having won a Pulitzer and a number of Tony awards.

As Landesman's announcement indicates, Jujamcyn wished to make a political statement as well as to produce an evening of theatre. Demographically, Landesmen had his eyes on an urban American market that had the largest amount of disposable income at its fingertips, the homosexual community. It was also a community that has suffered discrimination, a community that was finding it almost impossible to purchase health insurance. In New York more than any other American city, AIDS has become a scourge. This audience needs a play that unabashedly links the disease with public policy choices. AIDS is to New York's theatre community what the plague was to Oedipus' Thebes. The hope is that *Angels in America* can produce an equivalent catharsis.

During the 1980s, Broadway has also become home to women's plays. Beth Henley, Marsha Norman, and Wendy Wasserstein are playwrights who are now familiar and recognizable names to Broadway theatre-goers. Again, these writers have come to Broadway from the not-for-profit institutional theatres. However, in each case the size and scope of the work warranted a larger market. Wendy Wasserstein, author of the Pulitzer Prize-winning *The Heidi Chronicles* (1989)[23] seems destined to repeat her first Broadway success with *Sisters Rosensweig*.[24] Over the years, she has established a close working relationship with André Bishop, who headed the New York-based workshop Playwrights Horizon. Now that Bishop has moved to Lincoln Center, a cultural center that houses not only two dramatic theatres but the New York Philharmonic, the Metropolitan Opera, and the New York City Ballet, Wasserstein's iconoclastic humor is receiving a much wider exposure. The forty-five thousand subscribers to Lincoln Center Theatre are the same kind of audiences who used to come to the Theatre Guild. This kind of audience appreciates the economy and the certainty that can only be secured by buying a series. With resident writers such as Wasserstein, Bishop can delight his subscribers while speculating on future transfer possibilities. Bishop can rest assured that there are many who subscribe to his theatre simply to keep up with their favorite author. The secret to Wasserstein's success is not her ardent feminism. What Wasserstein counts on is the college-educated woman who is now at mid-life and undergoing the same kinds of dislocation and uneasiness as Wasserstein's semi-autobiographical heroines. *Sisters Rosensweig* is a portrait of three successful sisters in crisis. That Wasserstein is able to cull humor from what might in many angrier and less talented writers turn into overwritten melodrama is what makes her Broadway material. And it doesn't hurt that professional women with disposable income make up a large proportion of New York's population.

What gives Broadway a bright future is not its current financials but its vast number of gifted playwrights. Arthur Miller, Edward Albee, David Mamet, and Neil Simon are firmly entrenched as writers of distinction. They will tread the boards again. They will be joined by fellow veterans: Arthur Kopit, Herb Gardner, David Henry Hwang, John Guare, Lanford Wilson, Terence McNally, Marsha Norman, Steve Tesich, Beth Henley, August Wilson, Tina Howe, Harvey Fierstein, Richard Greenberg, Charles Fuller, David Rabe, Ken Ludwig, Thomas Babe, Jules Feiffer, and a host of others. And there are several significant new writers waiting in the wings destined for greater theatrical recognition. Roger Hedden, Robert Harling, Jerry Sterner, Janusz Glowacki, Jon Robin Baitz, Mark O'Donnell, Robert Patrick Shanley, Leslie Lee, and Alfred Uhry, to mention just a few who come readily to mind. There are veteran directors of the calibre of Mike Nichols, Daniel Sullivan, Gregory Mosher, Marshall W. Mason, Jose Quintero, John Tillinger, and Jerry Zaks, together with the hundreds of directors regularly working in institutional theatres. In short, there is no talent shortage.

For its part, Broadway seems ready to greet a change in its economic fortunes. Under the leadership of civic-minded professionals, Broadway has made a tremendous effort to rebuild her crumbling infrastructure. The already successful Manhattan Plaza development, which provides middle-income housing near Times Square for theatre artists, has long waiting lists for flats. Times Square itself now has its own Task Force, the Mayor's Midtown Citizens Committee. And there is the Office of Midtown Enforcement (OME) cracking down on street crime; forty privately paid uniformed officers are on hand working alongside the City

Police.[25] OME states that street crime in the area has declined consistently over the last three years. The once ubiquitous massage parlors have been closing shop. The Times Square Business Improvement District has improved sanitation by 100 percent. The Catholic Church, the City's largest religious denomination, has turned the Markwell Hotel into a home for seniors. The new center has an appropriately theatrical name, Encore 49.[26] And soon construction will begin on a new Times Square subway (underground) station.[27]

Even Forty-second Street, once a legendary theatreland and now virtually abandoned, is slated for a whole host of renewal projects. Nine of its theatres are to be rescued from oblivion, including the fabled New Amsterdam where Flo Ziegfeld once reigned supreme. The New Forty-second Street, Inc. under Cora Cahan has been established as a part of two and half billion dollar redevelopment project. The project is the largest ever undertaken by New York's public sector. Cahan has been mandated to bring six of the legendary theatres back to life: the Apollo, the Liberty, the Lyric, the Selwyn, the Times Square, and the Victory.[28] So far, two not-for-profit groups have met the strict guidelines, and it may not be long before the district will have a permanent children's theatre and a dance company to service its diverse ethnic community.

On the east side of the Square, there are now two institutional theatres devoted to the revivals of dramatic plays. The Roundabout Theatre is in the new Criterion Center. For years, the Roundabout was located downtown and specialized in mounting plays that had once graced the West End. More recently, it has taken to dusting off American classics such as O'Neill's *Anna Christie*. The other new resident is the National Actors Theater, the brainchild of actor Tony Randall. It now occupies the Lyceum Theatre,[29] a theatre that in days of yore was the esteemed home of Daniel Frohman. During its first seasons, it sold 88 percent of its subscriptions, indicating that there is an audience for plays by Chekhov, Ibsen, and Shaw on Broadway. The problem so far has been living up to the promise of the theatre's name. Whether it will develop sufficient momentum to outlast the critics is open to question. What Randall's theatre has going for it is the indirect subsidy of the German music company whose name graces the Bertelsman Building next door.[30] Through various zoning ordinances, New York City has made it possible for the builders of high-rise office buildings to purchase the air rights over the old theatres. It has also made it attractive for the builders to earmark a certain portion of their building for use as theatrical space. Both the American Place Theatre and the Circle in the Square Theatre in the district have benefited from these arrangements. In exchange for contributing to the maintenance of theatre buildings or for providing space for theatres, the builder is granted a variance allowing him to build higher. As the rebuilding of the Times Square area continues, the theatres are receiving what is in effect an indirect subsidy, not from the government, but from the private sector. Clearly, the future of Broadway depends on these kinds of innovative arrangements.

Even though Broadway theatre is belatedly receiving some much-needed assistance from the City and the State, the federal government has consistently turned a deaf ear on the industry's tax problems. As playwright Robert Anderson (*Tea and Sympathy*) once observed, "The theatre is a place where a playwright can make a killing but not a living."[31] What Anderson meant was that all too frequently playwrights only have one big money-making hit. The Dramatists Guild estimates that 90 percent of its members only have one Broadway production. Fortunately, there are the not-for-profit regional theatres. But even so, there need to be changes in the laws to even out the peaks and valleys of tax liability, not just for playwrights but for producers as well. In reality, ten-year fallow periods are commonplace in the business. The commercial theatre must find a way similar to the not-for-profits to reinvest in play development. A not-for-profit service organization called the Theatre Development Fund already exists. However, its main task is audience development.

For the past twenty-five years, the Theatre Development Fund (TDF) has helped to offset the high cost of Broadway tickets through a series of highly innovative programs. In order to give shows enough of a run to allow "word of mouth" to help build an audience, TDF purchases between four and ten thousand tickets for its eighty-thousand member mailing list. Half of the twenty-eight new productions on Broadway received this kind of assistance. TDF also operates three ticket booths which sell day-of-performance tickets for half price plus an added service charge.[32] In the 1991 season, TDF sales amounted to 22 percent of all admissions and 13 percent of the gross box-office revenues for all attractions, approximately $40,000,000. TDF has also provided some assistance to a new production plan called the Broadway Alliance. The Alliance is attempting not only to deal with the high cost of Broadway tickets but with one of the causes of that problem, the high cost of production. What the Alliance has done is to provide special concessions to productions that are budgeted at under $460,000. Salaries, fees, and royalties have all been reduced by 25 percent, TDF puts up bond for the talent unions, while the theatre owners provide "endangered" theatres, which lie near the fringe of the district, rent-free until the show becomes profitable. Unfortunately, the three shows that have attempted to use the Alliance formula have all lost money.[33] The most successful, *Our Country's Good*, lost $72,000 during its six-week run.[34] To remedy this situation the Alliance will allow producers to raise ticket prices to $30 and increase advertising and publicity expenses after the show opens by 15 percent. So far, producers are not flocking to take advantage of the plan. One reason is that a one-set seven-character show such as Neil Simon's *Lost in Yonkers* or Wendy Wasserstein's *Sister Rosensweig* costs over $1,000,000 to produce. Even with the 25 percent across-the-board reductions, the numbers don't add up. For the Alliance to really be successful, it needs to help set up a rotating fund that will supply some of the high-risk capital for theatrical producers.

Another area where Broadway needs to pool its energies is in getting the most out of industry-wide media coverage. About ten years ago, Broadway experienced a temporary boom in ticket sales due to the "I Love New York" campaign run by the State of New York on television stations all over America. Although the campaign publicized all of the tourist attractions in the State, it gave particular attention to Broadway. All the shows and productions on Broadway benefited from the increased exposure. Presently, Broadway has become the slave of network television's annual "Tony Award Telecast." The fact that this broadcast takes place in the late spring has meant that the entire season suffers. Obviously, the eligibility period for Tony nominations needs to end before early May.[35] Producers and theatre owners are now waiting until March to open plays so that they can garner the attention of network air time. As a result Broadway now has a three-month season which could just as easily be renamed the "Tony Festival." This practise negates the very idea of getting audiences into a theatre-going habit. Easily half of the available stock of theatres are now dark from September until March. If broadcast publicity is so important, then why doesn't Broadway collectively invest in a syndicated television magazine show? David Anthony, who once produced a local cable show entitled *Broadway Magazine*, has demonstrated that this kind of a show can be produced on a shoestring budget. And it may just be the gimmick to get audiences into the theatres, starting in September so that there is income throughout the winter months.

As the Alliance Plan indicates, Broadway is beginning to address the problems of high labor costs in its labor-intensive business. Age-old practices are apt to continue for some time. Bernard Jacobs, the President of the Shubert Organization, succinctly describes the situation, "Things change, but they are never different."[36] The musicians' union and the stage hands' union are more resistant to changes than the Actors Equity Association, but each of the unions has its own special work rules that inhibit rather than spur the growth of the art. Somehow the underlying philosophy of the unions has to change to meet the changed market conditions. Policies that defeat the free flow of productions from not-for-profit theatres and from Off Broadway theatres from easily converting to Broadway production contracts need to be re-examined. Plays and productions are highly perishable commodities. As Clurman stated, they are created out of a time and for a time. What needs to happen in this instance is the private sector's equivalent of government deregulation. The industry needs to gather as a group as it did in 1974 and put everything on the table, keeping only those regulations that are absolutely necessary for survival.[37] Only workable guidelines that truly protect talent should be maintained. A regular union arbitration procedure ought to be established which involves more than one union, since theatre is a collaborative art form. Recently, progress has been made in the production of *Falsettos*; the musicians union allowed producers to employ only four musicians although the theatre minimum recognized by the union work contract required five. This was a negotiated settlement since the producer had only wanted three. No matter, for the size of the compromise, it was a step in the right direction and should be applauded. It wasn't long ago that *A Chorus Line*, which only required sixteen musicians, paid the house minimum of twenty-six. The payment of these "walkers" went on for fourteen years of its run.[38] Perhaps it is the beginning of a more responsible attitude to safeguarding live theatre's continuance. For Broadway, the need for reform is an on-going imperative which both labor and management need to address on a daily basis.

Are new working agreements really possible? At midnight on January 18, 1974, Michael Bennett, an experienced director-choreographer, and eighteen dancers gathered in a studio on East Twenty-third Street in order to explore where they had come from, where they were going, in short – who they were. Out of a series of questions came a series of revelations about growing up in the world of Broadway dance. After hours of exposing and sharing the most intimate details of their lives, a common theme emerged about how dancing had transformed each of them. This was the birth of *A Chorus Line*. Michael Bennett's unique group creative process established a totally new way of working on musicals, patterned after the experimental techniques of Off Off Broadway's Open Theatre. Before *A Chorus Line* opened to the public on April 16, 1975, there had been two workshops, each lasting several weeks, and a regular rehearsal period as well. Under the artistic direction of the late Joseph Papp, the New York Shakespeare Festival committed more than $300,000 to the process while Broadway veterans such as Neil Simon contributed their time to help bring this seemingly spontaneous work to fruition.[39] Most importantly, in response to Bennett's process, Actors Equity Association evolved a new Workshop Agreement awarding individual contributors fractional percentages of the gross box-office receipts in lieu of receiving full salaries during a protracted creative period. In the case of *A Chorus Line*, many of these workshop participants became millionaires as the show made Broadway history, running for 6,104 performances. Today, many Broadway musicals have followed in the footsteps of *A Chorus Line* and workshopping has become so well established that it is taken for granted. Yet it represents the kind of creative inno-

136

vation which Broadway is capable of undertaking. Obviously this is the kind of creative partnership that management and labor need to restore dramatic production to the Great White Way.

Why Broadway? Because America worships fame and success. The fact is that America's live theatre needs an end market, a place where the industry can show its wares in front of large popular audience. In the 1920s, during the height of the Little Theatre Movement, the theatres that were springing up all over the country were thought of as tributary theatres. It was thought that significant plays would flow to Broadway from their stages just as rivers flow into a main stream on their way to the sea. Unfortunately, the Great Depression and the talkies put an end to all that. Today, a workable system of for profit and not-for-profit theatre is coming closer to realizing the dream. Intellectuals may complain that the Broadway theatre is now superfluous. This is certainly a short-sighted point of view. One has only to return to the era of the Little Theatres, when similar statements were made, to discover that out of the hundreds of theatres that depended on charitable donations, only one, the Cleveland Playhouse (1916), survived, while Broadway, for all of its invalid status, lost only half of its stock of theatres and continued to produce. When the times have demanded it, the Broadway stage has helped Americans defend their liberty. It has been comparatively free from government, church, and special interest manipulation. This is not because the high rollers are unimportant, but because the commercial theatre is pragmatic. If there is a buck to be made from producing something that others are too afraid to touch, Broadway will do it. Not for art's sake nor for the sake of liberty, God or country. But *for profit*! Audiences will flock to Broadway to find out what all the commotion is all about, and the long process of popularization and assimilation will have begun: from Broadway to Hollywood, to television, to cartoon, to children's board game, to the doll, etc. The idea will be marketed and merchandised to the hilt. No wonder that artists love and hate Broadway. It makes them well known while at the same time it makes them hand-maidens to the god of Mammon.

Why Broadway? Because there is still a Broadway audience. It is that simple. For critically acclaimed plays, there are more than eight thousand people a week willing to pay $50 a ticket in the City of New York. This is not because Broadway is the only place in New York to see quality theatre. There are 185 non-profit theatre companies there. In 1991, 103 of these companies were responsible for 459 productions, of which 85 percent were new works. In other words, there were 11,000 performances and an audience of more than 2,500,000 for other kinds of theatre.[40] Theatre is a vital part of New York life. New Yorkers love the theatre. And ultimately, it is this audience that makes Broadway great. They seem to have an uncanny ability to spot success and turn the events of an evening into a legend. For all the effort that is spent in denying the appeal of the Broadway audience, it is the sound of their applause that makes playwrights, directors, designers, and actors undergo the tortures of a life in the theatre. It is not simply the salaries, fees, and royalties. The financial rewards are ten times higher in Hollywood. It is something spiritual. There is a kind of warmth and affirmation that comes from playing in one of those old theatres where the lobbies are no bigger than a postage stamp and the dressing rooms are clearly an afterthought. There is an energy that comes from the hustle and bustle of New York itself, a city hungry for theatre. Where the City fathers will raise a statue to those who entertain them or burn the poor soul in effigy should he dare to disappoint. Broadway audiences are not there to perform a social function. It is not like being seen at the Opera or showing up at the Philharmonic. Going to the theatre is not merely chic. It's something akin to a revival meeting, *the* place to go and be counted!

The League of American Theatres and Producers has designated the 1993–1994 season as *Celebrate Broadway: 100 Years in Times Square.* There will be exhibits at the International Center of Photography, the New York Public Library for the Performing Arts, the Empire State Building, the Municipal Art Society, the Guggenheim Museum, and a traveling photo-poster exhibit for schools. The occasion will be marked by a "star-studded" network television spectacular and new outreach programs including discount student tickets for those holding International Student Identity Cards. Amidst all the hoopla and ballyhoo, a "Time Chamber" filled with memorabilia from the 100th Anniversary Season will be placed in an "undisclosed theatre district location" where promoters believe it will remain undisturbed until 2094, the 200th anniversary of Broadway. If Broadway holds true to tradition, one thing is predictable: there is not a chance of that happening!

APPENDIX: CALENDAR OF
PRODUCTIONS

The following calendar has been prepared from the best available sources for the major productions discussed in this volume. The following categories have been used:

Play: author(s) (a =), theatre (t =), date (o =), producer (p =), director (d =), designer (s =), (number of performances). Major prizes. Note: (T) following a name indicates a Tony Award. Original casts are given and major players of revivals.

Beyond The Horizon: a = Eugene O'Neill, t = Morosco Theatre, o = February 3, 1920, p = John D. Williams, d = Richard Bennett, s = Homer S. Saint-Gaudens (production was moved to the Little Theatre (now Helen Hayes)) (111 performances). Pulitzer Prize.

Richard Bennett (Robert Mayo), Robert Kelly (Andrew Mayo), Elsie Rizer (Ruth Akin), Sidney Macy (Capt. Scott), Mary Jeffrey (Kate Mayo), Erville Alderson (James Mayo), Louise Closser Hale (Mrs Akins), Elfin Fin (Mary), George Hadden (Ben), George Riddell (Dr Fawcett).

Broadway: a = Philip Dunning and George Abbott, t = Broadhurst Theatre, o = September 16, 1926, p = Jed Harris, d = George Abbott, s = Arthur P. Segal (603 performances).

Paul Porcasi (Nick Verdes), Lee Tracy (Roy Lane), Clare Woodbury (Lil Rice), Ann Preston (Katie), Joseph Spurin-Calleia (Joe), Mildred Wall (Mazie Smith), Edith Van Cleve (Ruby), Eloise Stream (Pearl), Molly Ricardel (Grace), Constance Brown (Ann), Sylvie Field (Billie Moore), Robert Glecker (Steve Crandall), Henry Sherwood (Dolph), William Foran ("Porky" Thompson), John Wray ("Scar" Edwards), Thomas Jackson (Dan McCorn), Frank Verigun (Benny), Millard Mitchell (Larry), Roy R. Lloyd (Mike).

Off Broadway: t = Lenox Hill Playhouse, o = October 1950, p = Equity Library Theatre

Pre-Broadway: t = Wilbur, Boston, o = April 15, 1978, p = Roger Berlind, d = Robert Allan Ackerman, s = Karen Schulz (24 performances). William Atherton (Roy Lane), Teri Garr (Billie), Chris Sarandon (Steve Crandall), Roy Poole (Dan McCorn).

Revival: t = Royale, o = June 25, 1987, p = Frank Goodman, d = George Abbot, s = John Ezell (transferred from Cleveland, Great Lakes Shakespeare Festival) (4 performances). Lonny Price (Roy Lane), Peggy Taphorn (Billie), Richard Poe (Steve), Joseph Culliton (Dan McCorn).

Strange Interlude: a = Eugene O'Neill, t = John Golden Theatre, o = January 23, 1928, p = Theatre Guild, d = Philip Moeller, s = Jo Mielziner (432 performances). Pulitzer Prize.

Tom Powers (Charles Marsden), Philip Leigh (Professor Leeds), Lynn Fontanne (Nina Leeds), Earle Larimore (Sam Evans), Glenn Anders (Edmund Darrell), Helen Westley (Mrs Amos Evans), Charles Walters (Gordon Evans, as a boy), Ethel Westley (Madeline Arnold), John J. Burns (Gordon Evans, as a man).

Revival: t = Hudson Theatre, o = March 11, 1963, p = Actors Studio, d = Jose Quintero, s = David Hays (95 performances). Geraldine Page (Nina), Franchot Tone (Prof. Leeds), William Prince (Marsden), Pat Hingle (Sam), Jane Fonda (Madeline), Ben Gazzara (Edmund), Richard Thomas (Gordon, as a boy).

Revival: t = Nederlander Theatre, o = February 14, 1985, p = Michael Gesler and associates, d = Keith Hack, s = Voytek with Michael Levine (63 performances). Glenda Jackson (Nina), Edward Petherbridge (Marsden).

Waiting for Lefty: a = Clifford Odets, t =Longacre Theatre, o = March 26, 1935, p = Group Theatre, d = Harold Clurman, s = ? (168 performances).

Russell Collins (Fatt), Lewis Leverett (Joe), Ruth Nelson (Edna), Paula Miller (Florrie), Herbert Ratner (Sid), Robert Lewis (Clayton), Dorothy Patten (Secretary), William Challee (Actor), Walter Coy (Irv), Roman Bohnen (Dr Barnes), Clifford Odets (Dr Benjamin), Elia Kazan (Agate Keller).

Pre-Broadway: t = Civic Repertory Theatre (Fourteenth Street), o = January 6, 1935, d = Clifford Odets, Sanford Meisner (1 performance). Significant cast changes: Morris Carnovsky (Fatt), Art Smith (Joe), Phoebe Brand (Florrie), Jules Garfield (Sid), Luther Adler (Dr Benjamin), J. Edward Bromberg (Agate Keller).

Off Broadway revivals: t = The Masque, o = December 13, 1967. t = Nat Horne Theatre, o = April 13, 1983.

Awake and Sing!: a = Clifford Odets, t = Belasco Theatre, o = February 19, 1935, p = Group Theatre, d = Harold Clurman, s = Boris Aronson, (209 performances).

Art Smith (Myron Berger), Stella Adler (Bessie Berger), Morris Carnovsky (Jacob), Phoebe Brand (Hennie Berger), Jules Garfield (Ralph Berger), Luther Adler (Moe Axelrod), J. Edward Bromberg (Uncle Morty), Sanford Meisner (Sam Feinschreiber), Roan Bohnen (Schlosser).

Revival: t = Windsor Theatre, o = March 7, 1939, p = Group Theatre 45 performances). Cast changes included Alfred Ryder (Ralph), Julia Adler (Bessie), William Challee (Schlosser).

Off Broadway revivals: t = Bijou, o = May 27, 1970, p = Willard W. Goodman, d = Arthur Seidelman, s = Ethel Green (41 performances). Robert Salvio (Ralph), Salem Ludwig (Myron), Phoebe Dorin (Hennie), Morris Strassberg (Jacob), Joan Lorring (Bessie).

Revival: t and p = Roundabout, o = April 19, 1978, d = Stephen Rosenfeld, s = Billy Puzo (45 performances). Hal Lehrman, Jr (Ralph), Joey Faye (Myron), Patricia Mauceri (Hennie), King Donovan (Jacob), Vera Lockwood (Bessie).

Revival: t and p = Circle in the Square (Uptown), o = March 9, 1984, d = Theodore Mann, s = John Conklin (61 performances). Thomas Waites (Ralph), Dick Latessa (Myron), Frances McDorman (Hennie), Paul Sparer (Jacob), Nancy Marchand (Bessie).

You Can't Take It With You: a = George Kaufman and Moss Hart, t = Booth Theatre, o = December, 1936, p = Sam H. Harris, d = George Kaufman, s = Donald Oenslager (837 performances). Pulitzer Prize.

Josephine Hull (Penelope Sycamore), Paula Trueman (Essie), Ruth Attaway (Rheba), Frank Wilcox (Paul Sycamore), Frank Conlan (Mr De Pinna), George Heller (Ed), Oscar Polk (Donald), Henry Travers (Martin Vanderhof), Margot Stevenson (Alice), Hugh Rennie (Henderson), Jess Barker (Tony Kirby), George Tobias (Boris Kolenkhov), Mitzi Hajos (Gay Wellington), William J. Kelly (Mr Kirby), Virginia Hammond (Mrs Kirby), Anna Lubowe (Olga), George Leach, Ralph Holmes, Franklin Heller (Three men).

Revival: t = Lyceum Theatre, o = November 24, 1965, p = APA Repertory, d = Ellis Rabb, s = James Tilton (240 performances). Donald Moffat (Vanderhof), Dee Victory (Penelope), Jennifer Harmon (Essie), Rosemary Harris (Alice), Keene Curtis (Boris), Sydney Walker (Paul).

Revival: t = Plymouth Theatre, o = April 4, 1983, p = Ken Marsolais, d = Ellis Rabb, s = James Tilton (312 performances). Jason Robards,

Jr (Vanderhof), Colleen Dewhurst (Olga), James Coco (Boris), Elizabeth Wilson (Penelope).

Death of a Salesman: a = Arthur Miller (T), t = Morosco Theatre, o = February 10, 1949, p = Kermit Bloomgarden and Walter Fried (T), d = Elia Kazan (T), s = Jo Mielziner (T) (742 performances). Pulitzer Prize.

Lee J. Cobb (Willy Loman), Mildred Dunnock (Linda), J. Arthur Kennedy (T) (Biff), Cameron Mitchell (Happy), Don Keefer (Bernard), Winnifred Cushing (The Woman), Howard Smith (Charley), Thomas Chalmers (Uncle Ben), Alan Hewitt (Howard Wagner), Ann Driscoll (Jenny), Tom Pedi (Stanley), Constance Ford (Miss Forsythe), Hope Cameron (Letta).

Revival Off Broadway: t and p = Circle in the Square (Uptown), o = June 19, 1975, d = George C. Scott, s = Marjorie Kellogg (64 performances). George C. Scott (Willy), Teresa Wright (Linda), Harvey Keitel (Happy), James Farentino (Biff).

Revival (T): t = Broadhurst, o = March 29, 1984, p = Robert Whitehead and Roger L. Stevens, d = Michael Rudman, s = Ben Edwards (146 performances). Closed and reopened September 14, 1984. Dustin Hoffman (Willy), Kate Reid (Linda), John Malkovich (Biff), Stephen Lang (Happy).

Cat on a Hot Tin Roof: a = Tennessee Williams, t = Morosco Theatre, o = March 24, 1955, p = The Playwrights Co., d = Elia Kazan, s = Jo Mielzner (694 performances). Pulitzer Prize.

Maxwell Galnville (Lacey), Musa Williams (Sookey), Barbara Bel Geddes (Margaret), Ben Gazzara (Brick), Madeleine Sherwood (Mae), Pat Hingle (Gooper), Mildred Dunnock (Big Mamma), Pauline Hahn (Dixie), Darryl Richard (Buster), Seth Edwards (Sonny), Janice Dunn (Trixie), Burl Ives (Big Daddy), Fred Stewart (Revd Tooker), R. G. Armstrong (Dr Baugh), Eva Vaughan Smith (Daisy), Brownie McGhee (Brightie), Sonny Terry (Small).

Revival: t = ANTA (Virginia Theatre), o = September 24, 1974, p = American Shakespeare Theatre, d = Michael Kahn, s = John Conklin, (160 performances). Elizabeth Ashley (Margaret), Keir Dullea (Brick), Fred Gwynne (Big Daddy), Kate Reid (Big Mama).

Revival: t = Eugene O'Neill, o = March 21, 1990, p = Barry and Fran Weissler, d = Howard Davis, s = William Dudley (149 performances). Kathleen Turner (Margaret), Charles Durning (Big Daddy), Polly Holliday (Big Mama), Daniel Hugh Kelly (Brick).

Who's Afraid of Virginia Woolf?: a = Edward Albee, t = Billy Rose Theatre (Nederlander), o = October 13, 1962, p = Richard Barr-Clinton Wilder (T), d = Alan Schneider (T), s = William Ritman (660 performances). Tony Best Play.

Uta Hagen (T) (Martha), Arthur Hill (T) (George), George Grizzard (Nick), Melinda Dillon (Honey).

Revival: t = Music Box, o = April 1, 1976, p = Ken Marsolais, d = Edward Albee, s = William Ritman (141 performances). Ben Gazzara (George), Colleen Dewhurst (Martha).

Revival: t = UCLA/Doolittle Theatre in Hollywood, o = October 5, 1989, p = Gordon Davidson, Center Theatre Group, d = Edward Albee, s = D. Martyn Bookwalter. Glenda Jackson (Martha), John Lithgow (George).

Revival: t = Alley Theatre, Houston, o = January 11, 1990, p = Gregory Boyd, Alley Theatre, d = Edward Albee, s = Jay Michael Jagim. Carol Mayo Jenkins (Martha), Bruce Gray (George).

American Buffalo: a = David Mamet, t = Ethel Barrymore, o = February 16, 1977, p = Edgar Lansbury and Joseph Beruh, d = Ulu Brosbard, s = Santo Loquasto (135 performances; concluded run at the Belasco). Critics Award for Best American Play.

Kenneth McMillan (Donny), John Savage (Bobby), Robert Duvall (Teach).

Revival Off Broadway: t = Circle in the Square (Downtown), o = June 3, 1981, p = Elliot Martin in the Long Wharf production, d = Arvin Brown, s = Marjorie Kellogg (259 performances). Al Pacino (Teach), Clifton James (Donny), Thomas Waites (Bobby).

Broadway Revival: t = Booth, o = October 27, 1983, p = Elliot Martin and Arnold Bernhard in the Long Wharf production (102 performances). Al Pacino (Teach), J. J. Johnston (Donny), James Hayden (Bobby). (Bruce MacVittie replaced Hayden October 11, 1983).

Pre-Broadway: t = Ruth Page Auditorium, o = October 23, 1975, p = Stage Two, Goodman Theatre and St Nicholas Theater Company, d = Gregory Mosher, s = Michael Merritt. J. J. Johnston (Donny), W. H. Macy (Bobby), Bernard Erhard (Teach). (Transferred to St Nicholas Theater, December 21, 1975. Cast change: Mike Nussbaum (Teach).)

Showcase Production (Obie Award, Distinguished Play): t = St Clements Theatre, o = January 23, 1976, d = Gregory Mosher, s = Akira Yoshimura. Mike Kellin (Obie Award) (Teach), Michael Egan (Donny), J. T. Walsh (Bobby).

Broadway Bound: a = Neil Simon, t = Broadhurst, o = December 4, 1986, p = Emmanuel Azenberg, d = Gene Saks, s = David Mitchell (756 performances).

Linda Lavin (T) (Kate), John Randolph (T) (Ben), Jonathan Silverman (Eugene), Jason Alexander (Stan), Phyllis Newman (Blanche), Philip Sterling (Jack).

Pre-Broadway: *The Kentucky Cycle*: a = Robert Shenkkan, t = Intiman Theatre, Seattle and Mark Taper, Los Angeles, o = June 1, 1991 (Intiman Theatre, Seattle), p = Intiman and Taper, d = Warner Shook, s = Michael Olich (Mark Taper Forum, Los Angeles: January 18 – March 29, 1992). Pulitzer Prize.

Lillian Garrett-Groag, Martha Hackett, Charles Hallahan, Katherine Hiler, Ronald Hippe, Gregory Itzin, Sheila Renée Johns, Roger Kern, Erik Kilpatrick, Matthew Kimbrough, Ronald William Lawrence, Scott MacDonald, Vince Melocchi, Tuck Milligan, Randy Oglesby, Jeanne Paulsen, Jim Ragland, Novel Sholars, Laurie Souza, Michael Winters.

The Sisters Rosensweig: a = Wendy Wasserstein, t = Ethel Barrymore, o = March 18, 1993, p = André Bishop and Bernard Gersten, Lincoln Center Theater, d = Daniel Sullivan, s = John Lee Beatty. (First produced in Workshop, Seattle Repertory Theatre and then at Lincoln Center.)

Julie Dretzin (Tess), Christine Estabrook (Pfeni Rosensweig), Jane Alexander (Sara Goode), John Vickery (Geoffrey), Robert Klein (Mervyn), Madeline Kahn (T) (Gorgeous Teitelbaum), Patrick Fitzgerald (Tom), Rex Robbins (Nicholas).

Angels in America, Millennium Approaches: a = Tony Kushner, t = Walter Kerr, o = May 4, 1993, p = Jujamcyn Theaters and Mark Taper Forum/Gordon Davidson with Margo Lion, Susan Quint Gallin, Jon B. Platt, The Baruch-Frankel-Viertel Group, and Frederick Zollo in association with Herb Alpert, d = George C. Wolfe (T), s = Robin Wagner. Tony Best Play, Pulitzer Prize.

Ron Leibman (T) (Roy Cohn), David Marshall Grant (Joe Pitt), Marcia Gay Harden (Harper Pitt), Joe Mantello (Louis Ironson), Stephen Spinela (T) (Prior Walter), Kathleen Chalfant (Hannah Pitt), Ellen McLaughlin (The Angel), Jeffrey Wright (Belize).

NOTES

PREFACE

1 Alexis de Tocqueville, *Democracy in America*, vol. II (Alfred A. Knopf, New York, 1953), p. 80.
2 Hallie Flanagan, *Arena, the Story of the Federal Theatre* (Limelight Editions, New York, 1985), p. 221: "Enemies made by the living newspaper were, I believe, powerful enemies, instrumental in the final closing of the project."
3 One could also mention the significant omissions of Maxwell Anderson and Laurence Stallings' *What Price Glory?* (1924) and Lillian Hellman's *Children's Hour* (1934).
4 For instance, with the play *Broadway*, the force was the producer, Jed Harris, while with Arthur Miller's *Death of a Salesman*, the force was the playwright.

1 CURTAINS UP

1 Allen Churchill, *The Theatrical Twenties* (McGraw-Hill, New York, 1975), p. 2.
2 Ibid., p. 5. With no air conditioning and New York's hot, sticky summers, closing down was virtually required. *The Follies* opened in July.
3 Ibid., p. 2. There were fifteen major dailies as opposed to the three today.
4 Ibid., pp. 5–6.
5 Brendan Gill (ed.), *States of Grace, Eight Plays by Philip Barry* (Harcourt Brace Jovanovich, New York, 1975), p. 35.
6 Kenneth MacGowan, *Footlights Across America* (Harcourt Brace Jovanovich, New York, 1929), p. 63. This was approximately three times pre-war costs.
7 Churchill, op. cit., p. 2.
8 Mary C. Henderson, *The City and the Theatre*, (James T. White and Co., Clifton, NJ, 1973), p. 15.
9 Martin Meisel, *Shaw and the Nineteenth Century Theatre* (Limelight Editions, New York, 1984), p. 18. MS letter to Siegried Trebitsch, September 16, 1920, Berg Collection, New York Public Library.
10 Henderson, op. cit., p. 29. From the writings of Grant Thorburn, owner of the feed and grain store next to the John Street theatre.
11 Ibid., p. 50.
12 Cooke was by far the most expensive attraction of the period. He was paid a princely salary of 25 guineas a week for ten months and 25 cents a mile for traveling expenses while in America. T. Allston Brown, *History of the American Stage* (1870, reprinted Burt Franklin, New York, 1969), p. 81.

13 Ibid., pp. 199–200.

14 John Augustus Stone's *Metamora; or, The Last of the Wampanoags* won the first prize. Barrett H. Clark published the play in *Favorite American Plays of the Nineteenth Century* (Princeton University Press, Princeton, 1943). The prologue contains the following couplet, "To-night we test the strength of native powers, Subject and bard, and actor, all are ours," p. x.

15 Garff B. Wilson, *Three Hundred Years of American Drama, from Ye Bare and Ye Cubb to Chorus Line* (2nd edn) (Prentice-Hall, Englewood Cliffs, NJ, 1982), p. 53.

16 Built in 1854. Henderson, op. cit., p. 103.

17 Ibid., p. 121.

18 John Gassner, *Best of the Early American Theatre* (Crown, New York, 1967), p. 186.

19 Adapted from Edouard Brisebarre and Eugene Nu's original. Produced in New York by J. W. Wallack, it ran for forty-two performances.

20 According to Davis, there had been fifty at the start of the 1870s.

21 Marvin Felheim, *The Theatre of Augustin Daly* (Harvard University Press, Cambridge, MA, 1956), p. 8.

22 Ibid., p. 17.

23 Ibid., pp. 14–15.

24 Ibid., p. 23.

25 Mary C. Henderson, *Theater in America, 200 Years of Plays, Players, and Productions* (Harry N. Abrams, New York, 1986), p. 24.

26 Alfred L. Bernheim, *The Business of the Theatre, an Economic History of the American Theatre, 1750–1932* (1932, reprinted Benjamin Blom, New York, 1964), p. 31.

27 Charles Frohman, not to be confused with his brother Daniel (also a producer), was the only individual among this group that regularly engaged in the creative side of the business. His spectacular rise to fame and fortune came with the production of Bronson Howard's romantic Civil War adventure drama *Shenandoah* (1889). He was killed when a German submarine sank the *Lusitania*, an event that helped to pave the way for American involvement in the First World War.

28 Brooks Atkinson, *Broadway* (Macmillan, New York, 1974), p. 14.

29 *Arizona* was a well-constructed melodrama produced by Kirk LaShelle and Fred Hamlin which ran for 140 performances. It had several successful revivals but a musical version, *The Love Call* (1927), failed.

30 E. F. Albee was the grandfather of Edward Albee, the playwright. Keith–Albee controlled the east while the Orpheum Circuit (Morris Meyerfeld, Jr and Martin Beck) controlled the west. According to Bernheim, east and west were joined by interlocking directorates.

31 Jerry Stagg, *The Brothers Shubert* (Random House, New York, 1968), p. 221.

32 *Norma's Affair*, renamed *Coquette* (1927) by George Abbott and Ann Preston Bridgers, is the clearest case in point, since it traveled the furthest distance from a social comedy to a tearful tragedy.

33 George Abbott, *Mister Abbott* (Random House, New York, 1963), p. 117.

34 Sam N. Behrman, *People in a Diary, a Memoir* (Little Brown, Boston, 1972), p. 39.

35 Martin Gottfried, *Jed Harris: the Curse of Genius* (Little Brown, Boston, 1984), pp. 47.

36 Abbott, op. cit., p. 118.

37 Jed Harris, *A Dance on the High Wire* (Crown, New York, 1979), p. 4.

38 Martin Meisel, *Realizations, Narrative, Pictorial, and Theatrical Arts in Nineteenth Century England* (Princeton University Press, Princeton, 1983). General reference to the concepts outlined in this volume.

39 Gottfried, op. cit., pp. 61–2.

40 Churchill, op. cit., p. 196.

41 George Abbott and Philip Dunning, *Broadway, a Play* (G. H. Doran, New York, 1927), pp. vi–vii. Preface is by Woollcott.

42 Cagney was cast as the lead for the London production but lost out at the last minute because his dancing was too good! Gottfried, op. cit., p. 73.

43 *Coquette* (1927) ran for 366 performances and starred Helen Hayes. The play closed after Miss Hayes revealed that due to "an act of God" she was pregnant. *The Royal Family* (1927) by George S. Kaufman and Edna Ferber ran for 343 performances and is loosely based on the Barrymores. Ethel Barrymore was infuriated by the play.

44 By Ben Hecht and Charles MacArthur ran for 276 performances. A vivid picture of the "madhouse on Madison Street" world of Chicago journalism. Frequently revived, the film versions are also well known, the earliest being *His Gal Friday* with Cary Grant and Rosalind Russell.

2 CHANGES IN THE ROAD

1 Jack Poggi, *Theatre in America* (Cornell University Press, New York, 1968), p. 91.

2 Kenneth MacGowan, *Footlights Across America* (Harcourt Brace Jovanovich, New York, 1929), p. 41

3 O'Neill contributed $1,000 in 1931. The money was important, but the fact that he supported this fledgling theatre was crucial in the Group's political dealings with their parent organization, the Theatre Guild. Wendy Smith, *Real Life Drama, the Group Theatre and America, 1931–1940* (Alfred A. Knopf, New York, 1990), p. 58.

4 MacGowan, op. cit., p. 96.

5 Ibid., p. 14, italics mine.

6 Ibid., p. 9.

7 Ibid., p. 12.

8 Ibid., p. 14.

9 This volume contained *Before Breakfast* and *Bound East for Cardiff.*

10 Arthur Gelb and Barbara Gelb, *O'Neill* (Harper and Row, New York, 1962), p. 408.

11 Ibid., p. 413.

12 Ibid., p. 413–14.

13 Allen Churchill, *The Theatrical Twenties* (McGraw-Hill, New York, 1975), p. 17. *Beyond the Horizon* (1920), *Anna Christie* (1923), *Strange Interlude* (1928), *Long Day's Journey Into Night* (1957).

14 In the 1923–4 season, the only new plays offered were by O'Neill. In future seasons other contemporary American playwrights were produced, notably Paul Green's *Abraham's Bosom* (1926). But it became commonplace to find the Provincetown mounting plays by Strindberg, Gozzi, Molière, and even Gilbert and Sullivan.

15 In 1929, Harold A. Ehrensperger, editor of *The Little Theatre Monthly*, drew a map in which he pinpointed 1,050 community and university theatres across the country (MacGowan, op. cit., pp. 10–11). MacGowan more conservatively estimated one hundred organizations offering from four to twenty-five

productions a season with admissions at the one million mark (p. 12). These organizations varied enormously with regard to resources and professionalism.

16 The Guild's Board of Directors were Lawrence Langner, Theresa Helburn, Lee Simonson, Helen Westley, Philip Moeller, and Maurice Wertheim. Langner and Helburn piloted the organization beyond the 1940s and into the 1950s after which time it became inactive as a theatrical producer.

17 Roy S. Waldau, *Vintage Years of the Theatre Guild, 1928–1939* (Case Western Reserve, Cleveland, 1972), p. 380. Although the Guild continued to grow on the road, adding cities and subscribers to a number close to a hundred thousand (1951), the period of its greatest importance as a producing organization were the fifteen years 1923–39.

18 Walter Pritchard Eaton, *The Theatre Guild: the First Ten Years* (Bretano's, New York, 1929), pp. 43–4.

19 The Fulton Theatre (built in 1911 as the Folies-Bergère, later renamed the Helen Hayes), together with the Morosco and Bijou, were demolished to make way for the Portman Hotel in 1982. The result was Save the Theatres, Inc. and the landmarking of thirty-two theatres in the Broadway district.

20 The Garrick Theatre, the Guild's Theatre on loan from philanthropist Otto Kahn, already had a history of Shavian productions. Richard Mansfield performed there in 1897. Later, Mary Shaw and Arnold Daly were arrested by the New York Police for daring to produce Shaw's *Mrs Warren's Profession* (1905). The theatre was located on the north side of Thirty-fifth Street, east of Sixth Avenue. It was built by Ned Harrigan in 1890 and demolished in 1932 after sustaining fire damage (Mary C. Henderson, *The City and the Theatre* (James T. White and Co., Clifton, NJ, 1973), pp. 167–8).

21 Lawrence Langner, *GBS and the Lunatic* (Hutchinson, London, 1964), pp. 20–31, *passim*. Richard Mansfield had already established Shaw as a money-maker with his successful production of *The Devil's Disciple* (1897, fifty-six performances in its first season in repertory).

22 Langner, op. cit., p. 21.

23 Waldau, op. cit., p. 13.

24 Several supporters who were involved with the Washington Square Players, felt the Guild had betrayed its trust and withdrew their support from the new organization.

25 Waldau, op. cit., pp. 18–19.

26 Ibid., p. 22.

27 Lawrence Langner, *The Magic Curtain* (E. P. Dutton and Co., Inc., New York, 1951), p. 212.

28 Eaton, op. cit., p. 93.

29 Langner, *Curtain*, op. cit., p. 217.

30 Waldau, op. cit., p. 28. The Guild was not without competition even in repertory. Eva La Gallienne's Civic Repertory Company produced Ibsen and Chekhov on Fourteenth Street. Unlike the Guild, La Gallienne ran fund-raising drives for as much as $200,000.

31 Waldau, op. cit., p. 33. Langner, a playwright and a patent attorney, was Welsh by birth. Being a foreigner, he was particularly sensitive to criticisms of his choice of repertory. He steadfastly maintained that the "quality" of the scripts he received was the sole issue. He stated, "We stuck to our principle, which was to produce important artistic plays regardless of their national origin." The few American works the Guild did produce were from established writers such as Sidney Howard and Elmer Rice.

32 Sam N. Behrman, *People in a Diary, a Memoir* (Little, Brown, Boston, 1972), p. 56.

33 George Jean Nathan, *Boston Transcript*, October 25, 1929.

34 Waldau, op. cit., p. 34.

35 The Guild was able to weather hard times due to a $750,000 capital accumulation and a redemption of over $200,000 worth of Guild Theatre bonds (Langner, *Curtain*, op. cit., p. 244).

36 Harold Clurman, *New York Times*, May 18, 1941, quoted in W. Smith, *Real Life Drama, the Group Theatre and America, 1931–1940* (Alfred A. Knopf, New York, 1990), p. 411.

37 Harold Clurman, *The Fervent Years* (Harvest, 1975), p. 46.

38 Smith, op. cit., p. 197.

39 Clifford Odets, *Six Plays of Clifford Odets*, (Grove, New York, 1935), p. 5.

40 Elia Kazan, *A Life* (New York, 1989), p. 112.

41 Ibid., p. 113.

42 Ibid., p. 114.

43 Odets, op. cit., p. 27.

44 Clurman, op. cit., p. 148.

45 Odets attended, the first Group summer in 1931.

46 Margaret Brenman-Gibson, *Clifford Odets: American Playwright* (Atheneum, New York, 1982), p. 321.

47 Frank Rich and Lisa Aronson, *The Theatre Art of Boris Aronson* (Alfred A. Knopf, New York, 1987), p. 53.

3 *YOU CAN'T TAKE IT WITH YOU*

1 Kaufman's record would eventually be surpassed by Neil Simon. See Chapter 8.

2 Both were produced by Sam Harris at the Music Box, a theatre designed for small musicals, long under the ownership of the Shuberts and Irving Berlin. *Once in a Lifetime* ran for 406 performances and *Merrily We Role Along* for 155 performances.

3 Scott Meredith, *George S. Kaufman and His Friends* (Doubleday, New York, 1974), p. 542.

4 John Boruff and Walter Hart did adapt the *Washington Jitters* for the stage. The play was produced by the Theatre Guild and Actor's Repertory in 1938. It was a failure (24 performances).

5 Malcolm Goldstein, *George S. Kaufman, His Life and His Theatre* (Oxford University Press, New York, 1979), p. 270.

6 This quote comes from a promotional brochure created by Sam Harris' office in the Billy Rose Theatre Collection, Lincoln Center.

7 The practice of casting ethnics against type has a long tradition in American theatre. In the early 1920s the Theatre Guild produced a translation of David Pinski's (1872–1959) Yiddish play *The Treasure* (1920). Although there were many Jewish actors available, the play was cast with Irish actors. Celia Adler, daughter of Jacob P. Adler (the famous Yiddish actor) and sister to Stella and Luther, was an exception. Obviously, she played the role of Tillie in English.

8 Typescript is located in the Frank Conlan file in the Billy Rose Theatre Collection, Lincoln Center.

9 It opened October 22 and ran for 169 performances. The film (RKO, 1937) has become famous for its incredible cast of feminine talent: Kathryn Hepburn

(the lead Terry Randall, played on stage by Margaret Sullavan), Ginger Rogers, Lucille Ball, and Eve Arden.

10 Quoted in Goldstein, op. cit., p. 271.

11 The material comes from a promotional brochure created by Sam Harris' office in the Billy Rose Theatre Collection, Lincoln Center.

12 Donald Oenslager, *Stage Design: Four Centuries of Scenic Invention* (Viking Press, New York, 1975), p. 251.

13 Geoffrey Arundel Whitworth, *Theatre in Action* (Whitefriars Press, London, 1938), p. 18.

14 Donald Oenslager, *The Theatre of Donald Oenslager* (Wesleyan University Press, Middletown, CT, 1978), p. 72.

15 William Carson, *Dear Josephine, the Theatrical Career of Josephine Hull* (University of Oklahoma Press, Norman, OK, 1963), p. 225.

16 Josephine Hull went on to create the stage and screen roles of Aunt Abby, one of the Brewster sisters, in Joseph Kesselring's *Arsenic and Old Lace* (January 10, 1941, 1,444 performances) as well as the role of Veta Louise in Mary Chase's *Harvey* (November 1, 1944, 1,775 performances).

17 Later the critic worked for the *New York Post*.

18 Built in 1913, this theatre should not be confused with Booth's own theatre on Twenty-third Street (1869) which was converted into a department store by James T. McCreery in 1883. The Booth on Forty-fifth Street has brown and ivory decor with mulberry upholstery, carpets, and curtains; this reflects the aristocratic taste of Winthrope Ames, a turn-of-the-century producer, who together with Lee Shubert built the theatre.

19 George S. Kaufman and Moss Hart, *Six Plays by Kaufman and Hart* (Random House, New York, 1972), p.234.

20 Ibid., p. 256.

21 Ibid., p. 315.

22 Ibid., p. 318.

23 John Peter Toohey, "Almost English and not quite Scotch, Irish by nature – that's Henry Travers," *New York Herald Tribune*, January 24, 1957.

24 He will no doubt be remembered by movie lovers as James Stewart's Angel in Frank Capra's *It's A Wonderful Life* (RKO, 1946).

25 Brooks Atkinson, *Broadway Scrapbook* (Theatre Arts, New York, 1947), p. 64. The article first appeared in the *Sunday New York Times*, December 20, 1936.

26 Interview with Donita Ferguson for the *New York Woman* (December 30, 1936).

27 Ibid.

4 *DEATH OF A SALESMAN*

1 *All My Sons*, produced by Harold Clurman, directed by Elia Kazan, opened at the Coronet Theatre, January 29, 1947, and ran for 328 performances.

2 *A Streetcar Named Desire*, produced by Irene Selznick, directed by Elia Kazan, opened at the Ethel Barrymore Theatre, December 3, 1947, and ran for 855 performances.

3 Harold Clurman, *Lies Like Truth* (Macmillan, New York, 1958), pp. 69–70.

4 Arthur Miller, *Death of a Salesman* (Viking Press, New York, 1949), p. 82.

5 Arthur Miller, *Timebends, a Life* (Harper and Row, New York, 1988), p. 182.

6 Arthur Miller, *The Theatre Essays of Arthur Miller* (Penguin Books, New York, 1978), p. 135.

7 Ibid., p. 136.
8 Arthur Miller, MS notebook: *Death of a Salesman*, Harry Ransom Research Library, University of Texas at Austin, dated 1948, sixty-six pages. The discussion that follows applies to this study for the play.
9 Ibid.
10 Miller, *Salesman*, op. cit., p. 133.
11 Ibid., p. 135.
12 According to Miller, this would have been more than a dozen years earlier.
13 Arthur Miller, *Timebends* op. cit., p. 184.
14 Ibid., p. 131.
15 Elia Kazan, *A Life* (Doubleday, New York, 1989), p. 356.
16 Ibid., p. 355.
17 Ibid., p. 359.
18 Ibid., p. 74.
19 Ibid., p. 360.
20 Miller, *Timebends*, op. cit., p. 186.
21 Kermit Bloomgarden, "The unfinished memoirs of Kermit Bloomgarden," ed. Christine Conrad, *American Theatre*, V, 8 (November 1988), p. 53. Material in this section is also drawn from Lynn Doherty, *The Art of Producing, The Life and Work of Kermit Bloomgarden*, dissertation, City University of New York, 1989.
22 Christopher Bigsby (ed.), *Arthur Miller and Company* (Methuen, London, 1990), p. 56.
23 Arthur Miller, *Death of a Salesman*, 2nd version, Manuscript #37, 122 pages at the Harry Ransom Research Library, University of Texas.
24 Jo Mielziner, *Designing for the Theatre* (Bramhall House, New York, 1965) p. 26.
25 Ibid., p. 26.
26 Miller, *Timebends*, op. cit., p. 186.
27 *Winged Victory* was basically a pageant designed to boost wartime morale. There were no opportunities for memorable performances.
28 Miller, *Timebends*, op. cit., p. 186.
29 William Stott and Jane Stott, *On Broadway* (University of Texas Press, Austin, 1968), p. 134.
30 *Children's Hour*, produced by Herman Shumlin, at Maxine Elliott's Theatre, opened November 20, 1934, and ran for 691 performances.
31 Miller, *Essays*, op. cit., p. 46.
32 Ibid., pp. 46–7.
33 Mielziner, op. cit., p. 43 The conversation took place on December 8, 1948.
34 Ibid., pp. 43–5.
35 Kazan, op. cit., p. 360.
36 Built in 1903 and located on the south side of Forty-second Street between Broadway and Eighth Avenue, it was the premier theatre of Erlanger's Syndicate and also the largest Art Nouveau theatre in the United States. Rehearsals were generally held in the Roof Garden Cabaret. In 1937, the theatre was converted to film. The building was sold to the Nederlander Organization (1982). Peter Brook considered staging *Carmen* there soon after, but was prevented by structural decay. This is one of the nine theatres slated for redevelopment by the Forty-second Street Development Project. At $2.5 billion, it is the largest effort ever undertaken by New York's public sector.
37 Miller, *Timebends*, op. cit., p. 187.
38 Ibid., p. 187.

39 Otis L. Guernsey, Jr (ed.), *Broadway Song and Story, Playwrights Lyricists Composers Discuss Their Hits* (Dodd Mead, New York, 1985), p.21.
40 Robert Garland, *Journal American* (February 11, 1949), "In *Death of a Salesman*, the present and the past of Willy Loman exist concurrently – the 'stream of consciousness' idea – until they collide in climax."
41 Miller, *Salesman*, op. cit., p. 56.
42 Mary McCarthy, *Sights and Spectacles, 1937–1956*, (Farrar Straus and Cudahy, New York, 1956), p. xvi.
43 William Stott and Jane Stott, *On Broadway* (University of Texas Press, Austin, 1968), p. 131.
44 Richard Watts Jr, *Post*, February 11, 1949; Howard Barnes, *Herald Tribune*, February 11, 1949; Hobe, *Variety*, February 14, 1949; Miller, *Salesman*, op. cit., p. 121.
45 Thomas R. Dash, *Women's Wear* (February 11, 1949): "from that point on [Biff's] disillusionment and bitterness are keen and sharp."
46 John Mason Brown, *Dramatis Personae, a Retrospective Show* (Viking Press, New York, 1963), p. 98.

> The quality and intensity of his writing can perhaps best be suggested by letting Mr. Miller speak for himself, or rather by allowing his characters to speak for him, in a single scene, in fact, in the concluding one. It is then that Willy's wife, his two sons, and his old friend . . . supply a scenery of their own.

47 Miller, Mielziner, and Kazan were highly praised in most of the reviews. Eric Bentley's review, reprinted in *In Search of Theatre* (Applause, New York, 1992), is alone in its negative statements about "bad poetry," "directorial legerdemain," and "vague" design.
48 Stott and Stott, op. cit., pp. 132–3.

5 CAT ON A HOT TIN ROOF

1 Tennessee Williams, *Memoirs* (Doubleday, Garden City, 1975), p. 168.
2 Tennessee Williams, *Cat on a Hot Tin Roof* (New Directions, New York, 1955), p. 152.
3 *Baby Doll* (Warner, 1956) directed by Kazan with Karl Malden (Mitch in *Streetcar*), Eli Wallach, Carroll Baker, and Mildred Dunnock. *Time* magazine: "Just possibly the dirtiest American-made motion picture" (quoted in *Halliwell's Film Guide*, 2nd edn (Charles Scribner, New York, 1983), p. 64. Certainly, it is a grotesque picture of the decadent south in all its sordidness.
4 John F. Wharton, *Life Among the Playwrights, Being Mostly the Story of The Playwrights Producing Company, Inc.* (Quadrangle, New York, 1974), pp. 20–35, *passim*.
5 Audrey Wood, *Represented by Audrey Wood* (Doubleday, Garden City, 1981), p. 164.
6 Don Shewey, "Gay theatre grows up," *American Theatre* (May 1988), 13.
7 Tennessee Williams, *Cat on a Hot Tin Roof* (James Laughlin, New York, 1955), pp. 108–9.
8 Ibid., p. 112.
9 Williams, *Memoirs*, op. cit., p. 168.
10 Williams, *Cat*, op. cit., pp. 149–50.
11 Ibid., p. 152.
12 Ibid., pp. 151–2.

13 Ibid., p. 169.
14 Ibid., p. 152.
15 Ibid., p. 169.
16 Ibid., p. 124.
17 Ibid., p. 159.
18 Ibid., pp. 162–3.
19 Ibid., p. 183.
20 Ibid., p. 184.
21 Ibid., p. 188.
22 Elia Kazan, *A Life* (Doubleday, New York, 1989), p. 541.
23 Ibid., p. 542.
24 *East of Eden* (Warner, 1954), directed by Kazan; the cast included Burl Ives with James Dean (his first starring role), Raymond Massey, and Julie Harris.
25 Richard Watts, Jr, writing for the mass circulation evening paper, the *Post*, also chose not to mention the issue of homosexuality. These two critics were responsible in no small measure for giving *Cat* a successful Broadway debute. At the other extreme John Beaufort, writing for the *Christian Science Monitor* (April 2, 1955), dismissed the play. Beaufort alluded to the homosexuality as being "abnormal" and stated that Tennessee Williams was "the poet laureate of degradation, decadence, and despair."
26 John Gassner, *Theatre at the Crossroads* (Holt Rinehart and Winston, New York, 1960), p. 360.
27 Eric Bentley, *What Is Theatre?* (Beacon Press, Boston, 1956), pp. 55–63.
28 Dakin Williams and Shepherd Mead, *Tennessee Williams, an Intimate Biography* (Arbor House, New York, 1983), p. 198.
29 Wood, op. cit., p. 169.
30 Ibid., p. 170.
31 Williams, *Memoirs*, op. cit., p. 169.
32 Ibid., p. 169.

6 *WHO'S AFRAID OF VIRGINIA WOOLF?*

1 Richard Amacher, *Edward Albee* (Twayne, Boston, 1969), p. 168.
2 Richard Barr, "You have to hock your house," unpublished MS, p. 185. The author wishes to thank Edward Albee for loaning him a copy of this manuscript.
3 Ibid., p. 203.
4 Ibid., p. 209.
5 Ibid.
6 Unpublished TS #89, Billy Rose Theatre Collection, New York Public Library at Lincoln Center. The author wishes to thank Edward Albee for his permission to consult these closed archives.
7 "End of Summer," unpublished TS #94, Billy Rose Theatre Collection, New York Public Library at Lincoln Center.
8 Barr, op. cit., p. 236.
9 Whether or not this use of the clock was intended to invite comparisons to Emile Zola cannot be determined.
10 Geraldine Page played Alma Winemiller in the 1952 revival of *Summer and Smoke* at Circle in the Square and the Princes Kosmonopolis in *Sweet Bird of Youth* (1959), a role she repeated in the MGM film (1961) opposite Paul Newman, with *Cat* veterans Mildred Dunnock and Madeleine Sherwood.
11 See Appendix for cast list and details of this revival.

12 The theatre was renamed the Nederlander in late 1980, after the late theatre owner David Tobias Nedelander, whose sons now operate the Nederlander Organization.

13 Fonda was furious that his agent did not show him the script. Eventually, Albee and Fonda discussed working together. Albee wrote the part of Charlie in *Seascape* for Fonda.

14 Uta Hagen did not originate the role of Blanche. She took over from Jessica Tandy in June 1949. Coincidentally, Hagen and Geraldine Page both attended the Goodman School of Theatre in Chicago at the same time.

15 Alan Schneider, *Entrances, an American Director's Journey* (Viking Press, New York, 1986), p. 319.

16 Ibid., p. 317.

17 Ibid., p. 326.

18 Barr, op. cit., p. 250.

19 Ibid., p. 254.

20 *A Delicate Balance* was produced by Barr–Albee–Wilder (Theatre 1967) at the Martin Beck. It opened on September 22 and ran for 132 performances. The cast included Jessica Tandy, Hume Cronyn, Rosemary Murphy, Henderson Forsythe, Carmen Mathews, and Marian Seldes. It was directed by Alan Schneider.

21 *Seascape* was produced by Barr–Charles Woodward–Wilder at the Sam Shubert Theatre. It opened January 26, 1975 and closed after sixty-five performances. The cast included: Deborah Kerr, Barry Nelson, Frank Langella, and Maureen Anderman. It was directed by the author.

22 Barr, op. cit., p. 257.

23 *Hair* moved to Broadway's Biltmore Theatre April 29, 1968, in a version substantially revised by Tom O'Horgan. It was the first rock musical to play Broadway, where it ran for more than seventeen hundred performances. It began its life at Joseph Papp's New York Shakespeare Festival, October 29, 1967, the first of three versions.

24 An example of this approach can be found in Martin Gottfried's *A Theater Divided, the Postwar American Stage* (Little Brown, Boston, 1969), pp. 264–72.

7 AMERICAN BUFFALO

1 David Mamet, *Some Freaks* (Viking Press, New York, 1989), p. 102.

2 Documents relating to the St Nicholas Theater are to be found in Special Collections, Harold Washington Library Center, Chicago, Illinois.

3 Gregory Mosher, program notes, *Goodman Theatre Program* (March 1982).

4 David Mamet, *American Buffalo*, TS, 1975. This copy is held in the St Nicholas Theatre Special Collection, Chicago Public Library.

5 Marion E. Kabaker, *Stagebill* (B.B. Enterprises, Chicago, March 1988), p. 30.

6 Interview with Michael Merritt, June 7, 1992.

7 Gregory Mosher, op. cit.

8 Quoted in Nesta Jones and Steven Dykes, *File on Mamet* (Methuen, London 1991), p. 21.

9 Ibid., p. 23.

10 *Chicago Reader* (October 24, 1975).

11 Jan Hodenfield, "A ping-pong hustler writes a play," *New York Post* (March 8, 1977), p. 38.

12 Warner, Academy Award-winning screenplay by William Inge with Natalie

Wood, Warren Beatty, Pat Hingle, Barbara Loden, Zohra Lampert, and Sandy Denis.

13 *The Subject Was Roses* (MGM and Lansbury) 1968. Jack Albertson won an Academy Award and Patricia Neal received a nomination. Martin Sheen also graced the cast.

14 Mel Gussow, "Ulu Grosbard pays a price for being a perfectionist," *New York Times* (April 13, 1977), C–23.

15 Judith Slawson, *Robert Duvall, Hollywood Maverick* (St Martin's Press, New York, 1985), p. 118.

16 Ted Morgan, "Robert Duvall, America's most famous unknown movie star," *Cosmopolitan* (November 1977), p. 223.

17 Duvall played opposite actress Rose Gregorio, Mrs Grosbard.

18 Hodenfield, op. cit., p. 38.

19 Mamet, TS, op. cit.

20 Mamet, *American Buffalo: A Drama in Two Acts* (Samuel French, New York, 1977), p. 74.

21 Gussow, op cit.

22 Ibid.

23 Ibid.

24 *New York Times* (February 11, 1977), C–2.

25 Clive Barnes now writes for the *New York Post*.

26 Gordon Rogoff, *Saturday Review* (April 12, 1977); John Simon, *New Leader* (March 28, 1977); Brendan Gill *New Yorker* (February 26, 1977); Douglas Watt, *Daily News* (February 17, 1977); Hobe, *Variety* (February 23, 1977); Rosalyn Regelson, *Soho Weekly News* (February 24, 1977); Alan Rich, *New York Magazine* (March 7, 1977); Martin Gottfried, *Post* (February 17, 1977); Howard Kissell, *Women's Wear* (February 17, 1977); Alan Havis, *Our Town* (February 25, 1977).

27 Barnes, op. cit.; Kissell, op. cit.; Feingold, op. cit.

28 *New York Sunday News* (February 27, 1977).

29 Morgan, op cit, p. 220.

30 Interview with Michael Merritt, June 7, 1992. Over the years the initial investors in *American Buffalo* did recoup.

31 *Glengarry Glen Ross* (1984) opened at the Golden, won the Pulitzer Prize and ran for 378 performances. The cast included Robert Prosky, James Tolkan, Joe Manegna, J. T. Walsh, Louis Smith, and Mike Nussbaum. Producer Elliott Martin directly transferred the show from the Goodman Theatre in Chicago.

8 *BROADWAY BOUND*

1 *The Goodbye Girl* (Warner/Ray Stark) directed by Herbert Ross with Richard Dreyfuss, Marsha Mason, Quinn Cummings, Paul Benedic, and Barbara Rhodes. Both *Jake's Women* and this musical lost money on Broadway.

2 Walter Pater, *The Renaissance* (London, 1888), pp. 111–14.

3 Eric Bentley seems to enjoy the self-conscious manipulation of such artificial writers as Shaw and Brecht. These playwrights are constantly visible on stage manipulating characters and plot. They seldom slip to stage realism except when they wish to emotionally move the audience at which times they are always berated for a lack of art.

4 Tadeuz Kantor actually appears on stage with his actors and manipulates their performances in an acknowledged anti-realistic fashion.

5 In *Chapter Two* (1977, 857 performances) with Judd Hirsch and Anita Gillette,

Simon had tried and succeeded in at least part of this play at being emotionally vulnerable. However, this quality in his writing is not sustained throughout the play.

6 *Long Day's Journey Into Night*, produced by Leigh Connell and Theodore Mann was directed by Jose Quintero. It premièred at the Helen Hayes Theatre on November 7, 1956, with Fredric March, Florence Eldridge, Jason Robards, Jr, and Bradford Dillman. It ran for 388 performances and has received several major revivals. Harold Clurman, in *Lies Like Truth* (Macmillan, New York, 1958, p.31), remarked "There is something moving, even great, in the impulse of the play, and no one can witness it without reverence for the selflessness of this extremely personal act." It is this quality of "selflessness" that is so frequently lacking from O'Neill's many imitators.

7 Eugene O'Neill, *Long Day's Journey Into Night* (Yale University Press, New Haven, CT, 1955), p. 7.

8 Ibid., p. 154.

9 Neil Simon, *Biloxi Blues* (Samuel French, New York, 1986), p. 48.

10 Neil Simon, *Broadway Bound* (Samuel French, New York, 1987), p. 89.

11 O'Neill, op. cit., p. 176.

12 Philip Weissman, *Creativity in the Theatre, a Psychoanalytic Study* (Delta, New York, 1965), pp. 113–46, *passim*. There are several interesting similarities including the fact that it took O'Neill fifteen years following his discussions with Barrett Clark (1926) to write his autobiographical drama. Judith Barlow (listed below) explores this process in depth. Although Simon has not divulged when the idea first occurred to him, he has indicated that it took him an unusually long period of six years to write *Broadway Bound*. Clearly, there were prohibitions within the artists working against the desire "to leave the remains of his victims spread out on a typewritten page with their names disguised, but their identities known to the world, exposed for all to see." This quote comes from Simon's introduction to his first volume of collected plays, *The Comedy of Neil Simon* (Avon, New York, 1973). The essay is dated March 1971.

13 Brendan Gill wrote, "For besides his own family memories the other indispensable source of material for a writer is every other writer's family memories; the past is not only what we spring from but who we are."

14 Neil Simon, *Comedy*, p. 3.

15 O'Neill's experiences did not prevent him from repeating the cruelty of his own childhood on his daughter Oona by cutting her off forever when she married a man of whom he did not approve: Charlie Chaplin.

16 Judith E. Barlow, *Final Acts, the Creation of Three Late O'Neill Plays* (University of Georgia Press, Athens, GA, 1985), p. 1.

17 *Lost in Yonkers*, presented by Emanuel Azenberg with Irene Worth, Mercedes Ruehl, Kevin Spacey, Danny Gerard, Jamie Marsh, Lauren Klein and Mark Blum at the Richard Rodgers Theatre (formerly the Forty-sixth Street Theatre) on February 21, 1991. At press time it had played more than 200 performances.

18 Neil Rosen, WNCN Radio, (February 22, 1991).

19 *The Gingerbread Lady*, produced by Saint-Subber at the Plymouth Theatre ran for 193 performances with Maureen Stepleton, Ayn Rumen, Charles Siebert, Alex Colon, Michael Lombard, and Betsy von Furstenberg. The critics did not care for this tale about an alcoholic lady.

9 ANOTHER OPENING

1 Tom Jacobs, "The sum and substance," *Performing Arts*, Greater Los Angeles edition, February 1993, XXVII, 2, p. 20

2 Steven Samuels (ed.), *Theatre Profiles 10, the Illustrated Reference Guide to America's Nonprofit Professional Theatre*, (Theatre Communications Group, New York, 1992). Non-profit industry data comes from this source.

3 *Variety*, March 9, 1966.

4 Interview with Sophy Burnham, Executive Director, Fund for New American Plays, February 13, 1993. Specific theatres have their own funds, such as the Harold and Mimi Steinberg Trust's $1,000,000 grant to the American Repertory Theatre in Cambridge, Massachusetts (*Variety*, January 26, 1993).

5 Interview with George Wachtel, American League of Producers, February 24, 1993. Much of the statistical information in this chapter comes from the League.

6 Interview with Gerald Schoenfeld, Shubert Organization, December 9, 1983.

7 The Impact of AIDS has been felt on Equity's health insurance fund, which is losing $1,000,000 a month. Changes in eligibility guidelines will be made which will leave as many as 4,500 part-time actors without health coverage (*Variety*, February 15, 1993), p. 89.

8 In terms of box-office receipts, a typical week shows 87 percent of the gross comes from musicals (*Variety*, February 9, 1993, p. 83). Owners of multiple theatres count on the long-running musicals for survival. Today's weekly grosses for musicals top out at about $700,000; for dramatic plays $340,000. Percentages paid off the top on a weekly basis to creative talents, etc. are: musical: 14–19 percent, dramatic: 16–17 percent. If a dramatic show can clear $50,000 above the break-even point, it will take twenty weeks to recoup the $1,000,000 up-front investment.

9 Publicity and advertising budgets for dramatic shows may run in the $20,000 range per week (approximately 10 percent of the gross) while musicals may run as high as $40,000 (slightly less than 10 percent of the gross). Interview with Bernard Jacobs, March 1, 1993.

10 Ibid. A large portion of these expenses are labor expenses. The manufacture of sets, costumes, properties, and electrics require the work of highly skilled artisans and artists.

11 Musicals such as *Phantom* or Neil Simon's musical of *The Goodbye Girl* cannot be stopped even by the *Times*. In the case of Simon's musical the advance sale before opening was already $12,000,000. Interview with Bernard Jacobs, March 1, 1993.

12 Japanese Corporations have invested on Broadway; see note on *The Heidi Chronicle* below.

13 Frank Rich, "The last of the one-man shows," *New York Times*, September 22, 1991.

14 Interview with Bernard Jacobs, March 1, 1993. On Broadway alone the gross was in the $280,000,000 dollar range. There is still a bus and truck road company touring the show.

15 *Fences*, produced by Carole Shorenstein Hays with the Yale Repertory Theatre, opened at the Forty-sixth Street Theatre, March 27, 1987. It won the Pulitzer Prize, the New York Drama Critics Circle Award, and the Tony Award.

16 *Zoot Suit* opened on March 25, 1979 at the Winter Garden, now the home of *Cats*. It was a massive undertaking and hopes were high.

17 Tony Kushner, "Playscript: *Angels in America*," *American Theatre*, June 1992, July/August, 1992.

18 Harold Clurman, *The Naked Image, Observations on the Modern Theatre* (Macmillan, New York, 1966), p. 151.

19 Michael Billington, "Nation built on guilt," *Guardian*, January 25, 1992. Christopher Hitchens, "*Angels* Over Broadway", *Vanity Fair*, March 1993, p. 72., Bruce Weber, "The Price of *Angels*," *New York Times*, January 29, 1993. John Lahr, "Beyond Nelly," *New Yorker*, November 23, 1992.

20 Jeremy Gerard, "Beating Broadway's odds," *Variety*, January 25, 1993.

21 The Walter Kerr, formerly the Ritz, is an old Shubert house now owned by Jujamcyn Theatres. It underwent a $1,500,000 renovation in 1983. It is located at 219 West Forty-eighth Street and seats 985. Because of its size and location it was designated an Alliance theatre, a designation that was supposed to save it from extinction. Jujamcyn currently owns the Virginia, the Eugene O'Neill, the Martin Beck, and the St James.

22 Gerard, op. cit.

23 *The Heidi Chronicles* opened March 9, 1989, at the Plymouth Theatre, produced by the Shubert Organization, Suntory International, and James Walsh in association with Playwrights Horizon. It was produced Off Broadway and at the Seattle Repertory before its transfer. It received the Drama Critics Circle Award for Best Play as well as the Tony Award and ran for 514 performances.

24 Interview with Susan Chicoine, Merle Debuskey Office, Lincoln Center Publicity, February 5, 1993.

25 Interview with Lee Silver, Shubert Organization, February 3, 1993.

26 Leonard R. Harris, (ed.), "Report: mayors midtown citizens committee," I, i, Autumn 1990.

27 Governor Mario M. Cuomo, "Press release," September 18, 1990, Site Plan Information Package, Office of Cora Cahan, President, The New Forty-second St, Inc.

28 These theatres are not suited to commercial production because of their size. They are all around the thousand-seat mark.

29 The Lyceum is one of the oldest theatres on Broadway. It was built in 1903. Frohman lived in an apartment atop the theatre which is now the Shubert Archives, administered by New York University. He could look out a window on to the stage and phone down his stage directions. During 1965–9, Ellis Rabb's APA Repertory company made a similar attempt to run an institutional theatre at the same address. The Lyceum is rich with tradition: Billie Burke, Ina Claire, David Belasco, and more recently John Osborne's *Look Back in Anger* with Kenneth Haigh, Alan Bates, and Mary Ure played the house.

30 Interview with Lee Silver, February 3, 1993.

31 Peter Stone, "Give my regards to Off Broadway and beyond," *New York Times*, June 21, 1988, p. 31.

32 The service charge is currently $2.

33 Interview with Jane Slotin, Manager, The Broadway Alliance, October 15, 1992.

34 Greg Evans, "B'way Alliance revamps, raises prices, budgets," *Variety*, October 14, 1991. Equity has agreed to designating seven more theatres to the list, *Variety*, January 18, 1993.

35 Interview with Peter Entin, Theatre Operations, Shubert Organization, August 19, 1992.

36 Interview with Bernard Jacobs, March 1, 1993.

37 This gathering called the First American Congress of Theatre (FACT) took place on June 2, at Princeton, New Jersey. Much of its attention was devoted to ways to build audiences through advanced marketing methods. It produced a book by Stuart W. Little, *After the FACT, Conflict and Consensus, a report on the First American Congress of Theatre*, Arno, New York, 1975. The Congress was successful in instilling a new spirit of co-operation into the industry. Obviously, something of this nature is needed again.

38 "Walkers" walk in, sign their names, and then leave without playing. The situation with the musicians' union (Local #802) is particularly difficult because of synthesizer technology. Dramatic shows used to have to pay musicians whether they needed them or not. The union now allows a show with less than twenty minutes of recorded music an exemption from the house minimums.

39 Ken Mandelbaum, *A Chorus Line and the Musicals of Michael Bennett* (St Martin's, New York, 1989).

40 Eugenia C. Cowan, Raffaela G. Pullo, and Jack L. Goldstein, *1982–1992–2002: A Generation of Theatre* (Exploring the Metropolis, New York, 1992), p. 17.

SELECT BIBLIOGRAPHY

Certain reference volumes such as *The Best Plays* series starting from its first volume in 1919 to 1991 have been frequently consulted. The original author is Burns Mantle, published by Dodd Mead, New York. The current author is Otis L. Guernsey, Jr, published by Applause, New York. Newspapers and periodicals are listed in the body of the text and unless otherwise indicated the place of publication is New York.

Abbott, George and Dunning, Philip. *Broadway, a Play*, G. H. Doran, New York, 1927.
——. *Mister Abbott*, Random House, New York, 1963.
Adler, Thomas P. *Mirror on The Stage, the Pulitzer Plays as an Approach to American Drama*, Purdue University Press, West Lafayette, IN, 1987.
Albee, Edward. *Who's Afraid of Virginia Woolf?*, Pocket Book, New York, 1962.
Amacher, Richard. *Edward Albee*, Twayne, Boston, 1969.
Atkinson, Brooks. *Broadway Scrapbook*, Theatre Arts, New York, 1947.
——. *Broadway*, Macmillan, New York, 1974.
Barlow, Judith E. *Final Acts, the Creation of Three Late O'Neill Plays*, University of Georgia, Athens, Ga, 1985.
Barr, Richard. "You have to hock your house," unpublished MS.
Bartow, Arthur. *The Director's Voice, Twenty-one Interviews*, TCG, New York, 1988.
Beckerman, Bernard. *Dynamics of Drama*, Alfred Knopf, New York, 1970.
Behrman, Sam N. *People in a Diary, a Memoir*, Little, Brown, Boston, 1972.
Bentley, Eric. *The Dramatic Event, an American Chronicle*, Beacon, Boston, 1956.
——. *What Is Theatre?*, Beacon Press, Boston, 1956.
Bernheim, Alfred L. *The Business of the Theatre, an Economic History of the American Theatre, 1750–1932*, Benjamin Blom, New York, 1964.
Bigsby, Christopher W. E. *A Critical Introduction to Twentieth-century American Drama*, I, II, III, Cambridge University Press, Cambridge, 1987.
——. (ed.) *Arthur Miller and Company*, Methuen, London, 1990.
Bloom, Ken. *Broadway, an Encyclopedic Guide to the History, People and Places of Times Square*, Facts on File, New York, 1991.
Bloomgarden, Kermit. "The unfinished memoirs of Kermit Bloomgarden," ed. Christine Conrad, *American Theatre*, V, 8 (November 1988).
Bordman, Gerald. *The Concise Oxford Companion to American Theatre*, Oxford University Press, New York, 1987.

Botto, Louis. *At This Theatre, an Informal History of New York's Legitimate Theatres*, Dodd Mead, New York, 1984.

Brenman-Gibson, Margaret. *Clifford Odets: American Playwright*, Atheneum, New York, 1982.

Brown, John Mason. *Dramatis Personae, a Retrospective Show*, Viking Press, New York, 1963.

Brown, T. Allston. *History of the American Stage*, Burt Franklin, New York, 1969.

Brustein, Robert. *Reimagining American Theatre*, Hill and Wang, New York, 1991.

Carson, William G. B. *Dear Josephine: the Theatrical Career of Josephine Hull*, University of Oklahoma Press, Norman, OK, 1963.

Churchill, Allen. *The Theatrical Twenties*, McGraw-Hill, New York, 1975.

Clark, Barrett H. *Eugene O'Neill, the Man and His Plays*, Dover, New York, 1947.

—— (ed.). *Favorite American Plays of the Nineteenth Century*, Princeton University Press, Princeton, 1948.

Clurman, Harold. *The Fervent Years*, Harvest, 1975.

——. *Lies Like Truth*, Macmillan, New York, 1958.

Cohn, Ruby. *New American Dramatists, 1960–1980*, Grove, New York, 1982.

Desmastes, William W. *Beyond Naturalism, a New Realism in American Theatre*, Greenwood, Westport, CT, 1988.

Doherty, Lynn. "The art of producing, the life and work of Kermit Bloomgarden," Dissertation, City University of New York, 1989.

Donohue, Jr, Joseph W. (ed.). *The Theatrical Manager in England and America, Player of a Perilous Game*, Princeton University Press, Princeton, 1971.

Downer, Alan S. *Fifty Years of American Drama, 1900–1950*, Henry Regnery, Chicago, 1951.

—— (ed.). *American Drama and Its Critics*, University of Chicago Press, Chicago, 1965.

—— (ed.). *The American Theatre Today*, Basic Books, New York, 1967.

Dukore, Bernard F. *American Dramatists, 1918–1945*, Grove, New York, 1984.

Eaton, Walter Prichard. *The Theatre Guild, the First Ten Years*, Brentano's, New York, 1929.

Eustis, Morton Corcoran. *B'way, Inc.!, the Theatre as a Business*, Dodd Mead, New York, 1934.

Evans, Abigail W. "The impact of labor relations on Broadway economics," unpublished M.F.A. thesis, Yale School of Drama, 1987.

Farber, Donald C. *Producing Theatre, a Comprehensive Legal and Business Guide*, Drama Book Specialists, New York, 1981.

Felheim, Marvin. *The Theatre of Augustin Daly*, Harvard University Press, Cambridge, MA, 1956.

Flanagan, Hallie. *Arena, the Story of the Federal Theatre*, Limelight Editions, New York, 1985.

Flexner, Eleanor. *American Playwrights, 1918–1938, the Theatre Retreats from Reality*, Simon and Schuster, New York, 1938.

Gaige, Crosby. *Footlights and Highlights*, E. P. Dutton, New York, 1948.

Garfield, David. *A Player's Place, the Story of the Actors Studio*, Macmillan, New York, 1980.

Garrison, Gary Wayne. "An examination of the comedic techniques found in selected works of Neil Simon," unpublished M.S. thesis, North Texas State University, 1980.

Gassner, John. *Theatre at the Crossroads*, Holt Rinehart and Winston, New York, 1960.

——. *Best Plays of the Early American Theatre*, Crown, New York, 1967.

Gelb, Arthur and Gelb, Barbara. *O'Neill*, Harper and Row, New York, 1962.

Gill, Brendan (ed.). *State of Grace, Eight Plays by Philip Barry*, Harcourt Brace Jovanovich, New York, 1975.

Goldstein, Malcolm. *George S. Kaufman, His Life and His Theatre*, Oxford University Press, New York, 1979.

Goodman, Randolph. *Drama, A View from the Wings* (2nd edn), Holt Rinehart and Winston, New York, 1978.

Gordon, Max and Funke, Lewis. *Max Gordon Presents*, Bernard Geis Assoc., New York, 1963.

Gottfried, Martin. *Jed Harris: the Curse of Genius*, Little, Brown, Boston, 1984.

Gottlieb, Polly Rose. *The Nine Lives of Billy Rose*, Crown, New York, 1968.

Gouran, Patrick Delburt. "Broadway comedy of the 1960's," unpublished Ph.D., dissertation, University of Colorado, 1975.

Guernsey, Jr., Otis L. (ed.). *Broadway Song and Story: Playwrights, Lyricists, Composers Discuss Their Hits*, Dodd Mead, New York, 1985.

——. *Curtain Times, the New York Theatre, 1965–1987*, Applause, New York, 1987.

Hanks, Nancy (ed.). *The Performing Arts, Problems and Prospects, Rockefeller Panel Report on the Future of Theatre, Dance, Music in America*, McGraw-Hill, New York, 1965.

Harris, Jed. *A Dance on the High Wire*, Crown, New York, 1979.

Hart, Moss. *Act One, an Autobiography*, Random House, New York, 1959.

Hay, Peter. *Broadway Anecdotes*, Oxford University Press, New York, 1989.

Helburn, Thersa. *A Wayward Quest*, Little, Brown, Boston, 1960.

Henderson, Mary C. *The City and the Theatre*, James T. White and Co., Clifton, NJ, 1973.

——. *Theater in America, 200 Years of Plays, Players, and Productions*, Harry N. Abrams, New York, 1986.

Herman, William. *Understanding Contemporary American Drama*, University of South Carolina Press, Columbia, SC, 1987.

Hirsch, Foster. *A Method to Their Madness, the History of the Actors Studio*, W. W. Norton, New York, 1984.

——. *Harold Prince and the American Musical Theatre*, Cambridge University Press, New York, 1989.

Hoogstraten, Nicholas van. *Lost Broadway Theatres*, Princeton Architectural Press, New York, 1991.

Houghton, Norris. *Entrances and Exits, a Life In and Out of the Theatre*, Limelight, New York, 1991.

Ilson, Carol. *Harold Prince, from Pajama Game to Phantom of the Opera*, UMI, Ann Arbor, MI, 1989.

Karpinski, Maciej. *Zycie I Smierc Na Broadwayu* (Life and Death on Broadway), Wydawnictwa Artystyczne i Filmowe, Warsaw, 1990.

Kasha, Al and Hirschhorn, Joel. *Notes on Broadway, Intimate Conversations with Broadway's Greatest Songwriters*, Simon and Schuster, New York, 1985.

Kaufman, George S. and Hart, Moss. *Six Plays by Kaufman and Hart*, Random House, New York, 1972.

Kazan, Elia. *A Life*, Doubleday, New York, 1989.

Langley, Stephen (ed.). *Producers on Producing*, DBS, New York, 1976.

162

Langner, Lawrence. *The Magic Curtain*, E. P. Dutton and Co., Inc., New York, 1951.

Lauf, Abe. *The Wicked Stage, a History of Theater Censorship and Harrassment in the United States*, Frederick Ungar, New York, 1978.

Lawliss, Chuck. *The New York Theatre Sourcebook, the Ultimate Guide to Theatre in New York and its Environs*, Simon and Schuster, New York, 1990.

Leiter, Samuel L. *Ten Seasons, New York Theatre in the Seventies*, Greenwood, Westport, CT, 1986.

Leon, Ruth. *Applause New York's Guide to the Performing Arts*, Applause, New York, 1991.

Lewis, Robert. *Slings and Arrows, Theatre in My Life*, Stein and Day, New York, 1984.

Little, Stuart W. *After the FACT, Conflict and Consensus, a Report on the First American Congress of Theatre*, Arno, New York, 1975.

Lowery, W. McNeil (ed.). *The Performing Arts and American Society*, Prentice-Hall, Englewood Cliffs, NJ, 1978.

McCarthy, Mary. *Sights and Spectacles, 1937–1956*, Farrar, Straus and Cudahy, New York, 1956.

MacGowan, Kenneth. *Footlights Across America*, Harcourt Brace Jovanovich, New York, 1929.

McNamara, Brooks. *The Shuberts of Broadway, a History Drawn from the Collections of the Shubert Archive*, Oxford University Press, New York, 1990.

Mamet, David. *American Buffalo*, Samuel French, Inc., New York, 1975.

——. *Writing in Restaurants*, Penguin, New York, 1987.

——. *Some Freaks*, Viking Press, New York, 1989.

Mandelbaum, Ken. *A Chorus Line and the Musicals of Michael Bennett*, St Martin's, New York, 1989.

Maney, Richard. *Fanfare, the Confessions of a Press Agent*, Harper, New York, 1957.

Mantle, Burns. *Contemporary American Playwrights*, Dodd, Mead, New York, 1939.

Marcosson, Frederick Issac and Frohman, Daniel. *Charles Frohman: Manager and Man*, Harper, New York, 1916.

Marsolais, Ken, McFarlane, Rodger, and Viola, Tom (eds). *Broadway Day & Night*, Simon and Schuster, New York, 1992.

Meisel, Martin. *Shaw and the Nineteenth Century Theatre*, Limelight Editions, New York, 1984.

——. *Realizations, Narrative, Pictorial, and Theatrical Arts in Nineteenth Century England*, Princeton University Press, Princeton, 1983.

Meredith, Scott. *George S. Kaufman and His Friends*, Doubleday, New York, 1974.

Mielziner, Jo. *Designing for the Theatre*, Bramhall House, New York, 1965.

Miller, Arthur. *Death of a Salesman*, Viking Press, New York, 1949.

——. *The Theatre Essays of Arthur Miller*, Penguin Books, New York, 1978.

——. *Timebends, a Life*, Harper and Row, New York, 1988.

Miller, Jordan Y. *Playwright's Progress, O'Neill and the Critics*, Scott, Foresman, Chicago, 1965.

—— and Frazer, Winifred A. *American Drama between the Wars, a Critical History*, Twayne, Boston, 1991.

Morden, Ethan. *The American Theatre*, Oxford University Press, New York, 1981.

163

Nelson, Stephen. *"Only A Paper Moon," the Theatre of Billy Rose*, UMI, Ann Arbor, 1985.

Novick, Julius. *Beyond Broadway, the Quest for Permanent Theatres*, Hill and Wang, New York, 1968.

O'Hara, Frank Hurburt. *Today in American Drama*, University of Chicago Press, Chicago, 1939.

O'Neill, Eugene. *Long Day's Journey Into Night*, Yale University Press, New Haven, CT, 1955.

——. *The Plays of Eugene O'Neill*, 3 vols, Random House, New York, 1955.

Odets, Clifford. *Six Plays of Clifford Odets*, Grove, New York, 1935.

——. *The Time Is Ripe, the 1940 Journal of Clifford Odets*, Grove, New York, 1988.

Oenslager, Donald. *Stage Design: Four Centuries of Scenic Invention*, Viking Press, New York, 1975.

——. *The Theatre of Donald Oenslager*, Wesleyan University Press, Middletown, CT, 1978.

Pater, Walter. *The Renaissance*, London, 1888.

Poggi, Jack. *Theatre in America*, Cornell University Press, New York, 1968.

Prince, Hal. *Contradictions: Notes on Twenty-six Years in the Theatre*, Dodd Mead, New York, 1974.

Rich, Frank and Aronson, Lisa. *The Theatre Art of Boris Aronson*, Alfred A. Knopf, New York, 1987.

Rogoff, Gordon. *Theatre is Not Safe, Theatre Criticism, 1962–1986*, Northwestern University Press, Evanston, 1987.

Roudane, Matthew C. *Understanding Edward Albee*, University of South Carolina Press, Columbia, SC, 1987.

Savran, David. *In Their Own Words, Contemporary American Playwrights*, TCG, New York, 1988.

Scheafer, Louis. *O'Neill, Son and Playwright*, Little Brown, Boston, 1968.

——. *O'Neill, Son and Artist*, Little, Brown, Boston, 1973.

Schneider, Alan. *Entrances, an American Director's Journey*, Viking Press, New York, 1986.

Selz, Thomas D. and Simensky, Melvin. *Entertainment Law, Legal Concepts and Business Practices*, Shepard's/McGraw-Hill, New York, 1983.

Shepard, Richard F. and Drechsler-Marx, Carin. *Broadway, from the Battery to the Bronx*, Harry N. Abrams, New York, 1988.

Shewey, Don. "Gay theatre grows up," *American Theatre* (May 1988).

Simon, Neil. *The Comedy of Neil Simon*, Avon, New York, 1973.

——. *Biloxi Blues*, Samuel French, Inc., New York, 1986.

——. *Broadway Bound*, Samuel French, Inc., New York, 1987.

Slawson, Judith. *Robert Duvall, Hollywood Maverick* St Martin's Press, New York, 1985.

Smith, Wendy. *Real Life Drama, the Group Theatre and America, 1931–1940*, Alfred A. Knopf, New York, 1990.

Sobol, Bernard. *Broadway Heartbeat, Memoirs of a Press Agent*, Hermitage House, New York, 1953.

Sobol, Louis. *The Longest Street, a Memoir*, Crown, New York, 1968.

Sponberg, Arvid F. *Broadway Talks, What Professionals Think About Commercial Theatre in America*, Greenwood, Westport, CT, 1991.

Spoto, Donald. *The Kindness of Strangers, the Life of Tennessee Williams*, Ballantine Books, New York, 1985.

Stagg, Jerry. *The Brothers Shubert*, Random House, New York, 1968.

Stanislavski, Constantin. *Building a Character*, Theatre Arts, New York, 1949.

Stevenson, Isabelle (ed.). *The Tony Award, a Complete Listing with A History of The American Theatre Wing*, Crown, New York, 1987.

Stott, William and Stott, Jane. *On Broadway*, University of Texas Press, Austin, 1968.

Strasberg, Lee. *A Dream of Passion, the Development of the Method*, Little, Brown, Boston, 1987.

Taubman, Howard. *The Making of the American Theatre*, Coward McCann, New York, 1965.

Waldau, Roy S. *Vintage Years of the Theatre Guild, 1929–1939*, Case Western Reserve, Cleveland, 1972.

Wallock, Leonard (ed.). *New York, Culture Capital of the World, 1940–1965*, Rizzoli, New York, 1988.

Weales, Gerald. *The Jumping-Off Place, American Drama in the 1960's*, Macmillan, New York, 1969.

Weissman, Philip. *Creativity in the Theatre, a Psychoanalytic Study*, Delta, New York, 1965.

Wharton, John F. *Life Among the Playwrights, Being Mostly the Story of The Playwrights Producing Company, Inc.*, Quadrangle, New York, 1974.

Whitworth, Geoffrey Arundel. *Theatre in Action*, Whitefriars Press, London, 1938.

Whyte, William H. (intro.). *The WPA Guide to New York City*, Pantheon, New York, 1982.

Williams, Dakin and Mead, Shepherd. *Tennessee Williams, an Intimate Biography*, Arbor House, New York, 1983.

Williams, Tennessee. *Cat on a Hot Tin Roof*, James Laughlin, New York, 1955.

——. *Memoirs*, Doubleday, Garden City, 1975.

Wilson, Garff B. *Three Hundred Years of American Drama and Theatre*, Prentice-Hall, Englewood Cliffs, NJ, 1982.

Wood, Audrey. *Represented by Audrey Wood*, Doubleday, Garden City, 1981.

Zeigler, Joseph Wesley. *Regional Theatre, the Revolutionary Stage*, Da Capo, New York, 1977.

BROADWAY THEATRE ON VIDEO

Many of the Broadway plays mentioned in this volume are now on video tape. Although tape provides one at best with only the shadow of the live performance, it is frequently better than no performance at all. The tapes mentioned below are generally available at rental houses some of which do an extensive mail order business such as Facets Video, 1517 West Fullerton Avenue, Chicago, IL 60614 (Tel. 800-331-6197).

You Can't Take It With You. Kaufman and Hart (1938)

James Stewart, Jean Arthur, Lionel Barrymore, Edward Arnold. The 1938 Academy Award-winning adaptation of the play has many delightful scenes. Two-thirds of this Frank Capra film is somewhat faithful to the play, but the ending is pure Capra.

You Can't Take It With You (1984)

Jason Robards, Jr, Elizabeth Wilson, Colleen Dewhurst. A video version of the Ellis Rabb 1983 Broadway revival. Although it was much livelier on stage, this television production evokes the spirit of the revival which stressed the sentimental aspects of the play. In the video, George Voskovec replaces James Coco in the role of Boris Kolenkhov.

Death of a Salesman. Arthur Miller (1986)

Dustin Hoffman, Kate Reid, John Malkovich, Stephen Lang. An excellent job of capturing the essence of the 1984 Broadway revival. Hoffman's Willy Loman is quite different from Lee J. Cobb's, less nobility and more petulance. Malkovich gives a very strong performance.

Private Conversations/On the Set of Death of a Salesman (1986)

A documentary about the Dustin Hoffman production. Interviews with Miller and Malkovich as well as Volker Schlondorff (director) add depth to the experience of viewing the revival.

Cat on a Hot Tin Roof. Tennessee Williams (1958)

Elizabeth Taylor, Paul Newman, Burl Ives, Judith Anderson. This adaptation manages to avoid the subject of homosexuality. Brick simply needs the reassuring love of his father. There are strong performances that do credit to what is left of Williams' script. Burl Ives is particularly worth seeing. However, if you want an idea about Kazan's direction see *Streetcar Named Desire* (1951), *East of Eden* (1954), and/or *Baby Doll* (1956) (with Mildred Dunnock).

Cat on a Hot Tin Roof (1984)

Jessica Lang, Tommy Lee Jones, Rip Torn. Directed by Jack Hofsiss (*Elephant Man* on Broadway) for television's American Playhouse. Although this version is closer to Williams' script, the performances lack authenticity. Rip Torn is miscast as Big Daddy, and everything about the production seems hollow and melodramatic.

Who's Afraid of Virginia Woolf? Edward Albee (1966)

Elizabeth Taylor, Richard Burton, George Segal, Sandy Dennis. An excellent adaptation of Albee's play. Taylor and Burton are at their best and Mike Nichols' direction is crisp and clean. Although there are some significant omissions from the play, this is a first-class effort.

Glengarry Glen Ross. David Mamet (1993)

Al Pacino, Jack Lemmon, Alec Baldwin, Ed Harris, Alan Arkin, Kevin Spacey. Although *American Buffalo* has not found its way on to the screen yet, David Mamet is represented by a star-studded cast including Jack Lemmon in this film version of his Pulitzer Prize winning play. Since Mamet writes screenplays (Brian DePalma's *Untouchables* (1987)), he knows how to convert his theatrical ideas into film.

Long Day's Journey Into Night. Eugene O'Neill (1962)

Ralph Richardson, Katharine Hepburn, Jason Robards, Jr, Dean Stockwell. Sidney Lumet directed this extraordinarily faithful rendering of the Tyrone family. There are strong performances all around. It captures the essence of the play.

Long Day's Journey Into Night (1987)

Jack Lemmon, Kevin Space, Peter Gallagher, Bethel Leslie, Jodie Lynne McClintock. Jonathan Miller brought the cast of his 1987 Broadway revival production to television. The differences between this television production and the 1962 film begin with the casting. Lemmon is better cast in *Glengarry Glen Ross*.

Brighton Beach Memoirs. Neil Simon (1986)

Blythe Danner, Bob Dishy, Judith Ivey, Jonathan Silverman. Gene Saks who directed the Broadway production turns the play into a Hollywood movie with

Jonathan Silverman as Eugene. It lacks the charm of the play and Eugene's angst here seems trivial. The sequel *Biloxi Blues* (1988) works better, in part due to Matthew Broderick's performance and Mike Nichols' direction (also stars Christopher Walken). A recent television production of *Broadway Bound* (1992) with Anne Bancroft will eventually find its way onto video tape. The TV adaptation is a bit sketchy and sentimental, but it has its moments.

INDEX

169